Are We There Yet?

CultureAmerica

Karal Ann Marling

Erika Doss

Series Editors

Are We There Yet?

The Golden Age of American Family Vacations

Susan Sessions Rugh

University Press of Kansas

Published by the University Press of Kansas
(Lawrence, Kansas 66045), which was organized by the
Kansas Board of Regents and is operated and funded by
Emporia State University, Fort Hays State University,
Kansas State University, Pittsburg State University,
the University of Kansas, and Wichita State University

Library of Congress Cataloging-in-Publication Data

Rugh, Susan Sessions.
Are we there yet? : the golden age of American family vacations /
Susan Sessions Rugh.
p. cm. — (CultureAmerica)
Includes bibliographical references and index.
ISBN 978-0-7006-1588-9 (cloth : alk. paper)
1. Vacations—United States—History—20th century. 2. Vacations—Social aspects—United States. 3. National characteristics, American. 4. Family—United States—History—20th century. 5. United States—Social life and customs—20th century. I. Title.
E161.R84 2008
973.92—dc22 2008007368

British Library Cataloguing-in-Publication Data is available.

Printed in the United States of America

10 9 8 7 6 5 4 3 2

The paper used in this publication is recycled and contains 30 percent postconsumer waste. It is acid free and meets the minimum requirements of the American National Standard for Permanence of Paper for Printed Library Materials Z39.48-1992.

For my parents

Contents

Acknowledgments

In homage to the late Hal Rothman, whose work inspired me, I write my book's final words in Hawaii where Asia and the Americas meet in a nexus of tourism. From my balcony overlooking the pool area, I notice the artifice of the exotic: the fake waterfalls spilling over the man-made lava mountain, the bright red and yellow tropical plants, the waving palm trees, the winding stone walkways, the thatched refreshment hut, and the resort workers in flowered shirts and dresses, wearing sturdy shoes as they serve the tourists drinks by the poolside. As a student of tourism, I know that behind the curtain of the resort's tropical paradise are workers pulling the ropes and pulleys of trash collection, changing sheets, laundering, cleaning, cooking, and pleasing the paying guests who consume their version of paradise here on the Garden Island. Beyond them are designers, planners, builders, and reservation agents, all spun together in an electronic web of global tourism that created this place for me to be on vacation far away from home.

But as I look over the pools, I also see families here on vacation like me, blissfully unaware of the machinations of the global tourism empire. A pair of besotted newlyweds stroke each other's arms as they soak up the sun. A young father pushes a baby in a stroller with one hand while balancing float toys on his other arm. In the pool, a lithe school girl balances on her father's shoulders to dive into the water while her mother watches. A straw-hatted grandmother gently warns two little boys to be careful and asks if they would like another drink. From my balcony I see families here to have a good time together, just as they have always done on vacation.

To write this history of family vacations, I am grateful for the assistance of those who helped me find sources. In particular, I am grateful to Marva Felchlin and Manola Madrid at the Autry National Center, where I spent a month immersed in the world of children's westerns. James Akerman at the Newberry Library graciously let me sit in on his maps seminar and guided me through the voluminous Rand McNally map collection. Pat O'Brian was tireless in making those maps available to me in the reading room. I appreciate Joseph Schwartz at the National Archives for making the newly processed set of National Parks Service records available to me. Tracey Panek at the California State Automobile Association and Morgan P. Yates at the Automobile Club of Southern California were gracious and efficient. I appreciate the efforts of librarians and staff at the Anaheim Public Library, Benson Ford Research Center, the Seaver Center for Western History Research, the YIVO Archives at the Center for Jewish History, the Schomburg Center for Research in Black Culture, and at the National Archives—the Jefferson Library, the Manuscripts Division, and the Prints and Photographs Division. For her generous hospitality while I did research at the National Archives, I thank my cousin, Michelle Derr. For their helpful service, I thank the staff of the Interlibrary Loan office at the Harold B. Lee Library at BYU.

For financial assistance, I am greatly indebted to the Charles Redd Center of Western Studies at BYU, which awarded me the Mollie and Karl Butler Young Scholar Award. I am also grateful to the Institute for the Study of the American West and its director, Stephen Aron, for a fellowship at the Autry National Center. At BYU, the College of Family, Home, and Social Sciences granted me a professional development leave and travel funds which made it possible for me to travel to archives and purchase photographs. I appreciate the encouragement of Dean David B. Magleby, who sets a brisk pace as a scholar and teacher.

My colleagues in the history department at BYU have been most supportive. I am grateful to former department chair Neil York, who not only nominated me for the Butler fellowship and provided course release time, but also loaned me his cache of historic Disneyland media. This book has benefited from the input of the Faculty Writing Group, especially the detailed comments supplied by Jenny Pulsipher, Brian Cannon, and Rebecca de Schweinitz. I am grateful to colleagues Kendall Brown, Craig Harline, Don Harreld, and Mark Choate for their encouragement. I thank Jeffrey Shumway for sharing his family Disneyland vacation photos with me, and Jenny Pulsipher for letting me read her diary of a family vacation to Alaska. Most of all, I am grateful to Richard Kimball, who read the entire book and made judicious suggestions for revision that brought out the best in what I had written. I am grateful for the efficient assistance of student research assistants, Hillary Poitier, Sarah Zupko, Melanie Bunker, and especially Tiffany Taylor, who has gone beyond the call of duty to bring this book to completion. The history department staff members—Julie Radle, Stephanie Lassen, and Michelle Stocking—have been unfailing in providing timely assistance.

I owe a debt to colleagues who graciously read parts of the book while it was in manuscript. For the many conversations while canoeing, I thank my dear friend Barbara Welke, who has taught me to see the people of the past more sympathetically as she assisted me in writing about race. Gail Radford's confidence in my project from the start means a great deal to me, and I thank her for insightful comments on several chapters. David Wrobel has been instrumental in launching the project, providing how-to advice, and broadening my understanding of western history. Kathleen Brosnan generously shared her scholarly expertise in environmental history, and Keith Erekson provided a critical reading of the chapter on pilgrimage. Donna Braden at the Henry Ford Museum provided stimulating direction from the start and made helpful suggestions for the first chapter. I appreciate the comments of Hal S. Barron, Eugene Moehring, and David Wrobel on papers presented at conferences. For help with choosing photographs, I am grateful to Susan Whetstone. Of course, I take responsibility for any errors.

At the University Press of Kansas, I am grateful to Nancy Jackson for providing early encouragement and acquiring the manuscript, and to Kalyani Fernando for bringing it to fruition. Series editors Karal Ann Marling and Erika Doss have provided insightful guidance and encouragement, and I thank the outside readers for their suggestions.

I wish to acknowledge those who have told me their family vacation stories. For many years this has been a delightful topic of dinner conversations, and I am grateful to Nancy Holt, Eugenie Tsai, Fred Woodward, Bud Scruggs, Brett Hammond, Pete Ellison, and Lyn Uhl. I am grateful to Andrea Corwin Weitzman, Nancy Freund Heller, and Ann Whiting Orton for letting me tell their family stories. I only regret I was not able to weave in all the stories I was told.

Writing this book has caused me to look back on the vacations my husband and I and our children took together, and I apologize now to my sons for our eating homemade sandwiches in the car when we could have eaten at McDonald's. Now that they are grown and have their own children, they are beginning to understand that we did it all for them.

I express deep appreciation for my husband, Tom, for his intellectual companionship, enthusiasm, and loving support. Finally, I dedicate this book to my parents, who took our family on vacation, from the beaches of Maine to the peaks of Peru. That I wrote this book without irony is a tribute to your love and dedication to your family.

Introduction

Perhaps the most famous family vacation in late twentieth-century America is featured in the 1983 feature film, *National Lampoon's Vacation.* On their summer road trip, the Griswold family—Clark and Ellen, daughter Audrey and son Rusty—suffers a series of mishaps. Thieves steal their hubcaps in St. Louis, they get lost in the Nevada Desert, and Walley World is closed when they arrive. The movie, which stars Chevy Chase as the father, struck a chord in the national consciousness and earned over $61 million. The movie inspired several sequels and has spawned a whole genre of family road trip movies, one nearly every summer. The tropes of the family vacation movie feature the American family—detached businessman dad, unappreciated housewife mom, indifferent children—whose misadventures culminate in calamity or a chase scene, pleasantly resolved by a contrived ending in which Dad, Mom, and the kids all come to their senses and realize there is nothing more important than the family.[1]

Americans have been making fun of family vacations from the time they came into style after World War II. The emergent medium of television captured some of the travails of the traveling family in late-night variety shows. Morey Amsterdam opened his show one evening in 1949 with a monologue reporting that he was just back from a vacation to Florida with his family: "I steered, my mother-in-law drove." He commented on the expense of the vacation: "It cost us $400—a day." It was "ten dollars for an aspirin." He suffered the usual fate of the New York tourist in Florida when he admitted he went out on the beach and "walked away one big beautiful blister."[2] Morey Amsterdam's jokes made television viewers feel better about spending the money and putting up with their families on vacation because they could laugh at themselves. Perhaps at least they recognized they weren't alone in their stupidity!

In their comedy show on NBC television in 1952, Bob and Ray satirized the summer vacation by offering for sale a summer vacation kit "for people who want to be uncomfortable without leaving home." It included a dozen items, among them "a bathing suit that makes you look kind of silly" and "a hard table so you feel like you have slept in a camp cot." It came complete with a beach umbrella, along with a "handsome lifeguard to divert your wife's attention while you are setting up the umbrella." Finally, the sound effects man added the sounds of a day in the country: bullfrogs, owls hooting, crickets chirping, waves pounding on the beach, moose calling, the horn of a passing train sounding.[3] Summer vacations were a lot of trouble and not really much of a vacation, but the men were caught up in this travel ritual for the sake of the family.

The family vacation parodies are based on the middle-class American vacation experience that many recognize as part of their own childhood memories. If the family vacation is such an ordeal, why do we go on vacation together? How did this madness get started? How has it changed from the days of our parents and grandparents, who stuck us in the backseat with our siblings? And why do we still spend our money and take time off work to go on vacation with our children? What does this say about us? Why do we do it?

This book is a cultural history of the American middle-class family vacation in its golden age. The era began as World War II ended in 1945, when family vacations became an established summer tradition, and lasted until the 1970s, when family road trips declined in popularity. Record numbers of parents loaded the luggage in the trunk of the family car, stashed the children in the backseat, and drove America's highways together. Unprecedented prosperity and widespread vacation benefits at work meant most middle-class families could afford to vacation. Rising rates of automobile ownership and the construction of new highways facilitated the family road trip. An ideal of family togetherness in the baby boom justified spending money on a vacation.

To say the era was the golden age of family vacations does not mean to suggest a rosy-hued portrait of the past. Although it may have been the golden age for the white middle-class family on vacation, it was hardly a golden age for African American families who had to sleep in their cars after being turned away from motels that refused to rent them rooms, or for Jews who saw signs that read "Gentiles Only" or "Clientele Carefully Selected," leading them to build their own resorts in the Catskills. Yet despite the discrimination, even these families joined the throngs on the nation's highways in pursuit of family time together on vacation during the golden age of American family vacations.

The modern family road trip had its roots in the auto camping of the 1920s, when one young couple from New York City piled their belongings and their six-year-old (dubbed "Supercargo") into their Ford and camped their way to San Francisco through twelve states in over thirty-seven days. In *The Family Flivvers to Frisco,* not much is made of the burden of traveling with a child who had a mind of his own. When they were forced by passing cars into a ditch near DeKalb, Illinois, the Supercargo "scrambled over the door and started, a small irate figure in yellow oilskins, to walk in the general direction of New York." By the 1930s, family vacations were curtailed somewhat by the Depression, but so strong was the habit, they did not disappear. In Edward Dunn's 1933 account of a western family vacation, *Double-Crossing America by Motor,* the four children were part of a traveling party of eight. As long as they stopped for their afternoon treat of ice cream, the children seem to have posed no problem at all. This family, who could afford a cross-country jaunt to Arizona for a month at a dude ranch, was far wealthier than most Americans, especially in the depths of the Depression.[4]

American involvement in World War II after the bombing of Pearl Harbor in December 1941 severely curtailed travel in America because the country's factories were producing for and families were separated by the war effort. The rapid resumption of pleasure travel surprised everyone in its scale. As Americans read in the papers about President Harry Truman fishing at Key West, Florida, they were planning their own summer vacations.[5]

Soon after war's end, the vacation became democratized by the popularity of the road trip. As rates of car ownership soared, Americans took the whole family on the summer road trip, traveling by car on newly paved roads built by the federal government, eating at roadside restaurants, and spending the night at motels. Families could choose from a variety of vacation destinations: amusement parks, national and state parks, or country resorts with their cool air and fishing ponds. Almost half of all Americans surveyed by the Gallup organization in 1954 said they planned to take a summer vacation, most for a week or longer. A 1962 government

The Farnsworth family ready to go on vacation in 1962. (Courtesy Tiffany Taylor.)

report on national recreation stated that during the previous year, Americans "took nearly 80 million vacations on which they spent $6.9 billion, traveled more than 100 billion passenger-miles and remained away from home more than 800 million person-days." By the 1970s, families still took summer vacations, but the family road trip was not as widespread. The three decades of postwar expansion fizzled with the 1973 oil embargo and a recession, squeezing family budgets. The family vacation, along with the nuclear family, had also lost its cachet. More middle-class Americans could afford to travel to Europe, and a new generation rebelled against the authority of their parents. The travel industry let go of the image of the white middle-class suburban family in favor of narrower niche marketing that played to countercultural themes.[6]

The family vacation as a middle-class custom emerged during the cold war era. Scholars argue that the 1950s were a time when Americans retreated to home and family, where they felt safe from threats of communism and the bomb. *Life,* America's most popular newsmagazine, presented political events through the lens of domesticity, the white nuclear family in the suburbs.[7] The grand scale of family vacationing poses a challenge to the ideal of domestic containment, of the image of the family huddled in its basement bomb shelter. If Americans were so fearful, why were so many American families on the road, exploring the country, dragging along their small children?

The cold war era may have been marked by fear, but it was also an age of robust consumerism. Historian Lizabeth Cohen has explained how what she calls the consumer's republic in the era of postwar prosperity was "built around the promises of mass consumption, both in terms of material life and the more idealistic goals of greater freedom, democracy, and equality." To these I add the ideal of family togetherness, which justified spending money to buy a suburban home and fill it with consumer goods: family car, modern kitchen appliances for the housewife, lawn mowers and golf clubs for the father, bikes and toys and clothes for the children. Spending money on a family vacation was a consumer choice, a way to buy experiences to promote family togetherness. Travelers consumed experiences prepackaged in national parks, amusement parks, or highway landscapes. Family consumerism was political in that it upheld the idea that consuming goods and experiences sustained national security. In an era of anticommunism, the ability of American families to afford new kitchen appliances or a summer vacation demonstrated the superiority of the free enterprise system.[8]

Placing the study of family travel within the framework of the consumer's republic allows us to resolve this apparent paradox of domestic containment by acknowledging that the family car was a home on the road. To sustain domesticity while away, families traveled together in the car—a cocoon of domestic space in which they felt safe. While on vacation, they stayed in motels that provided a home away from home, or they traveled in recreational vehicles that offered the comforts of home. Even when they camped, families took along the consumer products that helped them feel at home outdoors. Americans took domesticity on the road in the family car, with a modern faith in consumer technology that allowed them to quell their fears and explore America.

Family travel fits squarely into the study of the history of tourism, a field that has grown tremendously since Dean MacCannell's 1976 manifesto, *The Tourist.* Scholars in many disciplines have turned to the study of travel as a useful approach to understanding modern culture. The theoretical literature has focused on the idea that travelers are seeking an authentic experience, but no one has yet considered how group or family travel could alter the experience. We observe from studying the family vacation that the experience of tourism takes place in a human context, and that experiences are mediated through the interaction with members of the group. Family travelers chose the comfort, safety, and convenience of traveling with children over the quest for authenticity.[9]

Historians have examined the family vacation before the war but have not written about family travel after World War II. Cindy S. Aron argues that the American vacation, once the preserve of the wealthy, became a habit of the middle class by the end of the nineteenth century and of the working class in the early twentieth century. I take the story beyond 1940 to consider the archetype of domestic travel after World War II, the family vacation in a modern consumer culture. Marguerite Shaffer contends that travel was a way to discover America, a ritual of citizenship, but her story likewise ends before this study begins. In *Devil's Bargains,* Hal Rothman argues that tourism transformed the postwar West, but I am more interested in how tourism transformed the traveler. This book studies the important postwar period of travel in the context of consumer citizenship during the turbulent times of the civil rights movement, and at a time when the structure and definition of the family was transformed. I argue that Americans justified taking a family vacation out of their commitment to the idea that travel together would strengthen family bonds, and that travel provided a way to educate children as citizens.[10]

The history of family vacations highlights changing patterns of family life, such as the relationship between work and play, the increase in the number of working women, or the generation gap of the 1960s. Public policy debates about the decline of the family feature the so-called traditional family as a foil to family pathologies today. But historians realize that the family of the television sitcoms like *Father Knows Best* never really existed. Instead, a variety of families inhabited the world of postwar America—immigrants and African Americans, Catholics and Jews—and a middle class that encompassed a wide disparity in income levels.[11] The nightly news features about changes in family patterns, such as a decrease in the rate of divorce or an increase in the number of unmarried parents, raise concerns that call for a more nuanced portrait of family behavior in the postwar years. This book aims to contribute to the revival of family history as a field by linking the family as a social institution to broader historical change in the postwar period.[12]

Tracing the history of the family vacation allows us to set family history within the context of postwar culture. Looking at ordinary people and how they chose to spend their money and time helps us understand what they valued for themselves and their children. We see how war veterans took their children to the Lincoln Memorial to teach them about the ideals they had fought for in the war that had just ended. We see how African Americans called on the federal government to ensure equal access to roadside motels and restaurants. We see how parents took their children to the national parks to show them the natural wonders of America. We see how Jewish immigrants constructed their own resort culture of food and humor in the Catskills, only to see it rejected by their children.

These histories of private life inform inquiries about broader currents in public life in postwar America, when the personal became political. Civil rights activism empowered the federal government to battle racial segregation, imposing national ideals of justice on local customs even while local cultures resisted change. Lodging and dining corporations expanded through franchising to satisfy the demands of families for convenient quality on a budget, putting small mom-and-pop motels and resorts out of business. Conservationists who feared tourism would damage the national wilderness agitated for protection, resulting in a broader environmental movement supported by those who had camped in the national parks. The story of family vacationing in postwar America is a story of changes in private and public life, and the blurring of the two that changed family and society.[13]

Today's baby boomers (those born between 1946 and 1964) still remember the sights they saw and the squabbles in the backseat, and they still keep the souvenirs they treasured as children. Those memories can be found in the family photograph album, on home movies, or in an oral tradition of favorite family stories. Because memories of family travel are reconstructed later than the actual events, they are not wholly accurate representations of the past. However, memories hold a key to understanding how people see their family as shaping their identities. This book not only reconstructs the vacation habits of middle-class Americans in the postwar period, but it also interprets memories of family vacations to understand the broader cultural meaning of family travel.[14]

The importance of the family vacation can be traced in the reminiscences of those whose memories shaped their perceptions of their country, their culture, and their family. Author Calvin Trillin (though not a baby boomer himself) recalls his childhood travels with ironic humor: "I might have seen more of America when I was a child if I hadn't had to spend so much of my time protecting my half of the back seat from incursions by my sister, Sukey." His father, who owned a grocery store in Kansas City, took a few weeks off every summer because "he had decided it was important for us to see the country." Usually they drove west to California, where they concluded their drive with a few weeks in a tourist court in Santa Monica. Trillin treasured the stops at the roadside zoos his father favored that were "come-ons for filling stations or maybe even flimflam dice games," because "the stops were about the only time I could concentrate on what I was supposed to be seeing, relieved temporarily from the tension of maintaining a full border alert in the back seat."[15] Trillin's memories are couched in the dynamics of the family, sibling rivalry and a dominant father who controlled the vehicle and thus the itinerary. The mother is notably absent in his recollection, but surely she was sitting in the front seat reading the map or handing out cups of lemonade.

Reflecting on road trips taken when he was an adult, Trillin remarks, "Growing up tends not to cure Americans of the notion that the number of miles covered is an important gauge to the success of pleasure travel." Indeed, he realized "Americans drive across the country as if someone's chasing them." After his children had grown, he was sorry that "Alice and I and the girls never took the same sort of car trip that I used to take with my parents and Sukey." For him, those trips were about family and about America: "I still think back a lot on those trips I took as a child, especially when I'm driving through some part of the country I particularly like the looks of." At those moments, "I sometimes imagine myself at the wheel and my own girls in the backseat, in an air-conditioned car this time, but still, somehow, on Route 66." His sense of nostalgia, for a time and a place that cannot be recovered (and perhaps never really existed), is palpable.[16]

Not all family memories are so nostalgic. Like family life at home, family vacations could be fraught with tension and conflict. In "Compulsory Travel," poet Lucia Perillo remembers feeling trapped by family travel. Her family's yearly sojourn at the Jersey Shore is recalled as a needless frustration, symbolized by the fact that they were taken to a pool and could not even swim. Perillo remembers best the family fights while on the road: "Yet each year we made a ritual of this week/Spent yelling and cursing and swatting each other . . . /Back then a sock in the jaw could set anyone straight." The poet describes in detail the frustration of her father battling the weekend traffic jam and his aggressive behavior "changing lanes and leaning on the horn." Perillo's slow-moving family car did not even stir a breeze, so "the car would hold our body heat like an iron skillet." Uncomfortably hot, sunburned, and bored, "we hurled pretzels and gave the finger to kids stopped in cars beside us." Her parents fought, too, in subtle plays for power from which children learned about the tensions in a marriage: "My mother wouldn't mention the turn we'd missed/a few miles back; instead she'd fold the map/And jam it resolutely in the glove box while we crept on." Reflecting on their aggressive behavior by borrowing from Churchill's tribute to his people at war, Perillo muses, "Perhaps this was our finest hour, as the people/we were becoming took shape and began to emerge:/the honkers of horns and the givers of fingers." Perillo makes her point clear: vacations shaped the children into belligerent Americans claiming their rights as citizens on the road.[17]

Memories of vacations can provide glimpses of families that fractured in the stresses of the 1960s. Soozie Tyrell, a backup musician to lead artists like Bruce Springsteen, wrote a song about the family vacations of her childhood called "White Lines":[18]

On the wheels of a Chevy 1964
Dad packed the family and drove
From the Chesapeake to the bay of Frisco
All the way we camped beneath the stars
Unaware of my folks uncivil war
But life seemed good at seven years old
With my hand out the car window hair blowin' back
Scoopin' the wind and the white lines on the road.

Tyrell remembers the fights in the backseat and the long-armed threats of her father to behave. "My two sisters and me in the back seat/Fightin' cause we're bored to tears/Wooly-Bully blarin' on the radio, Dad yellin' I can swing from here." From the first verse the song has traveled in time and space to the parents' divorce, breaking up the childhood family: "Everything tore loose 1974/Dad packed his Chevy and drove/To a small apartment north of town." Tyrell concludes with her own statement on family travel: "A six piece band is my family/And home is where we can get some sleep." Her life on the road with her band simultaneously signifies her rootlessness and the freedom she finds in life on the road.

These recollections of family vacations tell us about the families taking the vacation. Each recollection is told from the vantage point of a child in the backseat battling for space with brothers or sisters. The children fought because they were bored. Even from the backseat, the father is seen as powerful and dominant, exercising his authority with corporal punishment. The mother is largely invisible, or she serves as the navigator, blamed for any wrong turn or wielding the bit of power she has by refusing to give directions. Whether the vacation is remembered as a happy memory, a portent of family disintegration, or both, baby boomers remember their vacations with nostalgia for a world that is lost, even if they hated sitting in the backseat.

Memories of family travel led some of those children in the backseat to choose their life's work. When he was eight years old, Robert Smithson's parents took him on a tour around the United States. The trip made a huge impression on him, and he later recalled putting on postcard shows for his friends. So great was Smithson's enthusiasm for travel that his parents allowed him to plan their vacations to Florida, California, and the national parks of the West. Smithson's love of travel developed in childhood was crucial to his art, which required him to travel to remote locations to find the materials for his famed earthwork sculptures, like *Spiral Jetty.* His sensitivity to locale—geography and climate, the light and feel of a place—was developed in childhood on family trips. And his nonsite installations provoked viewers to travel to the far-flung locations of his earthworks art.[19]

Family memories offer us a way to make sense of our family history. For one it was a journey of American family identity in the making. Nancy Heller's father left Nuremberg for the United States in 1937 at the age of eleven, just in time to escape the Holocaust. He worked as an economist at a large insurance company, married a woman who was also a German émigré, and had three children. He earned a second income doing taxes for people in the Washington Heights neighborhood where they lived in New York City. The money went to help support his widowed mother and for vacations. Nancy recalls, "We went on nice vacations but would only shop at sale racks."

Nancy remembers a family vacation from New York City to the West in 1967, when she was eleven years old, her brother thirteen, and her sister eight. The vacation took place after her brother's bar mitzvah, for which her grandmother had traveled from Haifa, Israel. The family flew to Salt Lake City, where they picked up a rental car for the rest of the two-week trip. Eight persons crowded into the station wagon: the two parents, three children, her two grandmothers (who were sisters), and Clairie, a friend of one grandmother from her days in photography school in Switzerland. The journey west may have been motivated by the German fascination with the Old West, which her grandmothers had always wanted to see.[20]

Her father drove, and her mother navigated. Her grandmother from Israel did not speak English very well, so the adults conversed in German, which Nancy did not understand. Her brother was prone to car sickness and had to sit near the front, so Nancy always sat in the rear-facing third seat with her sister or Clairie, and she read comic books. Nancy remembers the scene as "total madness" with the two grandmothers competing for the children's attention by bribing them with candy. "Father was a lamb and never hit us," recalls Nancy, but her mother was known to threaten the children with a ruler.

The trip was well organized because they followed an itinerary that they had ordered from the American Automobile Association. She remembers Clairie getting her up early at Bryce Canyon to take photographs of the sunrise. She remembers going to the Grand Canyon and visiting the Hoover Dam near Las Vegas. At the national parks they stayed in cabins; because they needed three rooms everywhere they went, staying at the parks kept costs down. The family avoided what they called "TTs"—tourist traps—and bought only a few souvenirs, but they did take photographs. Their frugality (and the fact they kept kosher) meant they ate breakfast in the motel and carried lunch supplies in a round Scotch cooler in the car (tuna or peanut butter and jelly). They stopped at picnic grounds for lunch and went out for dinner. After a visit to Disneyland (where they stayed in a nearby motel), they drove up the coast of California on Route 1 and visited Hearst Castle and the redwood forests. They saw San Francisco, then flew home.[21]

Their story is more than the story of an American family on a road trip west; it is also the story of becoming American through travel, of the transferal of the family, with all its cultural baggage, from Europe to modern America. At the time of the vacation, Nancy was the same age her father was when he escaped Germany. Her coming-of-age travel, the vacation to the West, was a measure of his achievement in becoming American and having an American family. Three generations were brought together in this cultural ritual of the American family vacation.

The family road trip as a form of vacation occurred as a result of specific economic and demographic forces in a culture that prized the family ideal. Although families had long been taking vacations, in the postwar period, family vacations became common as a national tradition. Economic prosperity and high rates of fertility were important in making the family vacation a dominant form of travel from the end of World War II in 1945 to the early 1970s. The 1973 oil embargo is just one of a cluster of events that signaled the end of an era of unparalleled abundance and a shift in cultural authority as baby boomers came of age in a time of sexual revolution, women's liberation, and youth radicalism.

The word *family,* like other social constructions of identity, is malleable and constantly evolving. In this book I focus on families who fit the family ideal of the period, the nuclear family of husband and wife with young children living in the same household. Obviously not all families fit the ideal, but the image of the nuclear family was nevertheless a dominant cultural force. Family patterns did change in the middle decades of the century, but changes in the popular ideal lagged behind changes in society.[22] I have purposely limited my study to exclude travel by families without children because taking children along alters the travel experience of the family vacation. Often other relatives joined the family—grandparents, aunts and uncles, cousins—so the notion of taking the whole family includes the extended family. To set my study within the middle-class family milieu, I have excluded discussion of travel by the wealthy because they are not representative of the mainstream family vacation pattern of domestic car travel. The poorest did not take family vacations, but I have included the working class because most of the middle class found ways to travel within their limited means. A vacation is defined here as a pleasure trip away from home for a week or more, although some families may have combined a vacation with a parent's business travel.[23]

The family vacations of postwar America were characterized by four broad patterns. First and foremost, they were road trips. Car ownership by families rose from 54 percent in 1948 to 77 percent in 1960, and 82 percent by 1970.[24] Every year Detroit churned out new models of sedans and wagons designed to meet the needs of family consumers. A 1962 government report found that 84 percent of Americans traveled by car on their vacations. Car travel remained popular because it was economical (the roomy cars could hold even the largest family) and flexible (they could travel any distance and change plans to suit a family's needs). Even when the oil embargo caused the price of gasoline to rise, auto travel was still the cheapest form of family transportation.[25]

Second, the entire family went on vacation together. The mass habit of family vacations took shape within a culture that prized the family ideal consisting of an image of the white middle-class family of a male breadwinner and his housewife spouse. Over one-third of all vacation trips of those surveyed in 1961 involved husband, wife, and children, and an additional number included other relatives as well.[26] Taking a family vacation was justified by adherence to the ideal of family togetherness, out of a belief that a vacation would strengthen family bonds. Even as families changed, the vacation served as a normalizing ritual asserting the importance of belonging to a family—any kind of family.

Third, the family vacation became a consumption habit of the middle class, even a badge of status. Spending money on a vacation was like buying a car; it advertised that one could afford to spend time and money for leisure activities away from home. In order to travel, Americans rode the wave of postwar consumerism, buying a roomy family car for the vacation or a carload of camping equipment, all necessary objects to make a comfortable trip for the whole family. Of course, the reality of vacationing as a family could never match Madison Avenue's portrait of family harmony, but consumers put faith in the products or places advertised in the pages of the nation's newspapers and magazines.

Fourth, family travel helped Americans understand their status as citizens in the American nation. From the earliest tourist trips to Niagara Falls in the 1830s, travel has been one way for Americans to claim a national identity in a ritual of "mobile citizenship."[27] American parents took their children on pilgrimages to national monuments, from the White House to Old Faithful, to cultivate a sense of civic identity and attachment to American history. In the postwar period, this was true for all, even excluded groups like Jews and blacks who created separate travel subcultures while they fought for their full rights as citizens to travel freely, including the right to use public accommodations.

This book explores these common patterns of the family vacation by first explaining why the family vacation became so popular and how it was a distinctively American cultural ritual. The first chapter explains the emergence of the family vacation as a product of mass consumerism and heightened sense of family togetherness. Spending money on cars, suitcases, and vacation clothes was justified by a domestic ideal that was both reassuring and good for the economy. In Chapter 2, I contend that in an era fraught with cold war tension, families relied on maps and guides designed to appeal to family travelers. Through travel to Washington, D.C., and other historic sites, parents tutored themselves and their children in American history and patriotic values. Chapter 3 examines travel and citizenship by showing how racial discrimination limited the mobility of African Americans who traveled in a segregated space while it privileged the needs of white travelers. Civil rights proponents paraded the ideal of the family vacation to argue for equality in public accommodations in the Civil Rights Act of 1964.

The second half of the book presents variations on the vacation ritual, accomplished by focusing on common types of family travel: the western adventure, the camping vacation, and summering at rural resorts. Chapter 4 argues that curiosity and a thirst for adventure stoked by the mythology of the Wild West lured families to the western United States. Some families sought authentic adventure by staying at dude ranches, but many tourists found virtual adventure more convenient by visiting theme parks with their mock gunfights and thrill rides. Chapter 5 explains how family camping was promoted as an affordable way to explore natural wonders, but vacations in crowded and hazardous national parks hardly measured up to the ideal. The last chapter explores the habits of families who favored rural recreation at family resorts at the lake or in the mountains, creating a home away from home. The epilogue comments on how family vacationing has been adapted to retain its vitality as a cultural ritual in a nation that has been transformed in the last half century.

This book is about families searching for America as they traveled. They looked for America on cross-country trips to historic sites and in pilgrimages to Washington, D.C., the nation's capital. African American travelers sought the justice America promised them in its founding ideals, an America of freedom and equality denied them on the road, where they traveled in racially segregated space. Families traveled to the West, the quintessential America where the attractions of cowboys and Indians of the Old West gave way to a New West of Hollywood and space-age technology. Families searched for America in the national parks, where nature's monuments were civilized for their enjoyment. And in summer's heat, they retreated to rustic lake and mountain cabins in search of an older America, a place where they could be welcomed with their families in a summer community.[28]

For the "greatest generation," those who raised families in postwar America, the family vacation was a way to school their children in their own values, to acquaint them with their own heritage, and to see themselves as citizens of a mighty nation. Travel helped children forge a personal and civic identity as they grew up in an era of cold war anxiety, mass consumerism, and racial tension. Thus it is also a story of how Americans navigated the transformations of the twentieth century through travel together as a family.

chapter one

Selling the Family Vacation

When I was twelve years old, my family went on vacation to Yellowstone National Park. We borrowed a friend's camper and the nine of us piled in. My parents sat in the cab with my younger brothers, and my three sisters and I traveled inside the camper that sat in the bed of the red truck. The camper was a nifty little house on wheels, with a table, cushioned benches that turned into beds, a little stove and fridge and tiny sink, and a large bed over the cab. For most of the drive, my sisters and I played cards. It kept us from fighting. We were so involved in our game that my father had to stop the truck, get out, and open the back door of the camper to tell us to look at the Tetons. We gave the scenery a quick glance and went back to our card game.

One of the reasons for going to Yellowstone was that my mother had some rich relatives who lived in a family compound of cabins. The women and children spent summers there, and the men joined them on weekends and for a week or two. The cabins (large houses, really) clustered around the beach of Hebgen Lake. I remember they had their own dock, and speedboats and rowboats were tied to the dock. My only other memory of the trip is walking on the wooden walkways around the Morning Glory pool at Yellowstone and Mother saying that it was her favorite sight. I don't remember seeing any bears, nor do I recall seeing Old Faithful.

If one symbol remains of the trip, it is not Old Faithful or the bears, but the card game in the camper. Maybe it is our only common memory because it is the most-repeated anecdote about the trip. It neatly symbolizes the way we see our family in three groups: parents, the four girls (born between 1949 and 1954), and the three boys (born between 1955 and 1963). We girls were baby boomers, children of the greatest generation, World War II veterans and their brides. Mom and Dad married in 1948 after knowing each other only a few months. Mother abandoned her college studies not long after marrying Dad, and as a farmer's daughter, she knew how to pinch pennies as a homemaker. Dad finished college and earned a business degree in New York City before joining his father at the small-town furniture store. The partnership did not last, and Dad went on to earn his doctorate in business administration from Harvard, five children in tow; a sixth was born in Cambridge. The Yellowstone vacation took place upon our return from the years of graduate school in the East, after Dad took a job in his hometown to be a professor at the local university, and after my youngest brother was born.

The family vacation had long been a popular practice by the time we took our trip to Yellowstone. Recovery from World War II was just underway when Americans resumed their habit of the summer vacation. In "America Takes a Trip," *Business Week* predicted that "In this summer of 1947, more Americans than ever before will get trout lines tangled in trees, upset canoes, and recuperate from sunburn. They are jamming highways, airports and railway stations to travel farther in greater luxury, stay longer—and spend more money." A large share of American travelers was made up of families on vacation, who did not let tight budgets or the prospect of traveling with their children stop them from gassing up the family car and setting out across the country. The American Automobile Association (AAA) noticed in 1950 that "there's a greater trend this year toward family vacations; more parents are taking their children with them." Indeed, the AAA declared that "typical American vacationers . . . will still climb into the family car to take a look at the continental United States."[1] In the years after war's end, American families were on the road.

The roots of the family vacation ritual can be traced back to the nineteenth century, when Americans found ways to justify leisure in a culture with a strong work ethic by "working at play."[2] But it was not until after World War II that family vacationing became a widespread practice accessible to the middle class, financed by an increase in paid vacation benefits to American workers and facilitated by the federal government's construction of new interstate highways. Automobile manufacturers, oil companies, and the hospitality industry tailored their products to American families on the road. Consumers became convinced that buying cars and toys, eating at fast food restaurants, or staying at roadside motels would make the vacation an enjoyable and memorable experience for the whole family. The family transformed the American roadside landscape as they hit the road.

Making Vacations Possible

More middle-class families could afford to take vacations because of the increasingly liberal vacation benefits awarded American workers in the late 1940s. A Department of Labor report in 1948 declared that "paid vacation clauses are now a standard feature of union agreements in most industries." By the end of 1944, 85 percent of union agreements contained vacation provisions for workers. The inclusion of paid vacation benefits in labor agreements resulted in part from the acceptance of vacations as beneficial to the worker "not only because it makes possible leisure and relief from everyday cares and duties, but also because the right to a vacation with pay is a mark of social status and a recognition of the worth and dignity of the ordinary laboring man." Unions argued that vacations were necessary "to combat fatigue and to maintain good health" and improve the standard of living for the workers. Furthermore, they were good for the employer because paid vacations had a "beneficial effect of relaxation and recreation upon labor morale [and] productive efficiency," and they were thought to reduce worker turnover.[3]

In the following decade, paid vacations became widespread (93 percent of collective bargaining agreements contained vacation provisions in 1949), and provisions were liberalized. Two innovations occurred: reducing the length of service required to earn vacation time, and awarding longer vacation periods for time of service. Vacation provisions thus expanded from one week for one to four years of service, to two weeks after as little as two years of service. And upper-rank workers could expect to be paid for a three-week vacation with fifteen years of service. By 1956, only 18 percent of hourly employees were held to a two-week ceiling of vacations, and paid holidays were more common. Management trade literature boasted that "longer vacations and additional holidays are giving the employee more leisure at no loss in pay." Vacation taking had achieved its acceptance because industrialists realized that "our people are human beings and planned time-off recreation is a vital thing. . . . From a selfish point of view, it pays off both to the employee and the company." Indeed, an economist pointed out that both workers and employers were so convinced of the benefits of vacationing that they sacrificed "possible greater gains in real income."[4]

The spreading network of interstates and the upgrading of highways paved the way for car travel. In the summer of 1956 President Dwight D.

Eisenhower signed the $25 billion Federal-Aid Highway Act, which authorized federal funding for constructing interstate highways and created an ongoing fund supported by a federal tax on fuel. The federal government would henceforth pay 90 percent of construction costs of highways set to exacting federal standards. The legislation stipulated that construction of the interstate highway system was to be completed by 1972. The legislation was met with immense enthusiasm by mayors, manufacturers, and consumers alike. In a series of articles in the popular press about highways and safety called Freedom of the American Road, Ford Motor Company linked the new roadways with the idea of American mobility. More roads meant more freedom for Americans to travel wherever they wanted.[5]

The popular press educated readers on how to adjust to the changes in the roads. Family magazines like *Better Homes and Gardens* featured articles explaining the new roadway system to their readers. "You'll be on one-way ribbons of highway so wide and safe your whole family can feel free from strain and worry," promised one writer. Some feared the higher speed limits made the new roads more dangerous, or that they were monotonous because they bypassed historic towns. Their merits were faster travel through better engineering: "You don't follow winding valleys—you zoom right across them." Safety was a big selling point: "you'll never meet a car coming your way." The new highways meant an "escape from roads that have dotted our landscape with death." Of course, drivers had to learn to drive differently at higher speeds, with plenty of distance between cars to avoid rear-end crashes. Still, readers were told that "your family is at least *four times safer* than on ordinary roads."[6]

Already 1,600 miles of highway were in use in eighteen states and another thousand miles were under construction in 1956. Ohio had opened a cross-state toll road that linked Midwest and East "for modern travel." Indiana's toll road connected Chicago with New England, and in Massachusetts, a road through the Berkshire Mountains tied it to New York State's Thruway. Route 66 was pushing from Chicago to Springfield, Missouri, and Oklahoma was constructing a turnpike to link Tulsa to Oklahoma City.[7] The building frenzy of highway construction transformed vacationing by allowing travelers to go further and faster on the new roads.

The Family Car

The family road trip took shape in a culture of automobility characterized by widespread automobile ownership. Car ownership by families rose from 54 percent in 1948 to 77 percent in 1960 and 82 percent by 1970. The family car was a home on wheels, an extension of the domestic space, and thus represented a sense of security for the traveling family on the road. Car manufacturers appealed to American consumers' sense of the car as part of home in their advertising. In 1949 Ford advertised its popular sedan as "a living room on wheels!" Even its seats were "sofa wide."[8] The family car was a cocoon that buffered the family from the outside world and increased their sense of security while they traveled to unfamiliar places.

Car ownership increased dramatically after the war. As factories switched from wartime to peacetime production, automobile companies reassured consumers that cars would soon be available for purchase. Wartime shortages of steel and rubber meant 25 percent would wait for a new car before going on vacation, and many would need to wait for new tires. Ford Motor Company's 1946 ad campaign declared "There's a Ford in your future" and featured illustrations of families gazing into a crystal ball to see a vision of themselves in the new vehicle. Families were thus asked to picture themselves in the car they could not yet buy. Ford made a strong pitch to the family with a scene of a mother and daughter dressed in traveling clothes watching Dad load luggage into the trunk. Its headline noted, "It's big new H.P. V-8 engine says: Let's Go!" The copy appealed to those who would take the family car on vacation: "You'll want to start packing your suitcases when you own the big new Ford!" Another ad emphasized that the ride was "smoother than ever." The family scene pictured in the ad showed the backseat of the car, where the ride was so smooth that Mother could knit, Son could color with crayons, and Little Sister could sleep soundly while cuddling her plush toy.[9] As families waited for a car, they could plan a vacation, promised an ad that pictured Dad in an easy chair looking at a travel brochure, with Son looking on and Mother perched on the armrest. The Ford would be worth the wait because "From start to finish of jaunt or journey you'll ride in gentle comfort. And as mile as carefree mile unrolls, you'll discover this new car is thrifty, too."[10]

Buying a car was seen as a decision involving the entire family. "FORD'S OUT FRONT WITH ALL THE FAMILY!" was the headline in 1947 as Americans were on the market for a new vehicle. The advertising copy was inclusive: it stressed the input of each family member in choosing a Ford. Dad liked the engine's power, Mother the "roomy interior" and "deep, soft seats," Sister "the smooth lines and 'baked-on' enamel finish," and Brother the "king-size brakes" and "Lifeguard" body. Ford Lifeguard's heavy-gauge body was a safety feature promoted in ads.[11]

Car manufacturers appealed to women, who were behind the wheel more often than before the war. Women's magazines featured Ford ads that declared, "Ford's out front with Mrs. America!" The ads appealed to women as mothers who would feel safe in the car or housewives running errands who liked the way the car handled. Working women were also featured in the ads, such as an interior decorator who said, "if I were paid to 'do' Ford interiors I couldn't do a better job." A schoolteacher boasted that the car got her to school on time, emphasizing its reliability. The car as an extension of home was used to justify women's use of cars, as one clever headline proclaimed, "A Woman's Place is in the ~~Home~~ FORD!"[12]

As auto production reached 6,672,00 passenger cars in 1950, an increase of 30 percent over 1949, men had the final say on buying a car, so manufacturers appealed to men in car ads. Ads that featured all members of the family pointing out the car's features to Dad reinforced his decision-making power when it came to buying a car. In "Pop played dumb about the new Ford," the children did the research and told Dad which car to buy before he admits that he already bought the car. Dad's pipe and armchair enhanced his authority as the children gathered at his knee. Ford ads dealt with men's concern about the value of a dollar by promising that you could "take an extra week's vacation on what you save" by buying a Ford.[13] Despite the family councils, Dad was the one who bought the family car.

The station wagon was the quintessential family car, roomy enough for the bigger postwar family and their gear. Ford began marketing the station wagon as a family car in 1947, but the decade of the 1950s was the heyday of the station wagon. Ford produced 29,000 wagons in 1950, and ten times that in 1955. Production peaked at 340,000 in 1956, and then dipped to 172,000 in 1960. The cost of a station wagon rose as amenities were added to the car, from just over $2,000 to $2,685 as a factory price in 1959. Customers could choose a base model or select from the City Squire models with heavier engines, greater capacity, and more doors.[14]

Advertisements for station wagons that appeared in family magazines emphasized their spacious interiors with illustrations showing how much (or how many) could fit in one car. "There's always room for one more in a Ford Ranch Wagon," declared a 1954 ad showing four children and a dog. The station wagon was big enough for Dad to load furniture or Mother to bring along a baby carriage. In 1957, Ford added a third seat to its Country Squire wagon, so it could accommodate nine passengers. By 1964, when those babies had hit their growth spurts, the wagon was the only answer to a growing family. One ad depicted the plight of a mother with a large family: "She had so many children she didn't know what to do—until she got a new Ford wagon." Plymouth wagon advertisements claimed, "you get more kid-and-cargo room than you'll ever fill up."[15]

Consumer choices about family cars were shaped by what buyers thought would work for the family vacation. Ford boasted that "There's no vacation like a Ford vacation" in its 1956 ad for Thunderbird. Advertisements set cars in beach or shoreline scenes, or pictured them in landscapes of the West. Ford's Ranch Wagon, pictured in a Colorado corral, was meant for the West. The western theme appeared also in discussions about the cost of a car. Ford boasted that its car was "Big Chief of the Low-Price Tribe," and that "never did so little 'wampum' buy so much car." Buyers were advised to "come in for a Pow Wow on the new kind of Ford." Chevrolet featured its 1954 Delray Coupe in a scene with mother unloading groceries at a woodsy cabin, while Boy plays with the dog and Sister carries a tennis racket. The copy read, "That family up there has everything it takes to enjoy a wonderful vacation—a fine place to go and a fine new Chevrolet to get them there."[16]

American Motors advertised its Rambler 1962 Cross Country Station Wagon as an "amazing vacation machine!" Equipped with "Airliner Reclining Seats" for sleeping or napping, "it makes travel less tiring." Air-conditioning kept the passengers cool, and "with luggage in the Travel Rack, the big cargo area becomes a king-size playpen." Rambler emphasized the car's ability on the road: "It performs better, and you can feel it. Starts. Hills. Straightaways. Every way. In short it makes the greatest vacation you ever spent."[17]

In an appeal to the instincts of parents to make vacations educational, in the summer of 1959 Ford advertised its car as "America's schoolhouse on wheels." The illustration depicted a Mercury Country Cruiser and called it a "home away from home for the whole family." The four-person family was surrounded by historical figures, and ad copy declared, "It's a big country, and our history was made all over it. The way to see it is by car. Traveling great distances is no problem in our full-sized, comfortable American cars." The educational appeal was also patriotic, featuring the car as a vehicle to the heroes of the past, from New England's forefathers to Abraham Lincoln's Illinois, and "across the great plains to the place where Custer stood against the Indians."[18]

Family cars were meant for family fun, and advertisements reinforced the idea that recreation improved family relations. An ad for the Plymouth Suburban station wagon in 1957 offered a testimonial: "Life has taken on a big lift for the whole family since we got our new Suburban."

There's always room for one more

in a FORD Ranch Wagon!

The Customline Ranch Wagon

Now four Ford quick-change artists...and each with the smooth, agile "Go" of Ford's modern V-8 engine!

If your family's young and rambling, you'll find room aplenty in Ford's new Mainline or Customline Ranch Wagons. Both are 6-passengers big, yet convert to cargo haulers by merely folding the "stowaway" seat into the floor. Ford also offers the 4-door, 8-passenger Country Squire and Country Sedan.

No matter which Ford "wagon" suits your needs, you may have the most modern V-8 engine in the industry (or most modern Six, if you prefer) . . . new Ball-Joint Front Suspension . . . colorful new interiors . . . and a host of other "Worth More" advantages which make Ford your *smartest* station wagon buy!

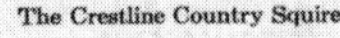

The Crestline Country Squire

The Customline Country Sedan

The Mainline Ranch Wagon

Worth More when you buy it... Worth More when you sell it!

Station wagons were roomy and comfortable for long vacations. Ford Ranch Wagon, 1954. (Author's collection.)

Auto companies like Ford promoted the educational value of vacations to sell cars. America's Schoolhouse on Wheels, 1959. (Courtesy Benson Ford Research Center.)

The illustration pictured the family at the beach with three children, Dad holding a picnic basket and daughter ready to toss a beach ball off the tailgate. The Suburban's third rear-facing seat made even more room for bigger families. Plymouth called it the "Observation Seat" and promised, "Kids love it!"[19]

The growing size of the family car satisfied a consumer appetite for size. In 1959 Ford proclaimed in its ads: "Our cars are family-sized—comfortable and roomy—because that's how America wants them." Ford advertisements boasted, "it takes broad-shouldered automobiles—our typical American cars—to fit our new ways of living in this country. Put the groceries in the rear, packages on the floor, put the paint in the trunk with the wallpaper, and be careful of the flowers." Ford cars were "America's family shopping cart," with "plenty of room." Advertisements like this one highlighted middle-class consumerism and the appetite for cars big enough to hold all the goods prosperity could buy.[20]

Although family cars of the 1950s had a sturdy auto body and good brakes, they were not equipped with passenger restraints. Some recommended seat belts for "comfort and safety" as early as the mid-1950s. One travel writer suggested, "they brace Mother when Dad's driving on winding roads." But critics warned that they could cause internal injuries or slow escape from a car on fire or underwater. A "safety pillow," a crude precursor to today's airbag, could be purchased and attached to the dashboard with suction cups. Safety equipment became more important with the 1966 National Traffic and Motor Vehicle Safety Act (effective January 1968), which mandated that manufacturers equip new vehicles with lap or shoulder belts, padded instrument panels, seat backs, sun visors, and armrests. The first child restraint standards in 1971 banned flimsy child car seats that hooked over the seatback, and it required that all child car restraints be anchored and pass tests for rigidity. With that law, child seats had to be designed to protect a child in the event of a crash. Still, car safety seats for children were not in general use until the 1980s, so most children were free to move around the car on family road trips.[21] The lack of safety restraints made taking children in the car a complicated challenge, as we shall see.

Planning the Vacation

The family vacation required careful planning and budgeting. Oil companies helped their customers get on the road (and consume their products) by publishing travel guides. Shell Oil Company created a travel guide written by their women's travel director, Carol Lane. This "invaluable guide book" was to "fit into the glove compartment of any car." The foreword makes clear that Lane is writing for women readers when she says that "traveling by car is like baking a cake. If you don't know how to do it, it can fall flat." Readers needed her guide just as much as they needed their cookbooks. Indeed, "this book contains hundreds of recipes for car travel." Lane guaranteed good results because her advice had been "road tested by thousands of inveterate car travelers." If readers used the guide, their next trip would be "more fun, more comfortable, and less expensive." Despite its womanly tone, vacation decisions were generally made by both husband and wife, with women making the decision more often at the lower end of the economic scale, and men more often for those with higher incomes.[22]

The Shell guide advised readers to plan but not overplan their trips. Sensitive to the limits of time and the family budget, the guide advised a brainstorming session and then narrowing the choice down to two or three alternatives. Of utmost importance was pondering the question of what a vacation was to accomplish. A vacation "should be a time to do all the things you don't ordinarily have the opportunity to do, to see some of the things you're interested in, but never get around to." Once the general destination was agreed upon, the guide advised using a map (from Shell, of course) to determine the radius of two hundred to three hundred miles a day. Then readers should write to the sources of information about the destination: "automobile clubs, state tourist bureaus, and local chambers of commerce." Only after receiving information should families make final plans.[23]

Next, the family should look at the budget. The largest expense was accommodations, estimated at $7 a day, for double occupancy ($4 for one person). Hotels rates varied from $5 to $30 a day, plus tips of 10 percent. Rates for children were less, but children were not free. Given the charges for children, it was not unheard of for parents to sneak children past the manager into the room so they would not be charged. To reduce expenses, travelers could choose to camp (about $1 a night) or stay in a tourist court. In 1954, when this guide was published, motels had not yet developed nationwide franchise networks, so the best alternative to an expensive hotel was a cheaper tourist court.[24]

Food was a variable expense, calculated at about $3.50 a day per person, with an additional $2.60 per person a day for entertainment and tips. Automobile operating costs were less variable. Fuel costs were projected to be 2.1 cents a mile, or about 28 cents a gallon. For a two-week vacation of 1,500 miles, auto maintenance costs (fuel and tolls) were estimated to be about $50. Finally, vacation planners were advised to take into account the costs of entertainment, such as entrance fees to parks, fishing license fees, rental of sports equipment, laundry expenses, and miscellaneous expenses for "those minor items that you meant to bring from home but forgot." To keep an eye on expenses, travelers should keep track of expenses so they would not run out of money, or so that they could afford a "splurge" at the end of the trip.[25]

WHAT TO PACK

Vacations required a special wardrobe, according to the Shell guide. Women should think of taking four "costumes" for a two-week vacation, outfits that were versatile and would fit into a twenty-six-inch suitcase. First on the list was a travel suit of skirt, jacket, and blouse. The jacket could be removed in warmer weather, and it should have a cut that allowed ease of movement. Straight skirts were to be avoided because they rode up while sitting or driving, so full or gored skirts were recommended. Fabrics should be lightweight wool or a synthetic blend in "medium tones of gray, beige, black, navy, and brown." For evening, the guide recommended a two-piece dress that could be worn informally or dressed up. The blouse should have a neckline "that can be worn prim or plunging," and the fabric should be a dressier synthetic, silk, or jersey. Rounding out the wardrobe was a "spectator sports ensemble" of a skirt, colorful strapless or halter top, and a bolero jacket in matching color. The jacket could be removed in the heat or worn "for the sake of propriety or for protection against the evening breeze." Finally, a woman on the road would need a "rugged-life costume" of sports blouse and shorts (or the flattering pedal pushers). Because "slacks are frowned upon" in many resorts, especially the East, women were advised to wear pants only when engaged in active sports.[26]

Women were advised to take along accessories of low-heeled shoes, one "roomy purse" and an evening clutch, two scarves, two sets of jewelry (daytime and glittering), and two belts. A stole might be added for evening. A "crushable, versatile" hat was essential, perhaps a velvet cloche or sporty beret. For bad weather, women should take along a light raincoat, sweater, and "drizzle boots." Lingerie should include a nightgown, robe, "two slips, two bras, two pairs of gloves or socks, three pairs of panties and stockings." What to pack depended on the destination. For a resort, she might also need a bathing suit, beach cover-up, extra shirt, shorts, and "play shoes." For outdoors, she should pack "dungarees" (denim trousers), a sport jacket, and hiking shoes. For a city trip, an extra dress and walking shoes would suffice.[27]

Men were advised to take a gray suit and a blue suit, a tan sport coat, and brown slacks for a total of nine outfits. Synthetic fibers meant men could reduce the number of shirts, sport shirts, and socks because they "are easily washable, require no pressing, and dry in from three to six hours." The guide contained much less detail for men than for women, but it did not trust men's fashion sense. It cautioned men against wearing "the wildest and brightest clothes they can find" because "garish" clothing would stand out and reduce the versatility of the wardrobe. Men were advised to go to a clothing store for advice and to "select garments which will not look as if they have been slept in after a few hours of wear." Presumably women bought men's clothes or store clerks told them what to wear because men could not be trusted to pick out their own travel wardrobe.[28]

Children's wardrobes were simpler. Most important was to pack washable and wrinkle-resistant clothing or the new synthetics like Orlon, nylon, and rayon, or good-quality cotton and wool. The goal was to "keep the squirming car rider looking reasonably neat" and to cut down on luggage space by packing less clothing. Slacks were appropriate for both boys and girls, and they could be made out of denim or other easy-care fabrics. Children should not wear dungarees in the car because "they're not suitable for wear even in a roadside restaurant. They should be packed only for emergencies." Girls could look more "feminine" in "wide, easy-to move-around-in skirts," and boys should have a jacket and both should have a sweater. Cotton T-shirts were best for both boys and girls, but parents should also take along "smartly styled" collared shirts for the children that would not require boys to wear a tie. Synthetic fabrics were promoted as easy to wash and iron. Nylon underwear for girls would dry quickly, but more changes of underwear would be needed for boys who wore "slower-drying cotton."[29]

Packing was a process that also required good planning, and again, it seemed to be best left up to the mother. Adults needed a large suitcase and an overnight bag, and rather than combining clothing, each child should have her own bag. Proper planning meant a dry run of loading luggage into the trunk or onto a rack on top of the car. Mother should write down a list of what was needed on the trip and check off each item as it was packed or purchased. Detailed instructions were given on how to pack a suitcase, including using cellophane tape and "pliofilm bags" for toiletries. Coats could be hung in the back of the car and "small items in a shoe bag hung over the back of the front seat." Toys, maps, sunglasses, booklets, combs, and brushes fit neatly in a shoe bag, making them more convenient for travelers. In addition to clothing, travelers should take items now standard in motels: alarm clock, folding ironing board and travel iron, and even clothes hangers. Toiletries like facial tissue, sewing kit, toothpaste, shampoo, and washcloth were on the list of what to pack, as well as medicinal items like aspirin and a first aid kit. Summer vacationers added "sun lotion" and sun glasses. The list was very, very long.[30]

DRIVING INSTRUCTIONS

While Mother was packing, Father's job was to have the car serviced. Lube and oil change were imperative, and brakes and steering should be checked for safety. Travelers should make sure the tires had proper pressure and were not too worn, that all lights worked, and that windshield wipers effectively cleaned the windshield. Equipment like a jack and car tools were a must, and a flashlight and flares were handy "if you get stuck on a lonely road." Before leaving, the final touch was having the car washed and upholstery cleaned.[31]

The *Guide* had a full chapter on how to care for a car in all seasons, but one of the most common problems for summer vacationers was an overheated engine. The solution was to pull over and wait until the temperature fell below 190 degrees. To prevent accidental burns from steam, only after at least a twenty-minute wait should the radiator cap be removed, and then by unscrewing it with a thick rag or towel. Water should be added slowly; ice cold water could crack an engine block.[32]

Driving in deserts required special instructions. Service stations were few and far between in the western deserts, so drivers were advised to carry an emergency supply of gasoline and water. Travelers commonly hung a canvas water bag on the front of the car to be air-cooled by evaporation. Because not all roads were paved, drivers should carry a shovel and a towrope. And because few cars had air-conditioning, travelers dealt with the heat by mounting shades on the windows, and perhaps by buying or renting an inexpensive evaporative cooler. Cheaper still were cardboard coolers loaded with dry ice that could be wedged into a partially open window. Unfortunately, the person closest to the cooler tended to be hit with flakes of dry ice, and those further away could barely feel the cold breeze. Another device was the "air scoop," which directed air from the window into the passenger space. For those with the money, by the early 1960s, FrigiKing air conditioners could be "easily and quickly installed in a new car or your present car."[33]

Mountain driving presented new challenges. It was wise to adjust the carburetor idle setting for the lower oxygen in the air at high altitudes. The guide stated, "The keynote to mountain driving is caution." Steep grades and sharp turns made it important to stay in one's own lane and pay attention to shifting gears at the proper time. Cooler temperatures posed the danger of icy roads, so travelers should check with the highway patrol to avoid being trapped by bad weather. Drivers were warned not to stop by the side of the road to admire scenery, but to use the turnouts provided. When parking, it was advisable to set the parking brake and block the wheel with a rock.[34]

Vacation driving was different from everyday driving because not only did one travel in unfamiliar terrain, one also drove for long stretches of time. To avoid boredom in flat terrain, drivers were advised to take breaks from hours behind the wheel. The driver confronted a different set of traffic regulations in each state, so the guide gave advice on how to deal with the "traffic officer" without crying, lying, or bullying. Driving advice concluded with instructions to passengers: don't be a backseat driver, and "keep children from climbing over the front seat" or blocking the view from the rearview mirror.[35]

The Backseat

The Shell travel guide admitted that travel with children could be a "nightmare" but assured readers that good planning could make a trip "a marvelous experience for the entire family." In addition to the educational value of the trip, "a car tour welds your family together through the sharing of new experiences." Just as at home, it was important to maintain a routine for children. Parents should take along toys, books, and games to entertain young children; older children would want to have sports equipment like a tennis racket or fishing rod. Women's magazines suggested toys and games to keep "squabbling and roughhousing by children" to a minimum. Everyone remembers the standard game of identifying state license plates and the game of putting together a menu from billboards.[36]

Travel guidebooks advised parents to control children's behavior by establishing firm rules like "Don't annoy the driver" and "Don't play with the dashboard controls or the cigarette lighter." Children should be warned not to stick their arms or heads out the window and not to play with the door locks. Parents were advised to load their suitcases between the front and back seats to create a level surface on which they could place a crib mattress. This "playpen" made a contained space for children where they could rest or play with their toys in the backseat. Other devices were available to make children comfortable or to constrain their movement, such as the Trav-L-Tot Hammock, which mounted on the windowsills of the backseat, "leaving the seats themselves free for passengers while moppets snooze or play." Straps on the hammock could be used to "keep energetic smallfry in place," but its usefulness was limited by the need to keep both side windows fully open at all times.[37]

Children routinely traveled in the front of the car, sitting between parents on the wide upholstered bench seat. One way to entertain them was to allow them to pretend they were driving. The Junior Steering Wheel cost only $3 and attached to the dashboard with suction cups. Car seats, made of a steel frame with rubber hooks that fit over the back of the front seat, contained children with a strap that prevented them from sliding out. "Sit and stand seats" allowed a child to stand up to "stretch his legs" and look out the front windshield.[38] Such seats were designed to contain and entertain children, not protect them in case of a crash.

Traveling with children meant stopping often to eat or sleep before children got too hungry or tired. The Shell guide advised, "If children get tired and cranky, stop and let them romp around for a while." Parents could travel with gadgets that allowed them to drive for longer periods, without rest stops for the children. Dee's Half-Pint was a portable plastic urinal for boys. The Car Jonn portable toilet had plastic throwaway liners, suitable for use by young girls. The invention in the early 1960s of Playtex disposable baby bottles eliminated the chore of washing bottles on

The Rothstein children shared the territory of the backseat on a family vacation in 1952. (Photograph by Arthur Rothstein, LOOK Magazine *Collection, Library of Congress, Prints & Photographs Division.)*

the road. Bottle warmers plugged into the car's cigarette lighter; bottles would heat in about ten minutes. In 1956 consumers could buy a "Baby on the go" traveling kit, with "baby oil, cream, powder, lotion, soap, and cotton buds." Perhaps the greatest invention for families traveling with babies was the disposable diaper, in common use by the mid-1970s for traveling.[39]

Taking the whole family could also mean taking along the family dog. The veterinarian who wrote the column "Your Pet and Mine" in *Better Homes and Gardens* advised readers to have the dog checked by the veterinarian before they left on vacation, and to obtain certificates and dog tags so they would not be delayed at borders. Dog owners were told to pack dog dishes, leash, comb, and blanket. Smart travelers checked ahead to see which motels welcomed pets. While traveling, dogs should sit in their assigned place in the car, with a break every few hours. The vet cautioned travelers not to leave the dog in the car alone on hot days because "the heat could make him sick." In a new place, a dog should be kept on a leash to avoid encounters with other animals, like skunks and porcupines.[40] Going on vacation meant taking the whole family, including the pets.

Children's books and toys prepared them for travel as they entertained. *The Golden Book of Automobile Stamps* (1952) boasted, "Today countless families take off for cross-country trips by car, with packets of free maps from oil companies marked with the preferred routes, with guide books to point out spots of historic interest or scenic beauty, and other guide books to suggest places for them to stop to eat and sleep." In fact, children were informed that they lived in "A Nation of Tourists," where "Sixty million tourists each year stop in the tens of thousands of motels, hotels, tourist homes, camps, and resorts of the country." By 1952 over 62 million licensed drivers roamed the 48 states in 50 million cars on 1,750,000 miles of highways, statistics recited to impress young readers. Indeed, children who licked and pasted the stamps picturing automobiles into the coloring book learned that they lived in "Our Automobile World."[41]

Activity books for children provided pencil games like connect-the-dot drawings of animals, matching, and crosswords. The *Travel Fun Book for Boys and Girls* (1954) included a grid where children earned points for spotting various makes of automobile, from Chevrolet to Studebaker, twenty-one in all. The games educated as they entertained, like the page on Missouri that included a crossword puzzle with clues such as "The Wizard of __" or "Mountain Range in Missouri." A nearly blank page provided a space for children to copy the Burma-Shave poems they saw along the roadway, and a "License Decoder" game showed children how to convert license plate numbers into "actual words." The one with the most words at the end of the trip was the winner.[42]

Car activity books also taught children how to encounter the environment by making collections of seashells, wildflowers, leaves, bottles of sand, or stones. Children were advised to choose carefully as they collected, and to discard all but the most interesting or perfectly formed objects. Collecting soil involved filling a jar with half-inch layers separated by cotton to make an "attractive" paperweight or gift. The book instructed children how to press leaves between pieces of tissue paper under a heavy object before pasting into an album. For all collections, the book told children to document when and where they found the object.[43]

Children's collections became souvenirs of the trip once at home: shells could be used as ashtrays or paperweights, glued around a picture frame, or strung together for jewelry. Maps could be pasted onto wastebaskets or trays and shellacked to make them shiny and waterproof. Postcards could be pasted together and cut into shapes to make a puzzle. Stones could become paperweights or doorstops; they could fill a jar to hold pencils; or they could fill a beanbag. Any object could be collected—matchbooks, bottle caps, menus, luggage stickers, or maps. By collecting, children made markers in their trip that they could narrate as they remembered it later.[44]

The activity book taught children how to take "snapshots" that would be lasting mementos of their travels. Rather than take pictures of "nearly everything," children were told to compose their pictures carefully before they hit the shutter button. For example, they should add a person to the foreground of a landmark for more interest. "Thus 'Mother looking at Niagara Falls' will be more enjoyed later, rather than just 'Niagara Falls' alone." The young photographer should also pay attention to the background: "In your interest in snapping Dad changing a tire, you may forget to look at what is behind him." No instruction was too basic: "pictures of things in motion will not turn out well." The limits of the black-and-white film of the era led to another tip: "Don't be fooled by color. It won't show in your snapshot." These instructions helped children translate the scope of what they saw into views within the frame of the finished photograph, teaching them to read the travel landscape and convert it into standards of what was pleasing and conventional in photography.[45]

Quiet games like "I Spy" or "I Went to the Store" were designed to keep children entertained without bothering the driver. "Motoring Games" involved reading license plates or maps, finding letters, or reading slogans on billboards, and they taught children reading skills or at the very least to be observant of their surroundings. Ideally, children played these games together in the backseat, but in reality, many travel games involved the cooperation of parents, if only to settle disagreements. A parent led the children in singing songs with actions, like "John Brown's Baby" or "Ten Little Indians." Because Dad usually drove, Mom would read stories like "The Bell," about a visit by two children to see their grandmother in New Orleans at Mardi Gras.[46]

Travel Fun for Kids updated age-old games with space-age themes in the mid-1960s. Crafts projects included a "flying saucer bonnet" made with two paper plates, with pipe cleaners for antennae. Children could make a "rocket control panel" from a paper plate, drive-in drink carrier, disposable cups, and lids. Connect-the-dot games were converted to "astronaut golf," where players had to avoid hazards like the "cosmic ray pond," meteorites, the Van Allen belt, or atomic sand. Like early travel activity books, games taught children how to identify states, solve riddles, fill in the blanks, or find "what's wrong here" in the pictures. *Travel Fun for Kids* added a child diary, with spaces for "relatives visited, names and addresses to keep."[47]

Travel games such as *Traffic Safety Bingo,* where children marked pictures of what they saw out the window, was marketed in many forms to families. *Zit Zango,* a version of travel bingo, was advertised as "educational" and "the ideal way to pass miles away" for "children of all ages and grownups too." The Family Travel Game of State License Plates promised "miles and miles of exciting fun."[48] Old-fashioned or modern, travel activity books and games were designed to keep children entertained—and educated.

Planning the family vacation required much more than getting the car tuned up and canceling the paper. Getting ready for vacation involved lists of what to pack, how to pack it, and most especially what to buy to be well-prepared for the vacation trip. Taking the entire family meant that Americans not only bought wrinkle-free clothing for themselves, but also an array of toys, activity books, and gadgets to occupy their children while on the road. The almost scientific planning for the modern vacation was a way to sell consumer products the vacationer would need while away from home.

What to Eat, Where to Stay

Before the advent of streamlined interstates, the American roadside was characterized by oddities: larger-than-life statues of folk heroes, petting zoos, and odd-shaped eateries.[49] Journalist Bill Bryson remembered that as a boy, "the highways were scattered with diversions" like billboards advertising glowing "atomic rock." Bryson recalled, "My big brother and sister, squeezed into the backseat with me and having exhausted all the possibilities for diversion that came with holding me down and drawing vivid geometric patterns on my nose, face, arms, and stomach with a felt marking pen, would set up a clamor to see this world famous attraction, and I would weakly chime in."[50] For Bryson, the value of such attractions, which invariably did not live up to their advertising, was a way to make the miles pass more quickly.

Bryson remembered the older roadside motels as "thrilling" for their horrors. They were of two types: the cottagelike good ones with a shady lawn edged by white painted rocks, or the "appalling ones" that his father chose because he was a "cheapskate." These had sagging springs in the mattresses, no air-conditioning, and frightening sounds of crimes being committed next door in the middle of the night. Remembering the nights spent in the run-down motels, he remarks ironically, "all of this, even at its worst, gave highway travel a kind of exhilarating unpredictability."[51] Interstate highways sidelined roadside oddities to the back roads as newer establishments clustered at the exits, making road travel more predictable but less exciting. In place of excitement, the newer roadside businesses promised a standardized experience of eating and lodging by depending on branded corporate chains.

Roadside restaurants that catered to the family traveler expanded to meet the needs of hungry families on the road in the postwar vacation boom. Before the invention of fast food restaurants, traveling with children required parents to plan ahead. Food costs could be cut in half by carrying food in the car for breakfast and lunch. The Shell guide recommended carrying sandwich supplies, milk, and fruit bought along the way. Before the era of fast food restaurants, the alternative to carrying food was to eat in roadside cafes or cafeterias, where a meal might cost $1 to $1.50. Feeding children meant "three-squares-a-day," but young children did not always like restaurants. The guide advised parents to choose a restaurant that served smaller portions for children and did not require a long wait in line. To eliminate embarrassment when a child was at "the banging-on-the-table stage," one parent could arrive first and order, while the other waited outside with the children. Snacks of fruits, raisins, and canned juices would be least likely to interfere with meals. If a child experienced car sickness, it was best to move him to the front seat and "give him a lemon to suck." To prepare for car sickness, parents should carry an empty ice cream carton and a rag to clean up the inside of the car.[52]

Howard Johnson's chain of highway coffee shops was among the first to welcome families with children. Founded in the 1920s, by the 1940s, the chain was operating 130 restaurants in New England and Virginia. By 1951, 255 Howard Johnson restaurants, with their trademark orange roof and turquoise cupolas, dotted the turnpikes, most in the eastern United States. Their pseudo-colonial design was based on the New England town hall or church, so it symbolized an American identity to the consumer. The atmosphere was wholesome, a blend of soda fountain and dining room. Families could get their food quickly because most of it was fried. Menus featured hot dogs, hamburgers, chicken, steak, and a New England dish, fried clams. Best of all, Howard Johnson restaurants served twenty-eight flavors of ice cream.[53] Families who stopped at Howard Johnson were counting on fast food in a friendly atmosphere at low prices, no matter what highway they were traveling.

Fast food restaurants revolutionized family travel. Former malt-machine salesman Ray Kroc opened his first hamburger restaurant in 1955, competing with proliferating roadside franchises like Dairy Queen, Kentucky Fried Chicken, and Insta-Burger-King. McDonald's opened its one hundredth restaurant in 1959 and operated 250 by 1960. By the late 1960s, McDonald's was the first choice of the "station wagon set." Their motto—Quality, Service, Cleanliness, and Value—summed up the needs of growing young families, at home and on the road. McDonald's cleverly placed their new restaurants in the expanding suburbs, with the result that when children went on vacation, they could eat out like they did at home. Because every McDonald's had the same menu and the same food products, it was a dependable choice, with no surprises on the road. The convenience of fast food and its low price catered to American families with many mouths to feed. No more tense moments with the cranky toddler banging on the table while the food was being cooked—at McDonald's, children's appetites could be satisfied almost instantly, and with food they (and their parents) liked. The informality of the roadside restaurant meant you could come as you are, with no need to even comb your hair before climbing out of the car. The clean restrooms were a bonus for road travelers; a family could make just one stop to buy food and go to the bathroom. Soon the family was refreshed and fed, ready to get back in the car and get back on the highway to get to their day's destination. And if you were behind in your itinerary, the people at McDonald's were happy to hand over the hamburgers and fries in a paper bag so you could eat in the car.[54]

The family vacation craze spurred the growth of the motel industry. The word *motel* was coined in San Luis Obispo, California, in 1926 but did not become a standard term for roadside lodging until the 1950s. The number of motels peaked in the 1960s with 61,000 in operation, and since then, the range of terms applied makes it difficult to distinguish motels from hotels. Motels replaced campgrounds or tourist homes because travelers valued safety, comfort, and convenience and were willing to pay more for amenities. John A. Jakle and Keith Sculle argue that motels are a "home away from home . . . an interface with the private automobile, further cocooning and protecting the traveler away from home."[55]

Consumers quickly converted to the commodified overnight experience offered by modern motels. In 1945, about half of AAA members preferred hotels with the rest staying in motor courts and tourist homes. In 1950 motorists could choose from among a half-million rooms in motels or tourist courts, a predecessor of the modern motel. By 1950 a building magazine claimed that two-thirds of all road travelers stopped at motels. Increased demand meant motels were constructed with "appealing design and landscaping" to attract travelers who viewed them from the road. As motels joined the AAA or other affiliates, motorists could reserve in advance, and roadside proximity was less important in finding lodging.[56]

Families were attracted to motels because they were less expensive than hotels, and motels allowed them to park near their rooms without going through a lobby or paying tips to a bellman. *Business Week* magazine featured the new motels in a 1952 article that featured photographs of a family checking into a motel. While the mother settled the baby in the room, the father and two sons unloaded the luggage from the trunk of the car right outside the door of the room. The photo captions explained: "Checking in is simple, involves no tips. That's one of the motel's best selling points. Checking out comes at any hour."[57]

The phenomenon of 30,000 motels was due to the wanderlust of the American family. "The motor court business grew with the American family's love to travel and vacation by car. Just as hotels grew up close to train and bus centers, motor courts have cashed in on the premise that motorists would like lodgings close by major highways." Families with tired children and hungry babies found it convenient to choose motels from the highway and unload on the doorstep to their room. An exhausted father need not worry when checking in because "the motorist can arrive with a day's stubble on his chin without worrying about disapproving glances." Motels offered amenities such as radios, televisions, air-conditioning, and laundry facilities. Nicer motor courts offered "almost all the extras and plush of the better hotels," at lower prices, such as "coffee shops, lounges complete with TV and writing desks, air-conditioning, tiled shower-bath installations, and mercury switches." Motels advertised wall-to-wall carpeting, ample lighting, and brand-name mattresses to attract guests. Motels may have been homelike, but the motel stay offered Americans a taste of luxuries like swimming pools and color television—amenities many could not afford at home. Thus motels appealed to consumers' aspirations to an upper middle-class standard of living in their accommodations.[58]

Families found motels convenient in part because they offered a cheap way to feed the family. Some offered free continental breakfasts, while many were equipped with kitchenettes. Motels allowed for more economical meals if one were prepared. *Better Homes and Gardens* suggested preparing a "motel feed bag" with an electric toaster, coffee heater (in which one could boil eggs), lightweight cups and plates, and condiments like sugar, powdered cream, instant coffee, and jelly.[59]

A growing number of motels featured swimming pools where children could get their wiggles out after sitting in the car all day long. *Business Week* noted, "Swimming pools are becoming a must" because "they may induce a tired family to spend an extra day or two at the motor court." Motels that installed pools saw their business increase up to 60 percent in some parts of the country, and some motel associations required members to have pools. By the 1960s, in the northern United States, motels were building indoor pools to attract guests. It was estimated that a pool would pay for itself in three and a half years, and that "there's a growing group of guests who like the luxury, the glamor and the image of quality and leisure which a pool creates."[60]

The old-fashioned tourist courts built in the 1930s were dingy and run-down—no place for a family with children to spend the night. The new modern motels were designed to fit the needs of the family on the road. By belonging to a chain or an association, motels could make reservations for the traveler for the next night, and guests could be assured that the motel met the standards of quality set by the association. In 1962 over half of all motels belonged to a referral organization (AAA, Quality Courts, Best Western, Master Host), and half belonged to a state association. Indeed, motels had become so successful that hotels were adopting the features of motels, further blurring the distinction between them. As expressways and city entertainment began to draw families to the city, city hotels took on motel features like free parking to meet their needs.[61]

Families seeking reliable lodging enthusiastically welcomed the development of franchise motor hotels in the late 1950s. Holiday Inn was the brainchild of Kemmons Wilson, who invented the nationwide branded motel franchise in Memphis, Tennessee, in 1953. He later recalled that his idea to build the franchise came from an experience he had while traveling with his family: "In 1951 my wife Dorothy and I loaded our five children into our station wagon and started on a vacation to Washington, D.C., from our home in Memphis. It didn't take us long to find that most motels had cramped, uncomfortable rooms—and they charged extra for the children. Few had decent restaurants and fewer still were air-conditioned. In short, it was a miserable trip." He realized that "the family vacation came into its own," and the money was to be made in developing motels.

Holiday Inn was the first major motel chain to allow children to stay free. Postcard ca. 1963. (Author's collection.)

After building the first 120-room Holiday Inn in Memphis, he sold the idea, and the blueprints, to builders, who paid a per-room, per-day royalty fee to use the Holiday Inn trademark. The success of the franchise operation depended on standardization, and as John Jakle points out, the company "developed comprehensive operational standards ranging from the details of the building design and materials, to the cleanliness of the restaurant, to the ways front-desk personnel were to handle guests."[62]

Holiday Inns were built for family travelers: "All had a swimming pool, air-conditioning, a restaurant on the premises, phones in every room, free ice, dog kennels, free parking, and available baby sitters." Wilson's mother designed rooms "which were bright and airy, with friendly, warm colors." Architects catered to the family crowd by designing "quiet, homelike accommodations rather than the hustle of the busy hotels or the rather commercial coldness of many motels." And in a stroke of brilliance, Wilson allowed children under 12 years to stay free. He recalled having to pay an extra $10 for his children when he traveled, and "I told my wife that I didn't think this was fair. It wouldn't encourage people to travel with their children. I told her I was going to build a chain of motels and I was never going to make a charge for children as long as they stayed in the same room as their parents."[63]

Holiday Inn steadily expanded by meeting the needs of the roadside traveler. In 1963 Holiday Inn offered a joint credit card with Gulf Oil and two years later set up a nationwide reservation system. By 1965, nearly 1,000 Holiday Inns were spread across the country. By 1970, Holiday Inn had 1,300 properties and had expanded overseas. Although its business plan had diversified beyond the family vacationer, still it appealed to families with the construction of Holidome Inns with indoor pools and fun centers. By raising the age at which children could stay free from twelve to eighteen years of age, Holiday Inn retained the loyalty of the family traveler. Holiday Inns set a pattern for family lodging that was imitated by other roadside chain motels.[64]

The postwar family road trip was made possible by paid vacations and affordable family cars. Experts advised families how to perform the common tasks of planning, packing, and budgeting to meet the needs of parents traveling with children. Automobile manufacturers, oil companies, and the hospitality industry all took advantage of the family road trip to sell their products. In turn, family consumers on vacation shaped roadside culture, from fast food restaurants to motels where children stayed free. The roadside material culture of family travel helped the family feel at home away from home, no matter their destination.

The optimism of postwar consumerism was linked with the ideal of family togetherness to sell products that promised to make the family vacation a time of love and harmony. Of course, in reality vacations could not possibly fulfill the sunny expectations of their promoters, from Madison Avenue to the family travel guides. Humorist Peg Bracken gently poked fun at the family vacation in 1959, acknowledging that getting through a vacation "is harder than it looks." Members of the family can never agree on what sights to see, and everyone looks like a mess when Mother decides there is no use traveling in good clothes. The photos of Buddy and Sis by the Hoover Dam can be unflattering, but pictures are necessary because "you must have something to show the neighbors back home." The worst part was returning home to open a huge stack of mail, to see the holes the moles dug in the lawn, or to make a meal from the half-empty box of wilted cornflakes, all that was left in the kitchen cupboard.[65]

A vacation was not only "harder than it looks," but it also threatened the very family togetherness that it was intended to foster. Women's magazines published advice from experts like the trusted Dr. Benjamin Spock, who asked, "Can parents and children share vacation fun?" But like the guidebooks, the dangers of family togetherness could be avoided with good planning, compromise, and the right equipment. The alternative—leaving the children at home—was almost unthinkable. In "Vacation for Two," a sentimental poem about a couple on a getaway without their children who discover that their children have secretly stowed a doll and a teddy bear in their suitcase, think fondly of home and realize, "we missed two treasures we could not go out and buy." The guilt of leaving the children behind with Grandma was worse to bear than the exasperation of taking care of the little ones on the road. Only if the whole family traveled together in the family car were they taking a real family vacation. To know where they went, and why, we must understand the America they saw.[66]

chapter two

Pilgrimage

In the summer of 1951 Ralph and Jean Gray and their three children, Judith (age eleven), Mary Ellen (nine), and William (five) took a family vacation along the Lincoln National Memorial Highway. In his article for *National Geographic,* Ralph Gray called their trip a "pilgrimage" to Lincoln shrines. By tracing Lincoln's migration route from his Kentucky birthplace through Indiana and Illinois, they hoped to teach their children about a man who for their family had "long been a hero and model." So they loaded their car with suitcases, camping equipment, cameras, and film. What did not fit went into a wooden box, fondly called "the attic," strapped to the top of the car. It was no easy trip. Like the ancient journeys of pilgrims to sacred sites who faced formidable challenges to reach their goal, the Grays faced modern obstacles on their road trip: "On its 425 mile length we bounded over rough trails that couldn't have been much improved since the Lincolns passed; we raised atomic-size dust clouds on gravel roads; we sloshed through fords and along flooded lanes."[1] In the decades after World War II, families like the Grays were pilgrims to historic sites and national landmarks, consuming the American landscape while tutoring their children in the history of their nation. Heritage travel boomed in the decades following World War II as Americans visited the authentic sites of historic events, presidents, and patriots.

Since its beginnings, tourism in America has been bound up in ideas of national identity, from the sacred spaces of the landscape like Niagara Falls to the grandeur of Yosemite Valley. In the early twentieth century, travel promoters (both private and state) tapped into feelings of national identity to sell tourism in the "See America First" movement.[2] What sets the postwar period apart is the increased scale of heritage travel. The linkage of education, democratic values, and travel reassured Americans of their superiority as they dealt with the insecurity of cold war politics. War veterans toured the United States as an affirmation of their own values and as a means of passing them on to their children. Travel to historic sites nurtured a commitment to the nation for which they had fought.

Visitors were searching for an affirmative national history better labeled as *heritage,* a selective remembering of what is "attractive or flattering" and ignoring all the rest. Historian Michael Kammen argues that the end of World War II "brought a pronounced sense of discontinuity between past and present," and Americans sought a "sense of continuity" by visiting historic sites and museums. About 49 million persons visited historic sites in the United States in 1954, and they could choose from about 1,000 historic restorations. Annual attendance surged 20 to 30 percent at historic sites and national parks until 1976, when it began to decline.[3]

We can label these travels *pilgrimages* because the destination is a special place, a place that has become set apart or "sacred." By going to those places, whether Washington, D.C., or a religious shrine, tourists strengthened their sense of national or religious identity. Central to pilgrimage tourism is the quest for authenticity, to see the actual site of a historic event, the same monument visited by all Americans, or the very spot a miracle took place. In that way, tourists can better imagine themselves as part of a larger community or can travel backward in time, to imagine that they too were a part of history. They sought no ordinary history but instead pursued a grand narrative of national greatness, or for African Americans, equality in a time when Washington, D.C., tourist homes turned them away. Parents who wanted their children to consider their citizenship, whether full or partial, took their children on pilgrimages to the sacred places of America. In the process, they strengthened their own sense of national ideals and reinforced their commitment to a nation with equal justice for all.[4]

Maps and guides facilitated civic pilgrimage by guiding travelers to national landmarks and historic sites in a landscape prepackaged for the traveling consumer. Map publishers, states, and automobile touring associations designed their products to appeal to the family on vacation, both by depicting families on maps and by mapping routes and listing sites that would most appeal to parents traveling with children. Maps and guides in hand, families set off on cross-country tours of historic sites or took their children to Washington, D.C., where children experienced a pilgrimage that did not always seem sacred.

Mapping America

Stories like Ralph Gray's travelogue in *National Geographic Magazine* inspired countless family vacations to American destinations. The magazine, which published many articles about travel destinations, was immensely popular and instrumental in shaping American views of the world. The National Geographic Society was at the forefront of educating Americans; the society had over a million members in 1940, and in 1950 it printed 1.9 million copies of each map it created. Americans subscribed to the magazine to satisfy their hunger for maps, for two-dimensional depictions of the world that imposed order through patterns and symbols and lines. Traveler-consumers needed instructions on where to go and how to get there (and back), and maps and guides provided geographic information that made the family road trip possible.[5]

While *National Geographic* made geography popular among all classes of Americans, the Rand McNally Corporation helped meet demand by publishing maps. Rand McNally was among the three large oil company map publishers, which also included General Drafting and the H. M. Gousha Company, which was begun by a group of cartographers who had left Rand McNally in 1926. Although H. M. Gousha would become the largest producer of oil company maps, Rand McNally had the most distinguished publishing history, having been in the map printing business since the middle of the nineteenth century. Its influence was extended in the 1920s when, long before the federal government created a national highway system, Rand McNally devised a standardized highway marking system and installed markers on roads throughout the country. In addition to printing oil company maps, Rand McNally printed its first national road atlas in 1924 and has produced one annually ever since.[6]

Road maps were an essential tool in directing family vacation travel, and their images and organization shaped travelers' perceptions of the American landscape. Vacationers depended on Rand McNally products, both their commercial atlases and the maps produced for free distribution by gasoline service stations. In a time of heightened international insecurity and fear of communism, Rand McNally maps and guides shaped Americans' notions of national identity. By facilitating travel to historic sites and cultivating an appreciation for the distinctiveness of America's regions, Rand McNally boosted patriotic commitment to a modern, atomic-age America. Maps helped alter travel habits from the adventure of local discovery to through travel on interstate highways systems, resulting in a transcontinental view of the nation.[7]

Atlases organized the national space into states and regions in formulations that changed over time. Rand McNally's 1949 *Cosmopolitan Atlas,* which transformed cartographic views of the world (such as a map of the world from the perspective of the North Pole) to emphasize global interdependence, sold out within a month. Maps and atlases presented a consumable America, what James Akerman calls a "national motorized space."[8] Road maps (whether bound into atlases or flat maps) were an essential tool in directing family vacation travel, and their images and organization shaped travelers' perceptions of the American landscape.

Free oil company road maps quickly became a staple of oil company marketing in the twentieth century. The road map's popularity can in part be attributed to the fact that it was free to consumers, but it was also attractive, useful, and contained the latest information on roads. Historians of the road map agree that by the 1930s, oil company road maps "had been brought to near-perfect harmony with the needs of the motoring public." Oil company maps were designed to promote travel to increase consumption of oil company products. In addition to handing out maps, oil companies formed internal travel bureaus to assist their customers. For example, Conoco provided Touraide guides to its customers, assembling custom guides (as many as 4,000 per day) from preprinted pages of maps. Conoco advertised its Touraides in national magazines like *Life,* with claims that "Now . . . there's a travel bureau in every Conoco station."[9]

The sites and routes on the map were continually changing, with extensive revisions in 1946, 1957, and in the late 1960s. Although technological improvements in mapping and printing obviously accounted for some changes, because maps were based on the U.S. Geological Survey maps, new surveys were instrumental in suggesting changes in the map's content. Map companies also relied on states for information about changes in roads or what sites to feature on their maps.[10]

The announcement of federal aid to the interstate highway system in 1956 further transformed the road map, which began to feature abstracted images of cloverleaf exits and entrances, or vistas of freeways cutting straight through the countryside. Ironically, the interstate highway system also made maps less necessary because travel between destinations was as simple as finding the freeway entrance and exit ramps. For example, maps of Wyoming erased local sites, like the site of the first Holy Mass offered by Father DeSmet, or the site of the Burnt Wagon Train near Glendo.

Such erasures made the state look more empty. Fewer secondary roads were mapped, so they effectively disappeared for travelers. The 1977 map showed only eleven points of interest and focused almost exclusively on Yellowstone, featured in an inset map with the Grand Tetons. Mapped travel routes became less adventurous and focused more on planned destinations than serendipitous discovery of roadside features.[11]

Service station map distribution reached its peak of 250 million in 1972, but as a result of intense competition from the Arab oil embargo, by 1980 gas stations found they no longer needed maps to attract motorists.[12] The end of free oil company maps made travelers more dependent on two other sources: the American Automobile Association (AAA) and state governments. The AAA, an umbrella organization of state and regional auto clubs, supplied maps and guides to its members in return for an annual membership fee. The AAA distributed 40 million maps a year in 1952, and by the mid-1970s was handing out 180 million maps yearly. The maps supplied by the AAA were not as commercialized as the oil company maps and had little promotional content. However, the AAA provided its members with detailed guidebooks in addition to maps, with listings of AAA-approved business establishments that catered to tourists. The ultimate AAA invention was the TripTik, a customized map showing a travel route lifted out of the surrounding landscape, with information about where to eat and where to stay.[13]

State governments handed out free road maps in hopes of attracting tourist revenue to their coffers. Each state created a brand or recognizable identity that distinguished it from other states. State maps generally promoted the historic and scenic attractions within the brand framework. And because state travel offices supplied publicity materials to other tourism promotion organizations, such as the AAA, the state brand characterized the image of the state on tourism materials *not* produced by the state. Tourists, responding to widespread advertising in newspapers and magazines, wrote to states for information while making travel plans, and they often picked up maps free at welcome centers at the borders.[14]

Maps and atlases were designed to appeal to family vacationers. Before the war, the illustration of the idealized traveler was a single figure or a couple, always white, and often of some means. The nuclear family made its appearance on maps after the war, usually a son and daughter with parents in a car, sometimes with the family dog. For example, the 1964 *Cities Service Washington DC* map cover illustrated a smartly dressed family in a late-model convertible car. Dad was at the wheel, chatting with Mom, who wore a dress and sunglasses. In the backseat, Daughter played with a red stuffed toy, while Son observed the attendant pumping gas. Their slogan, "For People Going Places" had the double meaning of travel and upward social mobility.[15] Map covers thus capitalized on the era's ethic of the family to harness the buying power of consumers.

Images of families accompanying the map reflected the rigid gender roles of the era. Men were featured at the wheel, buying gas, or as service station attendants. Women were most often seen taking children to the restroom. A 1952 road map showed a picture of Dad talking with the service station attendant while his son touched the car's headlight. Mom was behind the car in a summer dress, carrying the baby daughter. The oil company reassured its customers that family travel would not threaten the security of the domestic unit: "The road may be strange. The scenery may be strange. But when you drive up to the familiar Torch and Oval Sign of Standard, there's a cheerful welcome waiting from your friend on the highway—the local Standard Oil Dealer." Not until the 1950s were women pictured at the wheel on maps. And then they did not have to get their hands dirty, because attendants would fill the tank and check the oil.[16]

Oil companies knew that to please women customers, restrooms needed to be clean. The phrase *sanitary restrooms* became a mantra featured on nearly all road maps. A 1949 Gulf Oil map promised: "Sanitary Restrooms—this sign means added comfort and convenience." The use of the word *sanitary* may have served as code to women travelers who used menstrual products such as sanitary napkins. The map was illustrated by a picture of a woman in hat and skirt ushering her son and daughter from the car to the restroom. Gulf Oil assured its customers that "weekly and daily cleaning and maintenance schedules are followed, and hourly inspections made to further assure you and other members of your family of finding restrooms in the cleanest possible condition at all times." A Texaco map pictured a mother telling her daughter, "Look for the green and white sign that means clean Registered Rest Rooms." Images of women in maps always emphasized the feminine, with the women wearing dresses. In the Texaco map, the mother wore a red dress, matching heels, and a wide-brimmed hat. Her blonde daughter wore a pink dress with a bow, had a ribbon in her hair, and held a doll. With clean restrooms, women could uphold their standards of cleanliness and femininity even while on the road.[17]

Travel guides combined maps and texts to offer prepackaged travel itineraries that assured travelers of a safe and secure journey. The 1953 Rand McNally *Vacation Guide* listed seven "Transcontinental Tours" that

Free oil company maps featured images of the ideal family exploring America. Esso, Washington, D.C. and Vicinity Map and Visitors Guide *(General Drafting, 1957). (Courtesy Utah State Historical Society.)*

Service stations attracted families by advertising "Clean Restrooms" for their customers. Standard Oil, Road Map of Washington *(H. M. Gousha, 1962). (Courtesy Utah State Historical Society.)*

"take you over the best and most scenic highways and can be picked up or left at any point along the route." The Atlas provided a Transcontinental Tour Map and Transcontinental Mileage chart, along with more detailed routes of tours from Boston to Seattle, or New York to Los Angeles. The tours were broken down into units "so that it may be completed, with a moderate amount of sightseeing, in one day by the average driver." In 1955 Rand McNally renamed the cross-country tours "Beelines" because they were "the fastest, best, and often the most scenic routes to the Vacation Areas." The Beeline moniker stuck until the mid-1960s, when the guide no longer mapped transcontinental tours for its readers and instead marked "Go" routes "if you are in a hurry."[18]

A particular form of travel guide, the vacation guide, was organized so that travelers could target a certain geographic area for their trip. In 1953 the *Rand McNally Vacation Guide* introduced each section with an article that "gives you the flavor and character of the region as a whole." The regional approach allowed guides to highlight the history and culture of each area. For example, New England was where "colonial history comes alive for the traveler." Whether it was the Southwest or the Midwest, "Every region has a special appeal for the vacationer. It may be in the unusual and appetizing food—the exotic French cooking of New Orleans, the thick, rich steaks of the Montana cattle country, the sea food of New England, or the real farm meals of the rural sections." As late as 1970, commercial atlases organized the nation by region, complete with descriptions of regional character.[19] The idea of region was important to road travelers; air travel and a more homogenized American culture would later erase regional distinctions in maps and guides.

Atlases depicted popular understandings of American regions by relying on symbols of local culture. The 1960 *State Farm Road Atlas* featured a stylized map of the United States with pictograms located in various regions connoting local culture. An oil derrick in Texas, a lobster in Maine, and a cow in Wisconsin conveyed information about the state for travelers. The South's Atlantic coast was dotted with symbols of its growing importance as a vacation destination: palm trees and a waving bikini-clad woman. Iconography alluding to slavery dotted the South: black women in bandanas picking cotton, men dancing with a banjo. Other states drew on the iconography of the American Indian, with a tepee in Montana and an Indian in a headdress in Oklahoma. Such depictions of states and regions in shorthand that used lighthearted symbols to portray racial subjugation and conquest showed insensitivity to the struggle for racial equality then brewing in the South.[20]

The State Farm Road Atlas *(1960) depicted the regions of America with stylized symbols. (Courtesy Harold B. Lee Library.)*

Map cover art was also racialized, with other races "forming part of the landscape to be consumed, but never as consumers." The preoccupation with the white nuclear family excluded other races and family types. However, African Americans were not completely excluded in informational content of maps. Maps of the South reflected its segregated nature, as in the 1955 map to Atlanta that boasted "over 300 churches for the white population . . . in addition to 150 churches for Negroes" and seven "colleges for Negroes" that made Atlanta "the world's leading center for Negro education." Not until the 1984 Rand McNally *Vacation Guide* was black history featured; "those interested in Atlanta's unique black history" could visit the birthplace and home of Dr. Martin Luther King Jr.[21]

Maps and guides assisted travelers in negotiating cities as America became more urbanized. Cities became more common as tourist destinations, and the number of cities listed in the atlas increased, from 48 in 1949 to 147 in 1957. Flat maps featured more detailed urban guides, such as a 1956 map of Los Angeles that advised visitors to see the Civic Center, Exposition Park, the Griffith Park Observatory, the Spanish missions, the Motion Picture Industry, Olvera Street, and the Southwest Museum. An orange square on the map marked the location of the new Disneyland in Anaheim as a point of interest. Atlases featured cities in inset maps and in text that featured the many choices for sightseeing with children. "Visitors to New York City top the highest towers in helicopters, encircle Manhattan in excursion boats, and go aboard ocean liners docked at West Side piers. They take their children to see the Statue of Liberty, the United Nations, Times Square, the great museums, and the Central Park Zoo. They ascend the Empire State Building, still the tallest building in America."[22]

Oil companies promoted travel with advertising that tapped into feelings of patriotism. In the summer of 1959 Texaco provided a removable insert in *Life* magazine that readers could take along as a guide on their summer trips. Texaco's guide featured the "story of the flag and how to tour historic America." Its pages "picture and describe many of the historic points of interest and national shrines in America." As a bonus, it included "a beautifully illustrated story of the origins and changing designs of our American flag through the years." It suggested, "This year why not plan your motor trips to include stops at famous historic sites along your route? There are hundreds of these cherished spots that tell the story of our country's beginnings, and its growth into a great nation. Your trips will be more exciting and educational for the youngsters, too." This pitch to family travelers emphasized the educational value of travel for children, and considered the historic spots to be shrines worthy of a family pilgrimage. Lest readers forget, the advertisement repeated the commercial motto: "And wherever you go, *tour with Texaco!*"[23]

Commemorations of important historic events prompted map publishers to issue special editions to meet the needs of travelers. Rand McNally issued a Civil War centennial map in 1962, with a Civil War centennial schedule of events, such as battle reenactments, and several ceremonies, among them the Medal of Honor and Emancipation Proclamation commemorative ceremony at the Lincoln Memorial. The map featured three tours, including the northern theater of war, significant forts, the Confederate capital, and the western war theater from Mississippi to New Orleans. The cover featured photographs of two Confederate generals, Robert E. Lee and Stonewall Jackson, emphasizing events from the perspective of the South.[24]

Map makers heavily promoted heritage travel around the time of the nation's bicentennial celebration. Rand McNally's 1975 *Atlas* featured a pullout reproduction of a 1776 map of the theater of war, suitable for framing. It contained a special index to Bicentennial points of interest and a section on the "personalities" of the Revolution, with thumbnail biographies of female patriots like Betsy Ross. Notably it included a diverse cast of characters, like African American poet Phillis Wheatley and Mohawk chief Joseph Brant. Inside the back cover was a map of the town of Boston in 1775. The back cover twisted the national slogan to "Discover Historic America." States also issued special Bicentennial maps. The Massachusetts map bragged that "The Bicentennial Begins Here." Printed in the patriotic colors of red, white, and blue, it featured photos of historic sites such as the Paul Revere Monument and Old Ironsides.[25]

Even McDonald's, the fast food restaurant chain, got into the act during the Bicentennial. It produced a "Heritage Roads" map, a "guide to America's heritage, a summary of exciting places to go, what to see and do, so you and your family can enjoy these places of interest as you travel." The map conveniently marked locations of McDonald's restaurants, so when "mealtime rolls around, or you feel like a break, check it for the nearest McDonald's in your area."[26] By promoting national landmarks and historic sites, McDonald's not only encouraged patriotism but also boosted consumption of hamburgers and fries.

States likewise promoted their own historic landmarks by appealing to families traveling with children during the Bicentennial. Travel to New England's Revolutionary War–era landmarks provided an opportunity for families to inculcate patriotic values and nurture a sense of national identity in their children. The New England landscape had longed served as a primer for learning American history. The state capitalized on its history to promote heritage tourism. A 1970 Massachusetts map proclaimed that "Massachusetts men gave Americans a heritage of freedom, and today's travelers visit the sandy shore and the rustic inland valleys to dig for the origins of their democracy. Families, teaching their school-aged children American history from the storied buildings and streets of Massachusetts, are familiar sights on the state's highways." States like Florida boasted, "It's a grand family vacation project—brushing up on America's earliest history."[27]

Pennsylvania state maps featured Philadelphia as an important site for families making patriotic pilgrimages. In 1947 the Pennsylvania state map claimed: "In this historic shrine were formulated and signed the two documents which are the foundation of the Nation and upon which the whole world depends—the Declaration of Independence and the Constitution of the United States." The photograph showed a family, a man and woman with linked arms and their little girl, gazing up at the cupola of Independence Hall. Children could stand in line to touch the cracked Liberty Bell, or walk past Betsy Ross's house, or see where Benjamin Franklin once lived. The same family was pictured visiting a monument to Washington's crossing on the banks of the Delaware River.[28]

The search for a unified usable national past immediately after the war was challenged by the racial and social divisions in the 1960s. The astonishing success of Alex Haley's *Roots* and the associated television miniseries in 1977 was just one signal of a rekindled desire by many Americans to find their own roots by retracing the steps of their ancestors. The appearance of sites of black and immigrant history in maps and guides suggests that the idea of American heritage became multistranded. Atlases and guides in the 1970s depicted the national landscape as a mosaic created from an American immigrant heritage and highlighted the continuing presence of native peoples. The 1970 Texaco travel atlas announced that "Historic treasures, at long last, are cherished and restored. In the country and in small towns, as in the big cities, conservationists and history lovers now demand more than a statue in a park or a tablet on the sidewalk to record that X marks the spot." The historic consciousness led for some to a celebration of ethnicity and diversity that Rand McNally promoted by listing local festivals and reenactments. Noting that travelers could attend Norske Days in Wisconsin, rodeos in Wyoming, or Sioux powwows in Minnesota, the author remarked: "Whatever nationality your forefathers may have been, your fellow descendants will be recalling them at some frolic somewhere in this mosaic that is the Middle West."[29] The America presented in maps and guides in the 1950s was a regionalized nation, with distinctive subcultures and identities conveyed to travelers with symbols that sustained whiteness by depicting race as an artifact of history. By the 1970s, regional distinctions and signs of local culture faded from maps, replaced by the idea of America as an ethnic and racial mosaic. Maps and guides both reflected and shaped cultural change in ways unrecognized by the family travelers who used them to make the family vacation a pilgrimage.

Civic Pilgrimage

By traveling to the Lincoln sites or Civil War battlefields, American families could partake of the national legacy, praise its heroes, and internalize its democratic values. Through family vacationing, parents were inculcating patriotic values in their children, encouraging in them a loyalty to the nation for which many of their fathers fought in World War II. Civic pilgrimage combined education and emotion into one package. Tourism and religious pilgrimage share a concern with sacred space, a desire for authenticity, and a concern with the aesthetic elements of the destination.[30] Literature promoting the capital and tourists' accounts of their visits emphasized the notion of civic landmarks as sacred space.

American families undertook lengthy cross-country trips to see historic sites. If the journey of the Ralph and Judith Gray family outlined in *National Geographic* in 1952 is typical, American families who visited historic sites experienced the same sense of sacred pilgrimage. The Grays began their Lincoln tour at Sinking Spring Farm in Rockport, Indiana, where the National Park Service built a memorial building surrounding "what is said to be the traditional birthplace cabin." The park historian informed Ralph that attendance to the site had tripled since 1946, and he noted from car license plates that visitors came not only from adjacent states, but also from as far away as Wisconsin, Colorado, and Massachusetts. "Children had raced up and down the long inviting slope of steps outside the memorial but once inside, their shenanigans ceased without a word from their parents. A reverent mood gripped each visitor."[31]

The reverent mood persisted as the family visited the memorial to Lincoln's mother, Nancy Hanks Lincoln, a hearthstone, and her grave. Ralph cited the homage to Lincoln's mother on the hearthstone as "the altar of his home, a place of joy in times of prosperity, as a refuge in adversity; a spot made sacred by the lives of those spent around it." The Gray family walked the trail of Historic Stones to her grave site: "It heightened our sense of history at this hallowed spot when Judith looked down at the rocky path and by good fortune picked up a perfectly shaped Indian arrowhead." The sacred and civic meshed as they walked back to the cabin site from the burial spot and "the great flag at the top of a massive shaft rippled and snapped in the stiff breeze."[32]

The trip through southern Indiana took them back in time. Part of the appeal for children was imagining scenes from Lincoln's childhood and visiting Knob Creek, where a friend saved Lincoln from drowning. The surroundings were still rustic, with log cabins and tobacco fields; Judith noted, "You get a real 'Lincoln feeling' on this road." The family pitched a tent in Lincoln State Park, "headquarters for four days while we visited the shrines in the hills of southern Indiana." Ralph described the crude three-sided cabins in which early settlers lived and remarked, "By camping, we felt we were re-creating in small degree the rugged conditions the Lincolns lived under during their first winter in Indiana." The park was adjacent to the memorial, affording them a chance to dip in the lake created by damming Little Pigeon Creek, "in which hundreds of visitors swim every summer week end." A photograph depicted Judith fixing breakfast for the family. The trip was not without excitement: After a rainy night, Ralph discovered a stray dog had bedded down on his daughter's pillow, "a cold nose buried in her hair." Another day, both daughters awoke with "bloated faces and eyes swollen shut," a reaction to coming into contact with poison oak. They spent two days in Vincennes while their daughters were being treated.[33]

The Gray family took muddy back roads to New Salem, Illinois, a reconstructed village where Lincoln began his public career. The family walked the streets, and the children rode in a Conestoga wagon pulled by oxen and climbed a rail fence, just as in Lincoln's time. On the Fourth of July, costumed actors represented people from Lincoln's day, like his first love, Ann Rutledge, and Chief Black Hawk in a play, *Forever This Land,* in the state park. "Among the carefully reconstructed cabins, the made-up and costumed actors lent the final touch of reality." Judith commented: "The Lincoln feeling is strong here . . . you can almost imagine him walking around." Even Ralph got into the act by comically imitating Lincoln's favored reading pose, lying on the grass with his feet propped up on a tree. The Grays concluded their Lincoln tour at the restored family home in Springfield and toured "the massive tomb north of town . . . a constant reminder to native and visitor alike of greatness that once lived nearby and now, dead of an assassin's bullet, is come home to rest." The last paragraph concludes on a solemn note: "Having followed the mortal trace of Abraham Lincoln from the cradle to the grave, my family and I turned sorrowfully to leave Springfield."[34]

Perhaps few families made a pilgrimage as elaborate as the Gray's, but certainly other families were touring the Lincoln sites. The Grays made a vacation of history with camping, roaming the wooded sites, and just being silly by riding on oxen or pretending to be Lincoln reading under a tree. By traveling in space, they also felt they were traveling backward in time, which enabled them to imagine themselves in the world of Abraham Lincoln. Despite the mishaps of stray dogs and poison oak, by traveling in the footsteps of the great American president, they paid homage to him and to the nation he united by force of war. Notably, absent from the travelogue is a consideration of race—ironic in light of Lincoln's freeing of the slaves, but understandable in a nation still segregated by race.

While some families spent their vacations visiting historic sites across the country, others took their children long distances to Washington, D.C. Those cross-country trips to the nation's capital lingered in the memories of children in the backseat of the car. In 1950 young Ann Whiting made a three-week cross-country trip in the family car from rural Utah to Washington, D.C., with her parents, a brother, and a sister. Her father, Ray Whiting, was a farmer and raised livestock, so the family left in the spring after the lambs were sold. The children missed school, but her teacher assigned her to write something about the journey. Ann remembers sitting in the backseat with her sister, Gayle, playing card games and doing embroidery. Her mother kept a cardboard lunch box behind her seat stocked with bread, mayonnaise, tuna fish, and bologna for feeding the family along the road. When the family arrived at a motel, her father told the children to duck down behind the seat to the floor so they would not be charged more for the room. They took the blue highways across because the (red) interstate highways had not yet been built. She remembers being excited to cross the Mississippi River in St. Louis, after days of anticipation. There they visited the zoo, including the snake house, even though her mother was afraid of snakes. They visited Washington again in 1953 and took family snapshots at Mount Vernon, the Lincoln Memorial, and the Tomb of the Unknown Soldier.[35]

Travel east to see relatives and the historic sites was such a high priority that they lived in the basement foundation of their house until 1954, when they took out a mortgage to complete the aboveground living space. Ann remembers, "We never felt poor in any way" because "my Dad always had a new car." The family stopped at other destinations on their cross-country trips. On the 1950 trip they traveled via Memphis, where they visited

The Whiting children of Utah visiting the Tomb of the Unknown Soldier, 1953.
(Courtesy Ann W. Orton.)

the zoo and the Pink Palace. In 1957 they took the train to Chicago, where they caught a bus to Flint, Michigan, picked up a new Buick, and drove to Niagara Falls and New York City, where they visited Ann's aunts. Ann still has the souvenirs from those trips: a painted aluminum coaster from Nebraska, the Corn Husker state, and a guide to the observatory of the Empire State Building. Half a century later, she still has a Kodachrome pocket guidebook to Washington, D.C., on which she wrote her name in cursive. Each page contained a "Picto-Chrome" photo in "natural color," faced by a page with a short description of the site's significance.[36]

Washington, D.C., was the premier site of civic pilgrimage. Allied victory in World War II enhanced a sense of the importance of Washington, D.C., as not just a national capital, but as the capital of the world, its most politically powerful city. Taking the family to the nation's capital was thus not merely an educational excursion, but also a civic pilgrimage for both parents and children. Thus the nation's capital was the premier destination for families who wanted to teach their children about America's heritage. Printed maps and guides compared travel to the capital to the religious experience of pilgrimage: "For every American citizen the trip is not merely a dutiful pilgrimage but a tremendously inspiring, informative, and enjoyable experience."[37]

Heady with victory, an ad in spring 1948 for the Baltimore and Ohio Railroad boasted "our magnificent National Capital has become the hub of the world—where headlines made today are the history of tomorrow." The illustration pictured parents with their son ascending the steps of the Capitol and suggested that a trip to Washington would cultivate a feeling of patriotism in children. "Give yourself and the youngsters a holiday—and a new appreciation of our country. Come to Washington, the keystone of world security—and the key to a marvelous time!" Visitors should see the Declaration of Independence and recently built monuments like the Jefferson Memorial or "the amazing Pentagon Building."[38]

A postwar map and guide to Washington, D.C., recognized the power of the city to imprint a consciousness of American ideals:

> This city, a symbol of the greatness of our republic, stirs the very fibers of his heart as he reflects that it stands for "one nation, indivisible, with Liberty and Justice for All." No matter how lowly or humble he may be, when he experiences the majesty of the Capitol, or the strong simplicity of the White House, he will realize that Washington is, in part his, and he will feel as did George Washington, Thomas Jefferson, Abraham Lincoln with millions of other Americans, the strength and

> enduring permanence of those ideals of democracy forming the foundation of this city and this nation. He and generations of Americans to come will gain inspiration from this city to make those ideals a part of their lives and our nation's living history.[39]

The theme of sacred sites in a city home to Americans was common. A widely distributed guide in 1964 claimed: "Every American, from childhood on, is imaginatively and emotionally attracted to see his nation's capital. He knows he will feel at home, even before he gets there—for this wondrous, shining city belongs to all Americans." In Washington, tourists could see "the national shrines, the stately public buildings, the foreign embassies and the historic tree-lined avenues that appear so much in the news. And here is the glamour of a city where our country's history has been made and is in the making."[40] The appeal to democratic ideals was characteristic of postwar tourist guides and maps; such homage to national landmarks was seen as a way to preserve those ideals in an uncertain world. Elaborate and explicit tourist maps and guides allowed travelers, especially children, to imagine themselves as living history in the times of George Washington and Abraham Lincoln.

The national park system promoted heritage travel by restoring national landmarks like Independence Hall and battlefields like Gettysburg. Its Mission 66 initiative sparked a decade-long effort to refurbish visitor's facilities at the national parks and monuments to meet the demands of tourists, who numbered 56.5 million visitors in 1955. Creating civic awareness was an explicit rationale for the financing of the improvements, which were seen as a way of helping Americans rekindle the idealism of the patriots of their past. Five million visits were made each year to the national monuments in Washington, D.C. In 1960 the top draw on the Mall was the Lincoln Memorial, which attracted 2.5 million visitors, followed by the Washington Monument, which attracted 1.4 million visitors. Over 800,000 people visited the White House in 1960, and in 1961, 1.3 million visited. The Jefferson Memorial saw nearly 1 million visitors in 1962, part of a total of 6.3 million visitors to Washington, D.C., in 1960. In 1963 visits to national memorials totaled over 7 million persons.[41]

Special events like meetings, rallies, and marches swelled the crowds in the capital. Three million persons attended special events in the capital in 1957, a total that rose to 4.5 million in 1960. The number of events rose from 233 in 1957 to 366 in 1961. The 1963 civil rights march on Washington on August 28, 1963, reoriented the Lincoln Memorial as a place of protest. Park reports indicate that 150,000 persons were assembled at the memorial, and that over 3 million persons visited it that year—a new record. Encouraged by the success of the mass demonstration, various groups sought permits for meetings and religious events in the parks. In 1965, over 4 million visited the Lincoln Memorial and nearly 2 million visited the Washington Monument. Nearly 8 million persons visited the national park sites in the capital, an increase of 2 percent over the previous year. To cope with the crush of visitors, for the first time, the National Park Service erected informational kiosks and staffed them with employees to answer visitors' questions.[42]

The list of sites on maps and guides changed over time to reflect changes in the Washington landscape and in visitor consciousness. Free oil company road maps indicated not only the location of buildings, but also what they looked like in tiny sketches so the visitor could easily identify them. The 1945 Rand NcNally *Road Atlas* featured the capital with a one-page map showing the location and hours of major departments of government, memorials, gardens, museums, art galleries, libraries, and the zoo. A decade later, the 1955 Esso road map (which featured a family in front of the Jefferson Memorial posing for pictures) included an index of U.S. government offices and agencies, hospitals and institutions, schools and colleges, along with the usual tourist destinations of monuments and museums. In 1963 the Esso company map displayed the U.S. Marine Corps War Memorial (Iwo Jima) on its cover, adding it to the list of sites tourists were obligated to visit.[43]

Popular magazines published articles guiding readers with families to Washington. Marjorie Holmes wrote "This Is Your Year for Washington" in *Better Homes and Gardens* in May 1955. She urged readers: "While the children are still young, enjoy with them the thrill of discovering the city that truly 'belongs' to every American." She confided, "We live in Washington, and love it. Perhaps that's why we urge every American family to make at least one pilgrimage to the capital. Here, and in neighboring areas, are graphic concepts of history and government that can never be matched in school."[44]

Holmes carefully laid out an itinerary for a week-long tour of the city, Mount Vernon, Williamsburg, Virginia, and Annapolis, Maryland. Among major destinations in the capital, Holmes included the White House, the Capitol, and the Supreme Court Building. The Washington Monument was a good place to start, and "a ride to the top is the first thing that small fry generally clamor for." While visitors rose to the top of the obelisk in the elevator, a "recording tells of the man who became the Father of our Country." And children should not miss the Smithsonian

Institution: "Put on your walking shoes and prepare to spend the day with the first airships and the Spirit of St. Louis, with the former first ladies in their inaugural ball gowns, with life-size dinosaurs, Teddy Roosevelt's wild-animal collection, fabulous gems."

In her capsule descriptions of the sites, Holmes used language to convey their sacred qualities. At the National Archives "in lighted cabinets lie the hallowed documents that brought this nation into being," their words of freedom "preserved for eternity." She referred to the Lincoln Memorial as a "temple," where, in the words of architect Daniel Chester French, "the memory of Abraham Lincoln is enshrined forever." She claimed: "One of the most profoundly moving memorials ever designed is that to the immortal Lincoln." Visitors to the Jefferson monument could read his "immortal words . . . carved on its immaculate marble walls." The most sacred site was Arlington National Cemetery, where "sentries keep ceaseless vigil at the Tomb of the Unknown Soldier. And each hour, quiet crowds gather to watch the simple, impressive ceremony of the changing of the guard."

Holmes's theme of sacred space was interwoven with her argument that Washington belonged to the American people. At the White House, where "every citizen is a welcome guest to the main-floor rooms," one might see a tricycle or scooter left by the president's visiting grandchildren, just like at home. "One of the nicest things about visiting the White House is the feeling that it is your house, too, somehow. No pressure is put upon you to hurry; you can linger as long as you like." The Supreme Court, an "immense classic temple where knickered page boys scurry about and the solemn wheels of justice turn," offered visitors the opportunity to participate in government. Once seated in the chambers, "your most thrilling moments come when you are seated in the spacious courtroom." Visitors watched as the "ruby velvet curtains" parted and the judges entered, "nine famous personalities familiar from newsprint and television." Holmes emphasized the tourist as citizen: "In presenting their decisions, they address the audience persuasively, less reading than reasoning—with you!"

There was no better place to see government at work than in the Capitol, "where the laws are made." She asked tourists to imagine themselves in the footsteps of famous American statesmen: "As you climb the broad plaza steps on the east front, you'll be walking where every president from Monroe to Eisenhower . . . has been inaugurated." Her description of the Capitol building suggests its cathedral-like qualities: "Within the ornate bronze doors is a circular rotunda, man-dwarfing, breath-taking, as it soars up and up to a dazzling, resplendent dome." Children could learn history from what they saw: "This façade, the entire building, is rich with paintings, frescoes, murals, and statuary, much of which the children will recognize from their schoolbooks: The Baptism of Pocahontas, the Surrender of Cornwallis." Guides explained the history and lore of the artwork in the rotunda, telling stories that were lessons in national ideals. To show the acoustic properties of the dome, guides would customarily stand across Statuary Hall from their groups and speak in a whisper. A pass was required to enter the spectator galleries as a result of increased security after shootings in 1954 by Puerto Rican nationalists. "You've come a long way to see this arm of America in action; when you do so, be free to witness the hectic but fascinating goings-on to the full."[45]

The list of sites for the 1950s visitor was long and included sites not familiar to today's visitor, such as "the American Red Cross, with its celebrated Tiffany window, museum, and impressive Civil Defense exhibit"; Constitution Hall, headquarters of the Daughters of the American Revolution; and the Pan American Union building, "with its exotic Aztec gardens and magnificent hall of the Americas." Perhaps more appealing to children was a visit to the Federal Bureau of Investigation. "There, every half-hour, bright young G-men demonstrate every conceivable type of crime detection. You'll hear enthralling tales of the capture of 'most wanted' crooks, saboteurs, and spies, be led past laboratories where actual evidence is being analyzed; the whole show winds up with a 'bang' in the shooting gallery." Cold war politics was a feature of her recommended driving tour of embassy row: "Most people are curious to spot that of Soviet Russia, at 1125 Sixteenth." Holmes's detailed tour guide concluded that "this is the year for Washington. Renew the kinship every American has with these scenes. It will package the past into a permanent treasure, yet relate it to the present in which all have such a vital stake. Especially those citizens of tomorrow—our youngsters!" Maps and promotional literature aimed at the vacationing family headed for Washington, D.C., played on the theme of civic pilgrimage. They did so by depicting sites as sacred and as places where every citizen, even "youngsters," could participate in democratic government.[46]

The experiences of ordinary American families visiting the capital reflects the idealism of the tourism literature—with a personal slant. Nate and Bobbie Corwin of suburban Philadelphia took their three children to Washington, D.C., in the summer of 1963. A World War II army veteran, Nate was a skilled carpenter in a home remodeling business, and Bobbie was known as a good cook. Bobbie's mother, a Russian immigrant and expert seamstress, sewed the summer dresses worn by Bobbie and her daughter, Andrea. Nate and his sons, Alan and Gary, were comfortable but not casual in lightweight slacks and short-sleeved shirts, and Alan wore a tie. Bobbie carried a purse, Andrea carried her own camera, and Alan shouldered the leather case for the family camera.

The Corwin family photographs tell the story of their pilgrimage to the White House, approaching it first from the south across the lawn of the ellipse, and then pausing at the marker from which all highway mileages are measured, fittingly on the grounds of the president's home. Bobbie snapped a photo of the children and Nate against the iron fence, and Andrea stood on the bottom rail to be taller than her dad. The red tulips and fountain behind make a picturesque backdrop to the family framing the White House, home of the first family. Perhaps tired of the sun, they went to the Capitol, where Alan, the oldest, solemnly posed in statuary hall while Andrea and Gary, distracted, mugged for the camera. Nate's shot caught his wife's upward gaze at the inside of the Capitol's dome with its fresco of clouds and mythic figures.

Outside on the portico, Nate posed his family to frame his view of the National Mall with the Washington Monument in the distance. Later, at the Lincoln Memorial, they stood still for Nate, the photographer, who centered them exactly between the two columns framing the statue of seated Abraham Lincoln. Andrea looked down at her camera, maybe to take a picture of her dad; Bobbie has her hand on her youngest son's shoulder. Alan, the oldest son, is grown up enough to stand on his own, apart from his mother and his younger sister and brother.

The family visit to Washington, D.C., was documented by the father as photographer, except for the rare shot taken by Bobbie to include him in the memories they were creating of the trip. The Corwins, children of immigrants, were a thoroughly American family that had achieved the success of the American dream of home ownership in a prosperous middle-class suburb. Their pilgrimage was a way of cementing that American identity, of passing it on to their children by visiting the nation's capital. All the historian has are photos, the memories created of the trip. The pictures tell the story of their pilgrimage.[47]

The account of an adolescent girl also helps us see the city through young eyes and suggests that traveling without one's family made for a far different experience. June Calendar, a farmer's daughter from Versailles, Indiana, painted a detailed picture in her report of her senior class trip in May 1956 to the capital. She and her classmates traveled by train with two male teachers as chaperones. They stayed four to a room at the Hotel

The Corwin family of Philadelphia visiting the White House, 1963. (Courtesy Andrea C. Weitzman.)

Harrington and traveled by bus to sites in Washington. The temperatures were record-breaking, in the 90-degree range, and "I was becoming very hot in those wool slacks and that orlon sweater." Their first stop was the Washington Monument, where they waited "a half hour or more in the hot sun, swatting off knats—of which there seemed to be several million." They took an elevator to the top while listening to a recorded orientation. It was worth the wait: "The view from the top was spectacular. All of Washington seemed to lie at our feet and it was very, very beautiful." She was impressed by the changing of the guard at Arlington:

> I was amazed at the precise way the soldier on guard paced in front of the tomb and then would stand at attention for about a minute then pace to the other side. Then a bunch of sailors came and put on a ritual and then the Navy Band, or a part thereof, played the Star Spangled Banner, I managed to get Goosebumps, I was so impressed. Then after a little more parading a bugler played Taps which was very haunting. The whole crowd was quiet while the whole ceremony was going on except for the constant click of cameras.[48]

The reverence of the crowd, the military ritual, and the music inspired June's emotional response to the tomb. Her patriotic feelings were

The Corwin family at the Capitol, 1963. (Courtesy Andrea C. Weitzman.)

reinforced in her visit to the newly built Marine Corps war memorial: "I felt that I could reach out and feel the texture of the soles of their shoes and the cloth of their uniforms and I was struggling with the marines as they raised the flag." The memorial made her feel as if she was there with the soldiers, part of the military victory at Iwo Jima made famous by photographer Joe Rosenthal.[49]

The remainder of her tour of Washington did not provoke as deep a response. She and her friends saw the first ladies' ball gowns and documents in the National Archives, where she admired the handwriting of Thomas Jefferson. The Capitol's broad staircases, murals, and dome were "really lovely," but she "wasn't greatly impressed by the Capitol—except to think that I would like someday to get used to walking around it—on business." The trip inspired her to imagine a political career for herself in the Capitol. As they walked to the train station for the ride home, she confessed, "I was disappointed beyond words that I didn't get to go inside the Lincoln memorial but only went past it." She had spent her evening on a boat ride down the Potomac with friends, putting her social needs ahead of a tourist itinerary. The beauty of the capital awoke in her a desire to live there some day. "It is by far the most beautiful city I could ever dream of living in and is certainly a fitting city to be our nation's capitol."[50]

These accounts suggest that although logistical concerns about what to eat, what to wear, and Washington's summer heat may have muted their reactions, ordinary people did experience a civic pilgrimage to the sacred sites. The size and scale of the Capitol building, the triumph of the Marine Corps memorial to Iwo Jima, and the solemn site of the Tomb of the Unknown Soldier provoked an emotional response in visitors. As travelers remembered their visits, they recalled the moments of grace where they were moved to contemplate the greatness of their nation. Families took photos and children bought souvenirs to remember their pilgrimage to the White House, the Capitol, and the Lincoln Memorial. The photographs integrated their family into the national landscape of monuments and memorials. Traveling together as a family in a ritual of civic pilgrimage, parents and children reinforced their sense of what it meant to be American.

Heritage travel boomed in the decades after World War II as American families visited the nation's capital or constructed their own cross-country pilgrimage to historic sites. Travel writers portrayed Washington, D.C., or Lincoln's Salem as sacred sites that would impress a sense of citizenship upon the traveler. If family travelers experienced civic pilgrimage in fainter form, perhaps it was because the supposedly sublime experience of travel was in reality more mundane. Cardboard boxes of food, pesky insects, long lines, and rough roads had a way of muting emotional response to the sacred shrines. Whether because parents sought a sense of national community or because they wanted to imprint a national identity in their children through travel, making the journey is evidence of their strong belief in the value of the travel ritual. Family tourists depended on the consumable geography of road maps and guides designed to appeal to the family vacationer with happy portraits of the nuclear family of parents and two children—always white. Guides and maps suggested a freedom of the road for all Americans, but in reality, they shunted Americans toward prepackaged sites.

For African Americans, the civic pilgrimage was a bitter lesson in the limits of citizenship. Washington was a southern city with segregated hotels and rooming houses, evidence of racial prejudice in stark contrast to the ideals inscribed on the capital's monuments.[51] How African Americans resisted Jim Crow on the road is also part of the story of American pilgrimage, of claiming citizenship in the national geography.

chapter three

Vacation without Humiliation

On a hot day in July 1963, members of the Senate Committee on Commerce listened to testimony regarding the civil rights bill. Roy Wilkins, executive secretary of the NAACP (National Association for the Advancement of Colored People) began his testimony by reminding senators that "for millions of Americans this is vacation time. Swarms of families load their automobiles and trek across the country." He suggested the committee imagine themselves "darker in color" on an auto trip across the country and asked:

> How far do you drive each day? Where and under what conditions can you and your family eat? Where can they use a rest room? Can you stop driving after a reasonable day behind the wheel or must you drive until you reach a city where relatives or friends will accommodate you and yours for the night? Will your children be denied a soft drink or an ice cream cone because they are not white?

When questioned by Senator John O. Pastore as to what families did in these circumstances, Wilkins admitted, "You take your chances. You drive and you drive and you drive." Unable to stop when tired because there were no accommodations, he said, "You keep on driving until the next city or the next town where you know somebody or they know somebody who knows somebody who can take care of you."[1]

Wilkins's comments were supported by remarks from Senator Jacob Javits, who read into the record an article in *Hotel Monthly* about a black family denied accommodations at a motel in St. Petersburg, Florida. The "tired and hungry" family was riding in a "new Chrysler" and the father, Ralph Sims, owned an appliance business worth a half million dollars. When Sims asked the price of a room, the motel owner quoted the outrageous price of $50,000. Sims said he would pay double the rate that the proprietor charged others because "I've got two kids out there. They haven't had a good meal all day, we're all exhausted and we can't find any place to sleep." The motel manager refused, and the story concluded: "That night the Sims family, who were Negroes, tried to doze curled up inside their parked car, counting the minutes until sunrise when they would begin hunting a colored restaurant for breakfast."[2]

The family traveler was a common theme in testimony regarding public accommodations in the hearings for Title II of the civil rights bill of 1964. The remarks by Wilkins and Javits echoed the words of Martin Luther King Jr. in his Letter from Birmingham Jail, written a few months earlier. Defending the marches and protests against those who argued for patience, he wrote that it made him impatient "when you take a cross-country drive and find it necessary to sleep night after night in the uncomfortable corners of your automobile because no motel will accept you."[3]

The image of innocent children having to sleep in the car was aimed at public sympathy in an era of family togetherness. The comments of Wilkins and Javits were not mere coincidence but a calculated strategy to appeal to members of Congress, and to blacks and whites alike. In the face of Jim Crow laws in the South and persistent racial discrimination in the rest of the nation, the cultural icon of the family vacation was offered as persuasive evidence of the need for a federal law to ensure the rights of all citizens. Framing the experience of travel into a family narrative was essential to engendering sympathy for the civil rights struggle and led to the passage of the landmark Civil Rights Act of 1964.

In a nation where schools, housing, and society were segregated, vacationing was also segregated by race. Travelers in Jim Crow America—where whites and blacks were made to use different restrooms, drink at different water fountains, eat in different restaurants, and stay in different hotels—were citizens as well as consumers. Discrimination against black travelers meant that vacationing was a fundamentally different experience for them than it was for white families in cold war America. It was an uncertain, even fear-filled, experience because blacks never could be sure that they would find places to sleep and eat on the road. Indeed, African Americans often feared for their safety, even their very lives, as they traveled the dark highways of the Deep South. Historians of tourism have argued that travel was a way of affirming one's identity as an American and have argued that travel was a ritual of citizenship. By failing to acknowledge the meaning of race in the travel experience, we perpetuate "color-blind conceptions of national identity" of the culture of segregation.[4] Racial segregation and discrimination while traveling demonstrated the limits of citizenship and complicated the claims of African Americans to American identity. At the same time, whether they intended to or not, white travelers sustained segregation with their travel dollars and shielded their children from understanding the true legacies of slavery.

To resist Jim Crow, by the 1930s blacks had created an entirely separate tourist infrastructure, including their own travel guides and travel agencies that directed travelers to places where they would be welcome without fear of humiliation. Tourism's dual economy began to crumble as war veterans demanded their rights and as members of a growing black middle class claimed the privileges afforded them by their income. Because travel was bound up in consumerism and citizenship, both economic boycotts and political action were required for African Americans to become full consumers and complete citizens. The right to consume, to stay where you could afford to stay, eat where you could afford to eat, even to move freely on the highway, were inextricably bound up in rights of citizenship. As Roy Wilkins reminded the audience that hot July day in the Senate hearings, these "are people, human beings, citizens of the United States of America. This is their country."[5]

Although whites traveled freely to places they could afford, blacks were denied the right to travel the highways and eat and sleep where they pleased. To assert their rights as citizens, they drew on liberal ideals of fairness and on the principles of free enterprise in an expanding corporate economy. We may be familiar with the history of battles against discrimination on public transport, but how blacks battled the discrimination in public accommodations on the road, and how that was viewed through the lens of the family ideal, is an untold story.

Black Families on the Road

In July 1962, John Easterling of Denver, Colorado, wrote to the NAACP in New York City to lodge a complaint against the Mobil Oil Company. He and his wife and two children were on vacation together and were traveling through Shreveport, Louisiana. As he explained in his letter, "We have a credit card from Mobil Oil Co. so we stopped at Craigs Mobil Serv. To fill up our car & to use the rest rooms." Then, he recounted, "while the attendant was putting in the gas, we saw signs for ladies and men rest rooms, knowing the south we ask for rest rooms

Black travel guides like The Negro Travelers' Green Book *(1956) helped travelers avoid humiliation. (Photographer Peter Rugh. Courtesy Schomberg Center for Research in Black Culture, New York Public Library, Astor, Lenox, and Tilden Foundations.)*

& were informed they didn't have rest room facilities for coloured." The women and children "were on their way to the ladies rest room, that was in plain sight." He wrote that they "had to be called back, we then had to stop on the highway like animals."[6]

The Easterling family had the means to travel in their own car, and John Easterling earned enough to hold a credit card. However, their middle-class status meant nothing because of their racial status as "coloured" in the Deep South in the early 1960s. The proprietor of this Mobil Oil station was willing to sell them gas and take their money, but he adhered to Southern customs in providing restrooms for whites only. The refusal to let the Easterlings use the whites-only restrooms meant the family had to relieve themselves along the side of the road, "like animals." Humiliated and angered, Easterling pressed the NAACP to file a suit.

Such incidents were typical of the discrimination reported in letters to the NAACP, written by those who carefully constructed stories of their mistreatment on the road. By 1946, the membership of the NAACP had grown rapidly to about 400,000 persons in over 1,000 chapters. Its dues-paying members expected the NAACP to take action on the letters of complaint written to the chapter officers, who then forwarded them to the national organization. The NAACP staff relied on the letters to identify targets and craft strategies in the fight for civil rights.[7]

Those who wrote took care to point out that such incidents were doubly humiliating when family members were watching. Retired U.S. army captain Vance H. Marchbanks, who was returning from vacation with his wife and daughter in Los Angeles to Tuskegee Institute, Alabama, in June 1941, used that term to describe being denied the use of the restrooms and the water fountain at a Union Oil station in Opelika, Alabama. "I am a retired army officer, having served forty-four years in the army, and this is the most humiliating experience I have ever had, and we have traveled from coast to coast, and from the Great Lakes to the Gulf of Mexico."[8]

Children were often perplexed by the refusal of attendants to let their families use their restrooms. James Smith and his family stopped at a Texaco station in Bessemer, Alabama, in July 1962, and while his car was being refueled, he "asked permission to use the lavatory." An attendant "standing directly in front of the Men's Room told me that he didn't have a lavatory. My ten year old son, Dwight said, 'there's the bathroom right there.'" Dwight, a boy from Bridgeport, Connecticut, was unfamiliar with the segregated South, and he could not understand why his father was told there was no restroom when it was in plain sight.[9]

Because the family vacation in postwar America was primarily an automobile touring operation, black families who traveled by car depended on the services of gas stations. Filling stations were generally franchises of the larger oil companies, independently owned but part of a larger network of suppliers. Oil companies were huge promoters of travel in this period, supplying not only gas and oil at a reasonable cost and on credit, but also amenities like free maps, clean restrooms, and water fountains. Customers came to expect those amenities, and the sign "clean restrooms" was a code signifying that women and children were welcome to use the facilities. By supplying clean restrooms, oil company franchisees signaled their eagerness to attract family travelers. The quid pro quo of gasoline purchases for restrooms was obvious to Mrs. Annie Hayes, who motored from Dallas to New York City with her husband in June 1947. She claimed they were denied the use of restrooms in Texas, Arkansas, and Tennessee. She felt it was unfair that dealers would sell them products "and not provide these comforts for us also."[10]

Most letters of complaint sent to the NAACP about discrimination at gas stations focused on segregated restrooms (although water fountains were also segregated). In no case did the gas station attendant refuse to fill the car with gas, and in many cases, black customers chose a certain station because they had a credit card for that brand. Although paying customers were sometimes refused access to the water fountain, more common was the refusal to allow customers to use the restrooms set aside for whites. In Southern states, such restrooms were built in response to state laws that mandated segregation in public accommodations, but proprietors were not legally required to make toilets available to all customers. Indeed, when they were available, restrooms for black customers were invariably "around the back" and were not locked, presumably because they were not attended to or cleaned.

Discrimination persisted because gas stations were independently owned, and segregated restrooms were the rule in the South. As one Humble Oil Company official explained in response to a complaint, "We give these dealers advice on many phases of good business practice . . . [but] we are in no position to direct the manner in which these dealers actually conduct their business." When dentist H. Boyd Hall of Corpus Christi, Texas, wrote a letter to Humble Oil in September 1948 complaining that they were "putting up Jim Crow toilets," the oil company official responded with surprise. He claimed that he had received praise from "Negro friends for making modern sanitary rest rooms available for their use when they travel." He claimed they felt it was a good investment and attracted new customers. The disclaimers of oil companies that they were not responsible may ring hollow to our ears, but in legal terms, they were on firm ground in absolving themselves of the offenses committed by their independent dealers.[11]

Some black customers were not willing to be humiliated. Jewell Handy Gresham of New York City stopped in January 1960 at a Gulf Station in Macon, Georgia, with her brother, her husband, and their four-year-old daughter. While the car was being filled, as she related, "I took my daughter by the hand and went to the ladies rest room. Finding it locked, I stopped inside the station and asked the attendant for the key. He informed me that the rest room for 'Colored' was in the back. I told him that it was not my custom to use 'back' rest rooms, whereupon he took the key from the wall and turned his back on me." Perhaps because she was with her young daughter, Gresham refused to use the restrooms in the back. By so doing, she asserted her dignity at the expense of personal comfort.

Gresham, a doctoral student at Teachers College, Columbia University, in New York, complained in a three-page letter to the public relations officer at Gulf Oil of the "incongruity of denying the normal courtesy facilities which go along with paid patronage." She felt that humanitarian needs of Negro travelers were being ignored. "I cannot tell you what handicaps are endured by Negro motorists traveling through the South—often for long and weary miles—unable to be sure of finding adequate accommodations for taking care of the normal physiological functions of the body and for rest, relaxation, and refreshments."[12] Gresham stated what is so clearly implied: that to refuse access to restrooms, or to supply segregated restrooms, was an insult to the humanity of black customers. To deny services to black travelers was to suggest they were not human and did not have the need to deal with bodily functions in privacy.

Traveling families also faced discrimination at restaurants along the road, all over the country. In the late 1940s, blacks who wrote to the NAACP complained of being refused service in the Midwest (Bloomington, Indiana, and Zanesville, Ohio); the West (Reno, Nevada); and the Northeast (Port Jefferson, New York)—all outside the South. Even in 1961, so many black tourists from the South along Route 66 in Illinois were refused restaurant service that they took to bringing their food along and eating in their cars, "rather than chance being embarrassed."[13]

While African American highway travelers expected to have trouble in the South, they were frequently denied accommodations in the North.

On a bitterly cold night in Cheyenne, Wyoming, in 1949, Reverend Raymond Calhoun, his wife, and their two infant children were denied accommodation at eight different places. The reverend finally approached a state trooper, who told him that if he "was really interested in getting accommodations he would have no trouble across the railroad tracks at the Black and Tan." Fearful that such accommodations would be second-rate, he did not cross the tracks, but finally his family was taken in by a kind soldier. The president of the Syracuse, New York, branch of the NAACP who wrote the complaint letter stated he was "shocked at this Jim Crowism which took place, not in the deep south, but in the wide open spaces of the West." In another incident, lawyer Linwood G. Koger Jr. of Baltimore was surprised when his family was denied accommodations at the Bronx Park Motel near New York City in June 1961, especially because they had made reservations not twenty minutes earlier at another hotel on the New England thruway.[14]

One woman wrote at great length to the NAACP about her experience and claimed rights based on the recent military service of her two brothers, who were traveling with her. In 1945 Mrs. Bessye Brown was traveling from Chicago with her sister and brothers to check on family property in Bloomington, Illinois. They waited 25 minutes at the Woolworth's lunch counter before the manager told them they would not be served. Brown was incensed by their treatment: "Now mind you both of these boys have seen service. One had on his suit the other his discharge button but even that didn't phase them." The brother who had served in England had been in the medical corps, where he "had to minister to white soldiers, his hands probably touching every part of the human body and he comes back to this." Brown confronted the white manager about their treatment and asked, "Do you mean to tell me colored boys fought so smug people like you are saved and left behind. You probably have a colored cook home stirring up your biscuits with her hands!" Unusually vocal about her opinions, she zeroed in on what she thought made whites uncomfortable about eating with blacks: they might accidentally come into contact, skin to skin, light to dark. The formidable Bessye Brown concluded her letter by stating plainly how she felt: "I was never so humiliated or embarrassed in my life."[15]

War veterans thought that they deserved better treatment, given their service to the nation. Sailor Shirley H. Day wrote about an experience on his honeymoon in Nevada, a letter he typed on San Francisco Astoria Hotel stationery. He and his wife stopped at the Victor Coffee Shop on Virginia Street and sat in a booth together. As he wrote, "we was not

Prosperous middle-class blacks had the means to travel widely in the family car, 1959. (Frank Bauman, photographer, LOOK Magazine *Collection, Library of Congress, Prints & Photographs Division.)*

thir every long before a waters, come over and said 'we're verry Sorry but we dont Serve Colerd Peoples.'" Dispirited by the spoiling of his honeymoon, he marched down to the police station to make a complaint. The police answered that the city council had written the law that way and "that was nothing that thay could do about it, so I say *think.*" In an eloquent postscript, Day stated that he had been a prisoner of war in Japan and had been "over there" thirteen months. His brother had been killed in Nuremberg. He asked, "Why don't the American Peoples treat us like they did when thir was a War going on?" Day could not spell very well, but he could certainly think, and it did not sit well with him. Why should he serve his country and not be able to take his bride to lunch? It did not make sense to him.[16]

Whether those who wrote to the NAACP were denied the use of restrooms at a gas station, service at a lunch counter, or a place to sleep, the emotion they most often cited was humiliation. At home they might know how to avoid places that would treat them that way, but on the road they were in unfamiliar territory and especially vulnerable to humiliation. Their treatment was made even more humiliating because it was in front of their family. Members of their family could see that they were denied the privileges of citizenship, and that they were powerless to obtain their rights. And because they were on vacation and did not want to provoke a confrontation, parents were less likely to insist on fair treatment.

Avoiding Humiliation

Black travelers who were refused service in public accommodations had the option of patronizing black-owned businesses. The rise of black-owned travel businesses was a way to circumvent humiliation, and it recirculated tourist dollars within the black economy. Two travel guides attempted to spare black travelers that humiliation, the *Green Book,* published from 1936 to 1966, and *Travelguide,* which began in 1946. New York travel agent Victor Green began the *Green Book* as a local guide in 1936, and the next year it began national coverage. Green stated that the guide was modeled on Jewish travel guides, and it was for many years the sole travel guide for blacks. Perhaps as a way of deflecting criticism that they might be accommodating Jim Crow, in the introduction to the *Green Book* editors stated that someday "we can go wherever we please, and without embarrassment," but until then, the guide was published for the reader's convenience. As the driving force of the *Green Book,* Green's motto was, "If Negro-owned business is good, it can be better with advertising." In the twentieth anniversary edition in 1956, the foreword told readers that the guide "has made traveling more popular, without encountering embarrassing situations." Their goal was "Assured Protection for the Negro Traveler."[17]

Guides listed establishments by state and city in four categories: hotels, motels, tourist homes, and restaurants. Arranged by city within the state listing, each line listed the name and address of the business. Businesses paid extra to have their listing in bold print, or to have a star added denoting "recommended." For example, in 1956 a traveler headed to Arkansas could stay in Camden at Mr. Hugh Hill's Tourist Home and eat at the Harlem Restaurant in Fordyce. In the city of Hot Springs, a traveler of means would stay at McKenzie's Motel, "The South's Finest Motel," or for more affordable lodgings, one could choose from a list of four tourist homes or apartments. Travelers to Detroit, Michigan, could choose among two dozen hotels, but in Minneapolis, they would only find two hotels and one tourist home. Listings for New York State filled four pages, while New Hampshire had only three establishments that would serve blacks, including the Last Chance Motel in Twin Mountain on U.S. Highway 3.

In the West, travelers would be welcome at only four hotels and the YWCA in Utah, but New Mexico offered over a dozen motels or tourist homes and Aunt Brenda's Restaurant, which catered to black travelers, most along Route 66. Los Angeles boasted the starred Clark Hotel among the dozen hotels listed, along with three tourist homes, five motels, and five restaurants. The same edition's feature article, "Two Weeks With Pay," explained that "little racial friction" would be found in New Mexico, but that travelers would be judged on the basis of "cash not color." In addition to the listings, each edition contained a feature article, such as air travel, foreign travel, or a domestic travel destination, such as Louisville, New York City, or Chicago.[18]

Throughout its run, the *Green Book* remained a no-frills alphabetical listing handy to have in the glove box. In comparison, *Travelguide,* founded in 1946 and published through 1955, was a more racially assertive publication with the motto: "Vacation & Recreation without Humiliation." Edited by W. H. "Billy" Butler, *Travelguide* relied on advertising by its major sponsor, Blatz Brewing of Milwaukee, to pay the high production costs. Each edition sported a cover photo of attractive, well-dressed women in scenic vacation spots and featured full-page ads for Schenley whiskey and Philip Morris cigarettes. The *Pittsburgh Courier* and black radio stations advertised in its pages, as did prosperous businesses, like Roy Campanella Wines and Liquors, the Savoy Ballroom, Beulah Bullock's convertible traveling fashions, and Rose Meta's House of Beauty, all in New York City.[19]

More than just "a directory of accommodations unrestricted as regards race," *Travelguide* listed civil rights laws for each state and the addresses of the NAACP headquarters in each city. Every edition carried advertisements for the NAACP, the National Urban League, and the United Negro College Fund. In a feature called "*Travelguide* Salutes!" the guide published short biographies and photos of prominent black citizens like statesman Ralph Bunche, baseball star Roy Campanella, radio broadcaster Barry Gray, or theater director Margaret Webster. Heroes to the race, and exemplars of the American values of equality and fairness, the people highlighted in the pages of *Travelguide* reminded readers that they should take an active role in fighting racial discrimination.[20]

Black-owned travel agencies attempted to prevent the embarrassment black travelers encountered when reservations made through white agencies were not honored. In the summer of 1950 Miss Barbara Simmons made reservations to attend the Tanglewood Music Festival in Massachusetts. She and her group of friends arranged their hotel reservations through Ambassador Travel Agency of New York, but when she arrived and "it became obvious she was a Negro," the Festival House refused to accommodate her, and she had to stay in a rooming house "clearly for Negroes." When Simmons later lodged a complaint to the New York travel agent, he was "exceptionally abusive and unpleasant."[21]

To spare travelers embarrassment like that suffered by Barbara Simmons, in the mid-1950s, Admiral Tours and King Travel catered to the growing black travel market, and black travel guides operated their own travel referral agencies. More commonly African American travelers sought the services of a travel agent for foreign travel. Educators and black professionals favored affordable Bermuda and Mexico; they traveled there to avoid the segregation that they had encountered in the United States. Edwin B. Henderson, director of the Washington, D.C., schools' department of health for black students, promoted Mexico in an article in *Afro* magazine in April 1955. Noting the absence of racial discrimination, he stated: "During my recent trip there, for the first time in my life on the continent, I felt like a first-class American citizen." He argued, "colored Americans will find in Mexico more of beauty, culture, and friendliness than Miami or our Southern-most beaches will afford, even if or when vestiges of Jim Crow have disappeared." Henderson enjoyed traveling there because "you don't have to fear a barber's chair, or a 'no accommodations' stare by a hotel clerk in Mexico."[22] Ironically, to feel like a citizen, Henderson had to leave his country.

White Resistance

The letters of complaint to the NAACP were eloquent expressions of the humiliation felt by travelers who were turned away while traveling with their families. By writing a letter of protest, they were making claims to rights of public accommodation that they thought were due them as citizens of the United States. Those who denied them those rights argued that the rights of property ownership allowed them to choose their customers. Whites stayed in motels and ate at restaurants whose management turned away persons who were not white. A segregated travel infrastructure meant that whites would not have to sleep on the same sheets, swim in the same pools, or sit their bare bottoms on the same toilet seats as black travelers. Outside the South, most whites were probably oblivious to the fact that they were traveling within racially segregated spaces because whiteness stood as the norm. Yet evidence suggests that many white travelers chose to look the other way when they stayed in motels or ate at restaurants that would not serve black fellow travelers.

Cultural clues suggest that whites found the plight of black travelers comical, a funny joke. In 1953 an episode of the *Amos n' Andy Show* opened with a scene of Sapphire and her mother at the kitchen table making vacation plans with $400 from Sapphire's parents. At first they thought of Maine, where they could go "swimming, camping, [and] square dancing." Sapphire says, "I'm so excited I can smell the Maine pine trees." But unbeknownst to Sapphire, her husband, Kingfisher, has been withdrawing from their savings, and the $400 is gone. He and his pal Amos, the taxicab driver, talk it over, and decide he should sell his car to replace the money. He arrives home with the $400 just as the women have arranged to buy a travel trailer with the $400. They justify their purchase as a way to "stay away twice as long and see twice as much." Kingfisher attempts to earn back the money by charging a friend for taking him on a fishing vacation (actually Central Park), but when Sapphire and her mother discover his deception, they chase him out of the park.[23]

While whites may have found the situation laughable, any black viewer would have recognized that a trailer was a good solution to the problem of finding places to stay in the Jim Crow era. Despite the distasteful way in which the sitcom portrayed blacks (leading the NAACP to ask Blatz Brewing to cancel their sponsorship in 1953), the television show made light of a tragic truth. In 1953 blacks were not free to travel about the country because they were frequently denied lodging and refused service at restaurants. Maine, where Sapphire wanted to go, was an especially hostile place for travelers of color. Kingfisher's bumbling of the responsibility of the family vacation was just another reminder to white viewers that blacks neglected the family responsibilities held up as a national ideal in the 1950s.[24]

To understand the views of whites upholding Jim Crow, we can turn to arguments made to maintain racial segregation in the civil rights legislation of 1964. Although we do not have direct testimony from white travelers, we do have testimony by those who owned the establishments where they stayed. The owners' arguments were the other side of the coin of citizen consumers: they argued that owning property gave them the right to decide who should be their customers. And, they argued, if they admitted blacks, whites would stay away and their business would be ruined. Underlying their argument was an argument of fear, because they believed that white customers would stay away because they feared bodily contact with black customers.

Samuel J. Setta of Easton, Maryland, owned a mom-and-pop motel, typical, he said, of 85 percent of the motels in the nation. He opposed the civil rights bill "because it is aimed at businesses which are strictly private enterprise." Because "the customer is the boss," he saw his job as meeting their needs. "In my motel if my customers want TV, I provide TV. If my customers want room phones, I provide room phones. And if they prefer a segregated motel, I provide a segregated motel." He denied that he rejected a black customer "because of his color." He argued instead that "the Negro is rejected because he is an economic liability to our business." He buttressed his economic arguments with potent racism, arguing that segregation was "the law of nature." When Setta said that blacks were more likely to be diseased than whites, Senator Munroney pointed out that most of the fine dining establishments in the South relied on black cooks and servers. Upon further questioning about the inconsistency of hiring blacks but not allowing them to be customers, Setta admitted that all of his employees were African American. But he defended his logic of segregation by saying, "In my motel it is a lot more intimate for a man to jump in bed with his clothes off and sleep in it than it is for that maid to pick up those sheets and lay them on there." Setta argued that the fear of bodily contact, of whites touching the same sheets blacks had slept in, even though laundered, was a rationale for him to exclude blacks as customers.[25]

The same rationale, that fear of contact with blacks would scare away whites, was used by Edgar S. Kalb, manager of the Beverly Beach Club in Mayo, Maryland. He contended that segregated private beaches should be available to "persons who do not desire to bathe with the persons who patronize these public beaches." Senator Strom Thurmond probed further in his questioning by asking, "You feel this would hurt your business if this bill passes?" Kalb answered bluntly: "Senator, this wouldn't hurt my business; this would destroy my business." Because the private beach served a community of adjacent privately owned beach cottages, desegregation, he argued, "would be a rape of those communities, in plain language." The use of the sexual metaphor of rape appears deliberately calculated to conjure up the image of the black male preying on white "female" communities. His language insinuated the sexual politics that spawned and sustained the culture of segregation since Reconstruction.[26]

The conversation that followed made it plain that fear of the sexuality of black men was at the core of the custom of segregated beaches. Senator Hart asked if Kalb, who employed thirty-five to forty blacks, "would not object to swimming with them." Kalb replied, "Yes, sir; and I wouldn't want my wife to swim with them, and I wouldn't want my daughter-in-law to swim with them; no sir, under no condition." Kalb makes clear

Florida's beaches were racially segregated, 1959. (Frank Bauman, photographer, LOOK Magazine *Collection, Library of Congress, Prints & Photographs Division.)*

here his patriarchal duty to protect the women in his family from any possible contact with black men in the water. To Kalb, white women and black men in the same body of water was "just taboo, and it is taboo to the average white person I come into contact with." Because he feared breaking the taboo would cost him his white customers, Kalb thought that ending segregation would destroy his business.[27]

The hotel manager in Florida who turned away Ralph Sims and his family in 1955, forcing them to sleep in their car, cited the same fear as underlying his decision. The white manager, who was from Chicago, admitted he felt sorry for the Sims family but that he turned them away because if they were seen, it would disturb the regular customers. "I would kiss away a thousand dollars a year right there," he said. He continued, "And then just suppose they had wanted to use the pool this morning."[28] As swimming pools became a standard feature of roadside motels, the problem of race in motels was exacerbated, hardening the boundaries of segregation in accommodations. Owners of motels and beaches feared they would lose their white customers, who they believed would not swim in the same pools or sleep between the same sheets as black customers. While whites traveled freely and stayed where they could afford to, black

The family of Dr. John O. Brown swimming at one of the few black-owned motels with a pool in Florida, 1959. (Frank Bauman, photographer, LOOK Magazine *Collection, Library of Congress, Prints & Photographs Division.)*

families like the Sims either spent the night in their cars or stayed in the "black and tan" part of town at possibly inferior lodgings listed in the travel guides.

Challenging Jim Crow

The barriers of the segregation in public accommodations began to erode in the early 1960s. Within the black community, the question was, were the travel guides resisting or accommodating to Jim Crow? A rising middle class of African American professionals and educators protested that they would be accommodating Jim Crow by staying only in black-owned businesses. As early as 1953, NAACP public relations director Henry Lee Moon cautiously responded to a sample booklet for black travelers sent to him by a public relations firm "serving the Negro market." Moon thought that some would be happy to have it, but others "will look upon it as an attempt to steer them into Jim Crow quarters and, accordingly, might resent it."[29] Second, prosperous blacks felt such hotels to be second-rate, and wanted to stay in the higher-quality white-owned lodging. Many of the black-owned hotels were members of the Nationwide Hotel Association, a "great Negro Hotel" association, but many of its properties were at best second-rate. By the mid-1950s it suggested its members raise standards by modernizing their properties. In 1961 the *Green Book* urged black-owned businesses to raise their standards because today's traveler "is no longer content to pay top prices for inferior accommodations and services." Black travelers who could afford it preferred to stay in an integrated lodging establishment like the new interstate motels rather than detour to a black-owned motel in a remote highway location.[30]

The growth of the civil rights movement sharpened the rhetoric of rights in travel guides that catered to African Americans. The 1963 *Green Book* opened with an article called "Your Rights, Briefly Speaking!" that listed states that had salutary civil rights policies and where victims of discrimination could apply for redress. The article sent a clear message to readers that "the Negro is only demanding what everyone else wants . . . what is guaranteed all citizens by the Constitution of the United States." The *Green Book* acknowledged publicly that protests and demonstrations have "widened the areas of public accommodations accessible to all," but they created the listings because they realized "that a family planning a vacation hopes for one that is free of tensions and problems." The inside back page of the *Green Book* advertised Langston Hughes's history of the

NAACP, *Fight for Freedom,* a sign of a rising consciousness that would soon put the *Green Book* out of business.[31]

Responses to discrimination in business travel set the stage for broadening the battle to pleasure travel on the road. The NAACP had long brought incidents of discrimination to the attention of the parent companies of hotels, restaurants, and gas stations. Business travelers had always been quick to contact their local chapter of the NAACP in hopes that legal action would be taken. In the late 1940s these practices were brought to the attention of Thurgood Marshall, special counsel to the NAACP, who notified the offending hotels that they were in violation of state law and that he would ask the district attorney's office to intercede with the Hotelmen's Association. After a 1947 embarrassment when Negro delegates to the United Nations Educational, Scientific and Cultural Organization brought suit against a Denver, Colorado, hotel for denying them accommodations, the NAACP became proactive in checking out hotel procedures before conferences. During the 1950s professional and scientific organizations that had black members began to carefully investigate hotel practices and refused to schedule meetings at hotels that discriminated against their colored guests. By late in the decade, larger hotels in northeastern cities had open-occupancy policies, largely as a result of pressure put on hotel and motel chains by black travelers.[32]

As more black travelers refused to accommodate Jim Crow, the NAACP pursued a strategy of putting pressure on two national restaurant and hotel chains, Howard Johnson's and Hilton Hotels. Because they were a large and well-recognized chain, Howard Johnson restaurants made a suitable target. The NAACP had documented a consistent pattern of discrimination at Howard Johnson restaurants, and Thurgood Marshall had extracted an apology from the chain regarding an incident in 1941. In 1947 Marshall was refused service at the same Elizabeth, New Jersey, restaurant (certainly not a coincidental choice), and he lost patience with corporate executives' promises. In a letter to the company, he demanded that they not "tolerate this asinine effort to circumvent the policy of Howard Johnson's Restaurants, as well as the Civil Rights Law of the State of New Jersey." Unsatisfied with a reply from corporate headquarters denying that they were affiliated with the restaurant, Marshall and his traveling companion, Andrew Weinberger, sued for $500 in damages.[33]

As one would expect of an ice cream shop, children were involved in incidents at Howard Johnson restaurants. In August 1947 James Clair

Taylor of Paterson, New Jersey, and his eight-year-old son visited the Howard Johnson restaurant on the highway near Wilmington, Delaware. While Taylor was standing at the urinal in the restroom, a man interrupted him to tell him the restroom was for "white people." He replied the sign on the door read "Gentlemen," calmly washed his hands, and went back upstairs to pick up his order of sandwiches and ice cream.[34]

The problems at Howard Johnson persisted. In 1960 F. Weldon Younger and his wife were vacationing when they were refused service at the Howard Johnson café in Hagerstown, Maryland. According to his letter summarizing the incident, they waited a long time to be served and were glared at by the head waitress. Finally "a Negro wearing a white cap and an apron . . . stopped at our table and said, 'We can not serve you.'" Younger recalled:

> My polite assertions that we were very hungry; that we were U.S. citizens; strangers in the vicinity; that we had a Diner's club card; we were able to pay; we had Standard Oil and Texaco credit cards; are members of AAA, and they recommended Howard Johnson cafes to us; that it was undemocratic, unchristian and inhuman to turn us away hungry—all of this brought firm and positive answers that we or no other colored people would be served in this Howard Johnson café.

He would have expected discrimination "in the deep south," but not "eight miles south of the Pennsylvania border and about fifty two miles northwest of Washington, D.C., our national capitol."[35] In his complaint he was asserting his rights as a citizen consumer, arguing that he should be served in a place where he could afford to pay the bill. In essence, he was claiming rights due to him as a credit-card-carrying member of the American middle class.

In an atmosphere of rising racial tensions provoked by the 1961 summer Freedom Rides, CORE (Congress of Racial Equality) undertook a campaign in 1962 to integrate roadside eateries, primarily targeting Howard Johnson. CORE's press release calling for volunteers boasted, "Last year we virtually ran jimcrow out of the bus terminals. He still lurks on the highways of America and raises the 'whites only' signs too often when the Negro traveler stops at a Howard Johnson restaurant—and others in the South." Perhaps in response to the proposed sit-ins, Howard Johnson restaurants in Florida desegregated and were "tested" in major cities by CORE and NAACP volunteers.[36]

CORE was also involved in putting pressure on local hotels. In 1962 *Hotel Monthly* warned its readers that they could expect action if they discriminated against black guests. When famed jazz trumpeter Dizzy Gillespie was denied admission to the pool at a hotel in downtown Kansas City, he filed a complaint with CORE, which resulted in negative publicity for the hotel "from coast to coast." The author of the *Hotel Monthly* article suggests that the organizations were emboldened by court rulings against school segregation and warned hotel owners that these groups are "staffed with professionals, amply financed and in possession of both the machinery and power to force an issue in public." CORE chapters in Nashville, Atlanta, Richmond, Louisville, and New Orleans (whose hotels did not accept blacks as guests) planned protests to target these hotels. CORE leader William Larkins listed common arguments made by hotels to support their policies of racial exclusion but countered that "the quality of their clientele will not drop just because they remove the color barrier," because only blacks who can afford that hotel will patronize it. CORE battled discrimination by urging convention groups to boycott hotels that discriminated on the basis of race. Yet the economic pressure did not always result in hotels dropping the color barrier.[37]

The NAACP targeted Hilton Hotels when at the July 1962 NAACP conference in Atlanta, delegates from New York's welfare department were refused hotel accommodations they had reserved long in advance. On the spot the NAACP authorized an emergency resolution authorizing picketing of Atlanta hotels, and nearly one-third of the 1,237 delegates circled sixteen Atlanta hotels with picket lines. Their swift response resulted from advance planning of the conference as a test case of the hotel's policy in Atlanta, but they were unsuccessful in desegregating Atlanta's major hotels.[38]

When the delegates returned home, the New York State conference of the NAACP directed their ninety-five branches to "withhold patronage" from any of the Hilton hotels, and Robert L. Carter of the national NAACP and his staff assisted in filing complaints with the New York State Commission for Human Rights. Meetings were held between Hilton vice president Frank G. Wangeman and commission chairman George Fowler, and Hilton publicly issued a letter to Governor Nelson A. Rockefeller stating their policy: "to welcome all persons as its guests regardless of race, color or creed." Hilton admitted that two hotels were exceptions: New Orleans, where the state of Louisiana required segregation, and Atlanta, "where local custom has thus far prevented us from fulfilling our wish to accommodate Negro guests." The statement also protested the NAACP's actions by stating, "it seems scarcely fair to penalize the great majority of our properties whose record of observing human rights cannot be questioned." As a result of the complaint, Hilton was to show efforts to alleviate the situation during the month of October. On November 1 Hilton management reported to the commissioner that they had reiterated their policy of nondiscrimination to their hotels, and that they had directed the Atlanta staff "to convince the hotel interests of that city that their local custom is contrary to today's philosophies on human rights."[39]

Privately, Hilton Hotel personnel were not so willing to be made a target of boycotts. Clyde J. Harris, director of catering at the Waldorf-Astoria (a Hilton property) wrote to Kivie Kaplan, of Colonial Tanning Company and a member of the national NAACP board, to protest the boycott. He asserted that "we, in the Hilton Organization, probably engage more personalities such as Lena Horne, Duke Ellington, etc., than any other Hotel Organization in the Country." He thought it unfair that they would be singled out, especially because twenty-one other Atlanta hotels discriminated on the basis of race. Indeed, the NAACP had in its files a letter sent to all prospective guests by the Heart of Atlanta Motel explaining that they had a policy of not accepting Negro guests and had no intention of doing so in the future. But the Heart of Atlanta was not a national chain, so it was not as vulnerable to the economic pressure put on Hilton Hotels. By spring 1963, after a report from a NAACP member that her reservations at the Hilton Inn in Atlanta were honored, the NAACP issued a press release stating that the hotel was now accepting "Negro guests." And on May 18, the press release stated, the federal district court in New Orleans had ruled the Louisiana state law directing segregation in hotels to be unconstitutional.[40]

The Civil Rights Act of 1964

In the campaign to desegregate the nation's restaurants and lodging industries, organizations like the NAACP and CORE depended on their members to test the boundaries of Jim Crow. Without the carefully worded letters of civil rights activists, the NAACP would not have known what restaurants and hotels to target. The vehemence of the letters and the refusal of the writers to be humiliated, especially in front of their children, was powerful testimony of the pervasiveness of racial discrimination in travel that persisted long after the end of World War II. Not until black citizens and the NAACP put economic pressure on the larger corporate travel industry was action taken to assure them of their rights to a roadside meal and a good night's rest. But such actions, targeted at the national chains, were not enough to desegregate the many mom-and-pop motels and roadside eateries that routinely refused black guests. Roy Wilkins made exactly this point in the hearings for the civil rights bill: "The proprietors of small establishments, including tourist homes and gasoline filling stations, are no less obligated to render nondiscriminatory public service than are the proprietors of huge emporiums or hostelries."[41] Nor were the organization's tactics successful at desegregating hotels and restaurants in major Southern cities like Atlanta. Local efforts had failed; a federal law was required.

Months of tense and violent confrontations between civil rights activists and white segregationists in Alabama led up to President Kennedy's long-awaited call for civil rights legislation in June 1963.[42] After Kennedy's assassination in November 1963, President Lyndon B. Johnson boldly took steps to use his clout to get a bill passed. As a long-time senator from Texas who was against segregation, he had tried since 1957 to get civil rights legislation passed in Congress. Johnson's fight against segregation dated from an epiphany he had in the early 1950s in a conversation with Gene Williams, the husband of the Johnson's maid, Helen Williams. Each year, Senator and Mrs. Johnson would fly to Washington, D.C., for the congressional session, and at its end, they would fly back. The Williams and the Johnson's cook, Zephyr Williams, would drive. One year, Johnson asked whether the Williams could take his beagle in the car with them. Gene hemmed and hawed and said he would rather not. Johnson asked why, and Gene admitted that it was a difficult trip from Washington to Texas. As Johnson recalled in his memoirs, Gene said:

> We drive for hours and hours. We get hungry. But there's no place on the road we can stop and go in and eat. We drive some more. It gets pretty hot. We want to wash up. But the only bathroom we're allowed in is usually miles off the main highway. We keep goin' 'til night comes—'til we get so tired we can't stay awake anymore. We're ready to pull in. But it takes another hour or so to find a place to sleep. You see, what I'm saying is that a colored man's got enough trouble getting across the South on his own, without having a dog along.

Johnson said he had an awakening, that he realized for the first time the difficulties blacks faced in simple things, like finding a bathroom, a place to eat, or a place to sleep on the 1,300-mile trip from Texas to Washington, D.C. Johnson said, "That day I first realized the sad truth: that to the extent Negroes were imprisoned, so was I." Johnson told that story again and again to powerful men in the South to make his point, and he used the power of his presidential administration to fight for equal rights for African Americans.[43] In the end, it was the president's family experience that tipped the balance toward enacting federal legislation.

Members of Johnson's administration carefully prepared their testimony in the hearing on the bill. They made their case on the grounds that segregated facilities disrupted trade, rather than on grounds that black travelers needed to be protected. Secretary of Labor W. Willard Wirz focused his argument on how segregation was bad for the economy, but he too played on the theme of the black traveler. "If Negroes felt as free to travel and explore this country as white families of similar income, the economic stimulus would be very large indeed in the transportation, apparel, travel goods, sports, gifts, and camping goods industries, and in the full range of service industries—hotels, motels, and eating and drinking establishments." Beyond the economic multiplier effect, he commented on the dispiriting impact of segregation on black children. "I think there is no strain at all in relating to the fact that a child, a Negro child, will walk past a hotel or restaurant where he can't enter on his way to school, and he will enter the door of that school wondering whether it is worth spending the day working very hard."[44]

The image of the black family on the road trying to find a motel or a place to eat was at the center of the case made to the committee. The testimony of Franklin D. Roosevelt Jr., undersecretary of commerce, was based on extensive studies of the availability of accommodations for black cross-country travelers. He used the listings of accommodations in a black travel guide to predict that black travelers "would have an extremely slender choice in attempting to find overnight accommodations" at integrated hotels and motels along the route. He figured that the average distance a "middle class Negro family" would have to travel to find a place to stay was 141 miles on the route from Washington to Miami, and 174 miles on the route to New Orleans. His statistics, although only estimates, demonstrated "the tremendous problem faced by Negro travelers along the highways in the South." He cited statistics showing that blacks in Northern cities spent more on automobile operation, suggesting that blacks were traveling less and that "the absence of suitable facilities along our important national highways must be the discouraging factor."[45] Both arguments, the economic costs of Jim Crow, and the deprivations of the middle-class family with children, were linked in government testimony in favor of the bill.

Ultimately the testimony was successful in convincing lawmakers of the need for federal intervention, and President Johnson signed the Civil

Rights Act in July 1964. It did not ensure equality, of course, but it made discrimination illegal, and it provided citizens a tool to challenge discrimination.[46] The significance of the 1964 Civil Rights Act cannot be underestimated; although civil rights advocates had been successful in using the courts to fight Jim Crow on a case-by-case basis, and although some states enacted laws outlawing segregation in public accommodations, the act was the first congressional legislation to make discrimination in public accommodations throughout the nation illegal.

Traveling African Americans faced humiliation while simply trying to find a place to eat, to stop for the night, and to use the toilet. The growth of a separate travel industry that catered to black customers allowed black families to circumvent humiliation, but ultimately they fought to shed their second-class status as citizens. A rising black middle class that was prosperous and educated demanded rights equal to those held by white travelers. Many of them were veterans of World War II, and they demanded the same freedoms they had fought for in the war. They refused to settle for inferior accommodations on the wrong side of the tracks; they demanded their full rights as consumer citizens. Their fight for full citizenship while on the road led to a broader victory against discrimination against women and the disabled, who would ground their demands for equal treatment in the provisions of the same civil rights legislation that made it possible for African American families to vacation without humiliation.

chapter four

Western Adventure

By 1952, two-thirds of households in the nation owned televisions, and by 1960, nine out of ten American families were watching television. What were they watching? Westerns. Long a staple of radio and cinema, the new medium of television was quickly captured by gun-slinging cowboys fighting Indians or villains in black hats to save the frontier for the white man and his woman. By 1959, TV westerns took up almost one-fourth of the programming on television, and by 1960, westerns attracted over one-third of the television audience. Of the top ten shows on television, eight were westerns. The westerns' classic struggle of a heroic figure defending American settlers against the bad guys may have resonated with national viewers caught up in the cold war battle against the evils of communism. Viewing westerns offered the 1950s organization man and the trapped suburban housewife a way to escape their humdrum modern existence. The enthusiasm for westerns was inextricably linked to the family ideal since the mythic West provided a stage for reasserting masculinity in a domesticated family culture. Westerns served up a vision of the West as America, where the good guys always won.[1]

Children who grew up with television grew up with westerns. The first generation of television westerns in the late 1940s were juvenile shows and featured such well-known stars as Gene Autry, Hopalong Cassidy, and Roy Rogers. These stars of B western movies, along with radio veterans like the Lone Ranger, shrewdly jumped on the television bandwagon and helped create newer characters like Annie Oakley to attract female viewers. Children favored westerns; a 1949 survey found that over half the child viewing audience preferred them to shows like *Howdy Doody* or cartoons. Walt Disney's *Adventures of Davy Crockett* attracted over 40 million viewers in 1954, almost a quarter of the national population.[2]

Children's affection for their heroes set off a kiddie cowboy craze that helped make the West a prime vacation destination in the postwar era. In 1953 California ranked first in vacation choice, and Colorado came in second. The preference can be partly explained by Americans' desire to participate in outdoor activities, but the strongest lure of the West was the Old West. The American Automobile Association declared in 1945: "'Westward Ho!' will be the cry for nearly half of America's car owners now that the lights are on again all over the world." Calling up images of traveling in the Old West, "accompanied by the crack of a bull whip, the creaking of leather and chain oxen harness, or the rumble of heavy wheels under a Conestoga wagon," the AAA forecast that "the gold panned as a result of post-war travel and touring in the United States will make the rush days of '49 look like a penny-ante stack of chips." Like the settlers in their covered wagons, modern Americans conquered the West in their cars.[3] Powered in part by the astounding popularity of westerns, American parents loaded up their station wagons and drove west for adventure in postwar America. The children in the backseat were clad in cowboy gear, ready to shoot 'em up in a western vacation that blurred the boundaries between fantasy and reality.

Many Americans sought the adventure of the Old West by staying at dude ranches or following their own version of the Oregon Trail, stopping at Mount Rushmore along the way. Others found it more convenient and less expensive to visit Southern California's amusement parks, like Knott's Berry Farm or Disneyland, with their staged recreations of the Old West. Disneyland was the most successful at replicating the West of the westerns, relying on artificiality to create an Old West that was more appealing than the real West just outside its borders. As the western craze faded in the 1960s, Southern California amusement parks and movie studios offered modern versions of the West that attracted family tourists.[4] If we want to understand the West the tourists were looking for, we need to go back to the westerns they watched.

Kid Westerns

Watching westerns was about much more than entertaining the kids. Westerns were just the tip of the iceberg of a huge marketing enterprise to sell everything from peanut butter to pajamas to children. The fad for westerns crossed lines of gender, class, and race as it sold Americans on the idea of the West as the place where American character was built. Through their performances on the radio or television, in the movies, or on national rodeo tours, kid western stars insinuated themselves into every nook and cranny of children's consciousness, spurring a multimillion-dollar industry of adventure. The amusement parks were a natural outgrowth of the extension of the world of westerns—and of the tentacles of the westerns merchandising industry that were fueled by lucrative licensing fees paid to the producers of the westerns. To understand the huge enthusiasm for the West and its marketing machine, we must start with the kiddie western stars.[5]

The first kid western hero to recognize the enormous potential of television for his career was William Boyd, the actor who played Hopalong Cassidy. By 1948 he had mortgaged all he owned, including his car, to buy the rights to his early western movies. Boyd then sliced them up into television episodes, all without owing a dime to any studio. He was immensely popular. In 1950, 57 television stations showed his movies, and 151 CBS stations aired his Saturday morning radio program. That same year, he reportedly shook the hands of a million persons at one appearance on his twenty-five-city tour of department stores. He received 2,000 fan mail letters each week, and his Trooper Club for junior fans numbered over 2 million. His syndicated comic strip appeared in 126 U.S. and 24 foreign newspapers.[6]

At the heart of the enterprise was an ethic of goodness that resonated with cold war values of right and wrong. Hoppy looked like a kindly silver-haired grandfather, and his actions on screen were always heroic; instead of shooting the outlaws, he admonished them to change their wicked ways. *Coronet* magazine claimed the Hopalong character represented "classical virtues of honesty, modesty, and fair play." Because of his iconic status, he was featured on the covers of major news magazines. In 1950 he made the covers of both *Time* and *Look* magazines, and *Look* labeled him "Public Hero No. 1." *Time* acknowledged the power of television in children's cowboy mania: "The kiddies form a vast, commercial audience, almost as important to U.S. business as their soap-opera-loving mothers."[7]

All the publicity resulted in millions for Boyd. His real moneymaker was licensing over 100 products to manufacturers for a 5 percent take of the profits. In 1950 he held 65 percent of the market in western merchandising, earning between $80 and $100 thousand, not counting royalties. In one year, 3 million pillowcases with his name were sold, and his name was emblazoned on "suits, shirts, spurs, cameras, pistols and gun belts." His records, like "Hopalong Cassidy and the Square Dance Holdup," sold in the hundreds of thousands. Hopalong was a hero to America's children, and his multimillion-dollar income proved it.[8]

Gene Autry, the Singing Cowboy of radio and cinema, founded Flying "A" Productions in part to reach the kid's market in television. Sensitive to criticism that westerns were too violent for children, he came up with the Cowboy Code to promote moral values. These included guides for good behavior, such as "a cowboy always tells the truth" and "a cowboy is always helpful." Autry expected the heroes in his productions to portray ethical values and model them for the child viewing audience. While on tour he always included visits to children in hospitals; his handlers made sure these events got full media coverage. The Cowboy Code meant fans expected more of Autry; when his drinking became obvious on the rodeo circuit in 1955, parents sharply criticized him for not being a good example for the children.[9]

His success with children's audiences allowed him to spin his movies and television shows into a complex financial empire. Like his competitors, Autry lent his name to children's products. In 1953 there were over 100 products in the Autry line, and sales were estimated at over $6 million. Among the items licensed were cowboy suits that were highly flammable, and in 1949 a jury awarded $30,000 to the parents of a young fan who burned to death. Because his name was on the product, Autry was among those sued for damages in over twenty lawsuits that involved the cowboy outfit, most of which were settled out of court. His failure to publicly announce the problems with the apparel after he became aware of the hazards led to horrible injuries (one girl lost both legs) and in two cases, the deaths of his adoring fans.[10]

Autry realized that the kiddie western craze was not just for boys. In a stroke of genius, Autry invented the character of Annie Oakley, borrowing the name of the sharpshooter show woman of Buffalo Bill Cody's Wild West Show. Autry's decision to feature a female western heroine was a clever strategy to appeal to the girls in his audience. He explained to a reporter, "little boys have had their idols . . . why not give the girls a female Western star of their own?" Gail Davis (whose real name was Betty Jeanne Grayson) played Annie Oakley. Davis grew up as the daughter of a prosperous physician in Arkansas and had been a child performer and college beauty queen. To keep up with the action on the westerns, and to carry the title of the historical Annie Oakley of Buffalo Bill's Wild West Show, Davis had to be an expert markswoman and an excellent rider.

The character of Annie Oakley (here with her brother, Tagg, about 1957) became an idol for little girls who watched television westerns. (Courtesy Museum of the American West, Autry National Center.)

Davis's screen persona was built on her wholesome attractiveness coupled with her western riding and shooting skills. She was petite (five feet two inches and ninety-five pounds) and attractive without a trace of sex appeal that would make her inappropriate for child audiences. She wore her "golden brown" hair in braids or pigtails, and she was always modestly attired, either in fringed and bejeweled leather split skirt outfits or blue jeans and western-style shirts, along with the required Stetson hat.[11]

Annie Oakley may have been able to ride and shoot just like male western heroes, but her persona had a well-developed domestic side. Annie's chief responsibility was to care for her eleven-year-old brother, Tagg, who was left motherless at a young age. Annie's exploits were generally motherly, saving Tagg from runaway horses and foiling robberies. When not on a horse, Annie was in the kitchen baking pies for deputy sheriff Lofty (her love interest), cleaning house, and mothering Tagg. Such images reassured fans that despite her wilder exploits of racing a stagecoach, Annie Oakley still adhered to postwar notions of domesticity.[12]

Studio publicity emphasized Davis's conformity with gender ideologies of the period. The *TV Radio Mirror* feature spread in January 1957 portrayed her as having a split personality—"Annie Oakley the tomboy, and Gail Davis, the ultra-feminine woman." She wore western costumes at work but preferred "frilly feminine clothes" at home. The public spaces of her home were decorated in western style with saddle and Stetson motifs, but her bedroom was furnished in pink and white. However, her career choice contravened one of the basic tenets of womanhood because a grueling work schedule meant she was unable to care for her young daughter, from whose father she was divorced. Terrie, a "bundle of loving blue eyes and blond curls," lived in Arkansas with Davis's parents half the year, and for the other half, Davis's mother cared for her in Hollywood.[13]

Davis, who was Autry's lover, made multiple appearances in his rodeo tours in the United States and England. In 1955 alone it was estimated she drove 40,000 miles and flew 50,000 miles. Lured by advertising trailers on the Annie Oakley television shows, children filled the rodeo stadiums, dragging their parents along with them. While on tour she not only appeared in the performances riding and shooting, but also made appearances to crowds of children. To increase crowds, local venues would sponsor Annie Oakley look-alike contests, with contestants winning free movie passes or Annie Oakley lunch boxes.[14]

Autry's Flying "A" Productions worked hard to cash in on the Annie Oakley phenomenon. The Annie Oakley character was licensed to products like Sunbeam Bread, Gleem toothpaste, Hostess Twinkies, Laura Scudder chips, TV Time foods, and Wonder Bread. Children eagerly consumed storybooks, comic books, coloring books, paper dolls, lunch boxes, pencils, and drinking glasses—nearly any product imaginable that could be imprinted with an image of their favorite western television star, whether it was Hopalong Cassidy, Gene Autry, or Annie Oakley.[15] Such products allowed children to live in a world saturated with the images of their television heroes, images that projected a mythic West of heroes, high adventure, and the triumph of good over evil. As it made money for the stars and their companies, product licensing extended the reach of television westerns into new arenas of entertainment, such as amusement parks. Television westerns captured the imagination of parents and children and made the West a popular destination for a family vacation.

Promoting the Old West

To appreciate the rise of western-themed amusement parks, we must understand how car travel shifted promotion of western travel from the railroads to the states. Families who wanted to explore the West faced a promotional onslaught from the mass media. For almost a century, railroads had marketed the West to the American tourist, laying rails to National Parks and paying Native Americans to greet travelers. In the automobile era of family vacationing, tourists relied on state officials for information in vacation planning. States provided this free service to tourists because tourists spent money in the state and boosted the local economy. As rail ridership declined, states took over the promotion of the West by featuring their states as the best way to experience western adventure.[16]

Dude ranches offered vacationers a taste of western adventure, although the authenticity was contrived. Dude ranches had been promoted by railroads since the 1920s as a way to attract rail travelers, who had long frequented the national parks promoted by the railroads. Most ranches were clustered in Wyoming, Montana, and Colorado near the established national parks. The railroads were instrumental in starting dude ranch associations that encouraged owners to feature western furniture, upgrade their food, and advertise in the East. More dude ranch guests meant more rail passengers, and the railroads invested considerable sums in promoting dude ranches.[17]

The Colorado Dude and Guest Ranch Association beckoned visitors in their 1953 brochure titled "For a Real Vacation Come to a Colorado Dude Ranch This Year." Certainly it was an active vacation. Activities offered included fishing, riding, hiking, and swimming, as well as taking pack trips. Part of the appeal of dude ranches was their setting in the cool mountain air of the high Rockies. The Trail's End Ranch in Granby, Colorado, advertised its 8,700-foot elevation, "distant from noisy, treacherous highways." The Two Bars Seven Ranch boasted that it was "real 'cow-country' in mountain lands first pioneered by scouting parties and Overland Stage." Because cattle still roamed, "there's ridin' and ropin' to be done." Guests could ride out on the 7,000 acres in either a "buckboard ranch car" or their "trusty jeep." The accommodations were rustic, yet "modern." Buildings were constructed from "native rock with pine paneled, hand-hewn log interiors" and featured "massive fireplaces." Guest rooms had either private or adjoining baths, and one promised "excellent beds" and "modern baths."[18]

Dude ranches were selling an authentic western experience like the scenes vacationers saw in television westerns, but with the comforts of home. The ranch advertised the essence of western hospitality: "We aim to keep you comfortable and give you home cooked meals while you enjoy these WESTERN EXPERIENCES." Chuckwagon cooking featured trout and outdoor "steak fries." Back at the ranch, menus were more elaborate, with "the best of food served family style, ranch oven bread—rolls—pastry, crisp vegetables, fresh fruit." Family-style and "home cooked meals" were designed to convey that informal, out-West atmosphere. "Typical ranch wear, for both men and women, may include jeans or saddle pants plus bright shirts, comfortable boots and big hats." In the evenings, guests gathered at the spacious lodge where they could play bingo, pool, or cards, or participate in square dancing. More sedate activities included croquet or horseback rides in the moonlight.[19]

Dude ranches catered to families on vacation by offering "special family rates" with reduced rates for children and providing extras like a children's playground. Rates ranged from $63 to $77 a week, including horses and meals. One brochure bragged, "Nothing thrives on a ranch like young Americans growing up. Bring them by all means! Most ranches cater to families, and a great many of them have children's playgrounds, trained counselors and supervised programs." Parents saw ranches as places that offered healthful activities that promoted self-reliance in their children. The ranches were perfect for a family with teenagers, who could exercise some independence while vacationing with the family. Teenagers read about dude ranches in young adult books like *Cherry Ames: Dude Ranch Nurse* in the popular series by Julie Tatham. In her stint as a nurse at an Arizona dude ranch, Cherry solved the mystery of a hidden inheritance and fell in love with a handsome stranger.[20]

With the increase in automobile travel, railroads did not find it profitable to promote dude ranches at prewar levels. Auto travelers were less likely than rail travelers to visit dude ranches because it took longer to drive to them. Cars allowed them the flexibility of staying for shorter visits because dude ranching was rarely the entire purpose of their western vacation. By the late 1950s, railroads ceased their advertising campaigns for dude ranches, and dude ranches found it impossible to afford to advertise on the same scale. At the same time, rail travel was becoming less popular as vacationers preferred the convenience of driving.[21]

As railroads cut their advertising budgets, states took over the role of promoting the West. States sold their destinations by convincing tourists that their state would treat them to a taste of the Old West. Magazine feature articles on various states in the West were complete travel guides, with budgets, itineraries, and a list of must-see sites. Common to these articles was the pitch to the family vacation traveler. In 1954 a feature article in *Better Homes and Gardens* on the Black Hills of South Dakota touted the destination as the epitome of the West: "What would your family say to a vacation where it could: Ride horseback up the highest peak east of the Rockies? Inspect the richest gold mine in America? Pass buffalo along the highway and dine on them at night? Watch Indian dances . . . and [sing] cowboy songs around a campfire?" All this was available for the low price of $160 for the entire vacation for a family of four, provided they stayed in cabins and picnicked occasionally to hold down costs. South Dakota argued that it was "where the Old West still lives in a surprisingly noncommercial setting and comes in whatever degree of wildness you and the wife and the kids can take." This was the Old West on a budget, family style. At the end of these articles, and at the bottom of each advertisement, readers were directed to contact state travel and tourism offices for more information. State advertisements emphasized Old West themes coupled with an appeal to family travelers. Idaho boasted that "The REAL West is still here!"[22] As family rail travel declined, states took over the selling of the West to the family in the station wagon headed west.

Old West Theme Parks

The cowboy craze and the selling of the West as a vacation destination made western-themed amusement parks in Southern California popular destinations for families on vacation. Knott's Berry Farm, Corriganville, and Disneyland each offered a different version of the West, but only Disneyland's Frontierland successfully meshed the imaginary worlds of the West with the entertainment media to make it the top choice for amusement park adventure. With its array of "lands" inside the park, Disneyland was able to adapt to a decline in enthusiasm for westerns and to substitute a new West for the enjoyment of tourists.[23]

Knott's Berry Farm owed its success to capturing the West of the California Gold Rush and repackaging it for tourists. The Knott's Berry Farm theme park originated as a berry stand during the Great Depression when Mother (Cordelia) Knott began serving chicken dinners to boost profits. In 1940 Walter Knott bought the ghost town of Calico in the Mojave Desert and carted back its buildings to create a replica of a mining town in Buena Park. Knott built a three-block-long Main Street with a general store, Chinese laundry, the Silver Dollar Saloon, the Birdcage Theater, veterinarian's office, barbershop, blacksmith shop, bank, tintype gallery, drugstore, and the Ace-in-the-Hole Gambling House. A travel writer described the Ghost Town as a place of "color and lift and laughter—where the people can catch, if only for a brief hour or two, the true spirit

A Filipino American family posed in headdresses with an actor in traditional Indian dress at Knott's Berry Farm in 1964. (Courtesy Shades of L.A. Archives, Los Angeles Public Library.)

of the Old West."[24] It is no small irony that Walter Knott had to literally remove Calico from its authentic western landscape to a false setting to sell the "true spirit of the Old West" to visitors.

By 1945, two or three thousand persons a day were visiting Knott's Berry Farm, and by 1947 Mother Knott and her staff were serving up more than a million chicken dinners a year. What drew them? Not just the fried chicken and the boysenberry jam they bought as souvenirs. Knott built his amusement park as a tribute to his grandmother, who as a child made the pioneer journey from Texas to Azusa, California. The old ghost town was meant to be "an honest tribute to our pioneer forefathers." The goal was to make visitors feel as if they were back in the days of the California forty-niners. Children enjoyed panning for gold in a millrace, watched over by a grizzly prospector, or posing with Indians who wore feathered headdresses.[25]

By 1953 Knott's Berry Farm covered 40 acres and provided enough parking for 4,000 cars. That year there were more than 1.2 million visitors.

The souvenir guide promised, "today you may relive some of the heroics, pranks and deeds of violence that were part of the life of our forefathers." Daily attractions such as Mark Smith's horse show featured the movie star and stunt men performing a bareback "Ballet on Horseback" in a 3,000-seat arena. Part of the attraction was the Ghost Town and Calico Railroad, which made six trips a day and was regularly held up by outlaws, to the delight of the visitors. Western movie star John Wayne visited, giving Knott's Berry Farm his stamp of approval. Visitors were fond of posing for snapshots with the statues of the gold miners or saloon girls in Ghost Town, creating a memory of their visit to the Old West at Knott's Berry Farm.[26]

Part ghost town and part family farm, Knott's Berry Farm was the first of Southern California's amusement parks. Knott's Berry Farm owed more to myths of the Old West than to reality, but its imaginary world of the gold rush was grounded in the reality of the actual mining town buildings, overlaid with the whimsy of a crooked jail, wandering goats, and mock gunfights that made it fun for families. The Old West of Knott's Berry Farm reinscribed racial stereotypes of Chinese workers and Indians in ceremonial dress to entertain visitors.[27] Knott's Berry Farm sold the Old West, but because it was founded before television's emergence as a mass medium, it did not have any direct ties to western stars or productions.

Kiddie western star Bill Boyd (Hopalong Cassidy) funneled some of his profits into Hoppyland, an amusement park with only faint traces of the Old West of his shows. The park, which opened in May 1951, was primarily a promotional vehicle where Boyd made frequent appearances to promote Hopalong Cassidy. Hoppyland had places to picnic, pitch horseshoes, or play baseball. Children could go on carnival-like rides or get a taste of the Old West by riding in a pony cart or on a miniature railroad. Boyd's priority for Hoppyland was self-promotion, which explains why the park closed in 1954, a year after Boyd retired from films. Without a western frontier theme, and without a connection to an ongoing western show, Hoppyland could not successfully market itself to tourists.[28]

Ray "Crash" Corrigan, a now-obscure western actor, was the first to directly link westerns to amusement parks when he opened Corriganville Movie Ranch to visitors. Almost half of all Hollywood westerns filmed between 1937 and 1951 made some use of the Corriganville Movie Ranch located in Santa Susana in California's Simi Valley. Corrigan founded the ranch as a place to film TV and movie westerns for smaller, independent operations who did not have their own filming locales. Corrigan set up

Freddy Rubio and Geraldo Villegas pose for a snapshot with the statues at Knott's Berry Farm, 1961. (Courtesy Shades of L.A. Archives, Los Angeles Public Library.)

his ranch with production equipment and a variety of sets, including a fort, Main Street, Mexican street, frontier cabins, and a ranch house.[29]

After Corrigan established the ranch, he invited the public to see how westerns were made. Corriganville Movie Ranch opened May 1, 1949, and until Universal reopened their doors to visitors in 1964, it was the only motion picture studio open to visitors. Billed as a romantic western frontier, it offered "the romance of the Old West and the physical genius of the Motion Picture industry as a thrilling living story." Flooded with visitors that first Sunday, the admission ticket took the form of a printed Dixie Cup ice cream lid. The ranch attracted as many as 10,000 visitors on typical Sundays, and sometimes double that number visited. Corrigan staged special events to attract the public, but the standard fare was a Sunday afternoon rodeo with a burning stagecoach, stunts on horseback, and an "Apache flaming arrow attack on covered wagons." Local television station KNBH broadcast the Sunday afternoon rodeo as *"Crash" Corrigan's Round-up.*[30]

The western theme was carried out in live-action dramas for visitors who could pretend they were part of the action. Every half hour on Silvertown's Main Street, stuntmen would stage such classic western true-

Television western star Hopalong Cassidy (Bill Boyd) at opening day of Hoppyland in 1951. (Courtesy Herald-Examiner *Collection, Los Angeles Public Library.)*

life events as the beating of Joaquin Murietta, the gunfight at the O.K. Corral, or Billy the Kid's jailbreak (all presumably edited for children). Visitors could ride or hike eleven miles of trails, where they could explore caves and catch a glimpse of the filming. On the trails they could even pretend to be Indians and find planted arrowheads. The ranch had stables and corrals, and children and their parents could ride the old train on a track encircling the ranch. The old west facades concealed a merchandising operation where visitors could buy sandwiches and souvenirs, and have their pictures taken with the stars. Crash Corrigan himself posed for photos with visitors for a $1 fee.[31]

Television western hero the Lone Ranger took over Corriganville in 1955, when Outdoor Amusements Inc. (whose majority stockholder was Jack Wrather, owner of the Lone Ranger franchise), contracted to manage and expand the park. Renamed the Lone Ranger Ranch in January 1957, the *Lone Ranger* television show shot thirty-nine episodes there in the next two years. Publicity went nationwide, commanding the attention of children at the breakfast table. Sponsor General Mills advertised the Lone Ranger Movie Ranch Wild West Town on boxes of Wheaties and Cheerios cereal. Dell's *Lone Ranger* comics encouraged visits to a place where its readers could "relive the past where legendary outlaws come to life, banks are held up, and stagecoaches are robbed." The Lone Ranger Ranch came to an end when the Corrigans successfully sued to reinstate their name in summer 1958. In 1965, with Corrigan's health failing, they sold the ranch to comedian Bob Hope for $2.8 million, who closed it shortly afterward.[32]

Knott's Berry Farm and Corriganville recreated the Old West of ghost towns, saloon girls, bandits, and cowboys and Indians that children saw on television. At both parks, children could insert themselves into the imaginary scene of the Wild West, watching a gunfight, panning for gold like a forty-niner, or tracking Indians while picking up arrowheads. The amusement parks provided a stage for children's fantasies of the Old West in a wholesome way, without the blood and gore but with the good guys and the bad guys, just as the kid westerns did. Ironically, these early parks became imprisoned within their version of the West, and as children's westerns faded in importance, the parks were unable to adapt to newer representations of reality as seen on television.

Disneyland

No amusement park better combined the medium of television and amusement than Disneyland; indeed, the Disneyland amusement park was funded by the *Disneyland* television show, which aired on the ABC network. And no other park would achieve the popularity of Disneyland for the family on vacation. Disneyland opened on July 17, 1955, to instant success. Within a month, over 20,000 persons visited each day, and it was said to have attracted about half of the tourists to Southern California. Disneyland achieved its success by combining nostalgia and futurism, the Old West and the New West, as it tapped American values. Its "architecture of reassurance" appealed to families in postwar America because of its optimism, its convenience, and its attractions, which both young and old could enjoy together.[33]

The idea for Disneyland came to Walt Disney one Saturday while he was sitting on a park bench eating peanuts while his two daughters were riding a merry-go-round. As he recalled, "I thought there should be something here . . . some kind of a place where the parents and the children could have fun together." Disneyland became not just a better amusement park but "a full imaginative universe that could provide a unified experience." Disney biographer Neal Gabler argues that Disneyland exhibited Disney's desire to have control, to "craft a better reality than the one outside the studio." Indeed, Disney described each of the "lands" in the park as a scene from a movie. Disney films had provided comfort during the Depression; Disneyland provided an ordered, reassuring imaginary world during the cold war. Even the dirt berm that surrounded the park effectively walled off the outside, making the real world disappear for those inside the Magic Kingdom. Within Disneyland was a world like the one seen on television, a contrived environment carefully scripted as tourist space.[34]

Frontierland featured the adventure of the Wild West for children and their families. When Davy Crockett, "King of the Wild Frontier," debuted on the *Disneyland* show in late 1954, it set off a mania. Ten million Davy Crockett coonskin caps and 7 million copies of the record of the theme song were sold, a licensing coup that helped bring in over $300 million in 1955–1956. The western adventures of Davy Crockett attracted thousands of children to the theme park, many of them wearing their coonskin caps. Disney's Frontierland blurred the lines between reality and fantasy in its western adventure environment replicated from its television shows and movie westerns. American children, wearing their cowboy outfits to the park, played out their television fantasies at Disneyland's version of the Old West.[35]

The Disneyland guide promised that in Frontierland they could "experience the high adventure of our forefathers who shaped our glorious history." Children and their parents could board a stagecoach or ride in a Conestoga wagon. They visited the western saloon, Injun Joe's Cave, and Fort Wilderness. Visitors traveled aboard a sternwheeler like the ones that plied the Mississippi to Tom Sawyer's island, or toured a western mining town.[36] The mule pack ride allowed children one of their most vivid experiences of the Wild West. On the mule pack, a trail boss led each train of seven to eight mules, with smaller mules and child riders at the front. The trail bosses were experienced animal handlers who knew how to handle children as well. Sometimes the children's feet did not reach to the stirrups, so they held onto rawhide straps.

Alongside the mule train ride was the stagecoach ride, where riders could pretend to be in the days of Wells Fargo. To accommodate more riders, visitors climbed tall ladders to the tops of the stagecoaches. The three rides took visitors into a carefully designed recreation of a western desert environment of Disney's film, *The Living Desert.* Designers planted 156 varieties of trees, imported rocks and boulders, and set up animated animals that looked just like the ones children saw in western movies. The mechanized animals interacted with passing visitors: "Bears beg for handouts. Rattlesnakes pursue prairie dogs. Mountain lions crouch for a lunge at the passing mine train." A rider recalled, "Fantastic rock formations with balancing rocks and stone Indian dwelling atop could be glimpsed, bleached dinosaur bones lay exposed to the sun." Recorded sounds in the town buildings grew fainter as the riders ascended the trail, contributing to a sense of leaving civilization for the desert wildness.[37]

The use of audio animatronics allowed Disney to create an artificial desert with technology, an environment promoted as more authentic than the real West. Disney publicity featured the recreated Old West in its public relations materials: "If all you trailblazers of '62 been settin' back in your new Fords, skee-daddlin' across our Western freeways just a wonderin' where all them wild critters went to, an ol' straight-shooter can fill you in: You'll see a sow-belly full more 'wild animals' in a 10-minute mine train or mule pack ride through Disneyland's Nature's Wonderland than you'll set eyes on all across the 'civilized' West of today!"[38] As the deserts of the Old West were being "civilized" by freeways or built into subdivisions, tourists could find the West, carefully lifted from movies, at an amusement park.

Disneyland offered an immersion in the Old West in Frontierland. "It's like the wilderness West was back in the days when there weren't need for historical landmarks 'cause the history tales was bein' written in the minin' camps an' wide-open towns . . . an' the forests an' deserts were reckoned in hundreds of miles, not acres." In ten minutes visitors could see more of the Old West than they could driving the highways, including the "Old Unfaithful Geyser" and the Rainbow Caverns.[39] Frontierland rides not only took visitors to another place, they also took them back in time, to the days of the forty-niners and the pioneers. All of this was immensely entertaining to children, who slept with their boots on and toted cap guns in their holsters.

As in most amusement parks, Indians were an important part of the attraction. In Frontierland, children could dance with Indians at the "authentic Indian Village where true-to-life, honest-to-goodness Indians from throughout the Great Southwest perform daily." In 1958 Disneyland publicity proclaimed that the "Highlight of the show is the 'Friendship Dance' in which youngsters are invited to join the Indians in performing." Such cross-cultural friendship was a far cry from the portrayal of Indians as enemies in John Wayne westerns, although the Lone Ranger did have an Indian sidekick, Tonto. A decade later, Disneyland avoided confrontation with the American Indian political movement by obtaining permission from tribes for Indian performances for over 1.5 million visitors yearly. The *Disney News* boasted, "All are talented youngsters, whose underlying purpose in working at the Park is to erase a long-held impression here and abroad that all Indians are war-whooping savages, capable of little else than forever galloping across television and movie screens." Indeed, park publicity made it clear that instead of simply pleasing park visitors, the performers "contribute to a broader understanding of Indian traditions, while at the same time dedicating themselves to preserving the customs and arts of their people." Horse Stealer, Whitecloud, Red Eagle, Little Deer, Whirling Wind, Little Buffalo, Beaver, and Princess Morningstar put on continuous thirty-minute shows every week during the summer, and on weekends throughout the year.[40]

Staged gunfights added to the authenticity of the wild west in Frontierland. The performers studied the history of the famous outlaws and sheriffs they portrayed before they even chose a wardrobe or choreographed their moves. "Together with the other sights and sounds of America as it was a hundred years ago, the Gunfighters help re-create an exciting chapter in history for Disneyland guests." Saloon girls, dancers, and bartenders in the Golden Horseshoe Old West Revue, presented by Pepsi-Cola, rounded out the cast of characters recreating the Old West for western-crazed kids and their parents.[41] In Disney's version of the Old West, women were featured as entertainment, saloon girls and cancan dancers, in contrast to the sober pioneer mother of the less popular Knott's Berry Farm. The saloon girls and dancers made the Old West fun—and added a tinge of eroticism to the Frontierland experience.[42] In Frontierland, western adventure was not simply watched, it was experienced.

Davy Crockett may have set off the enthusiasm for the new Disneyland, but its family-friendly features kept them coming. The compact design with its central hub made navigation easy for the stroller set, and Disneyland offered special services for parents with children. In 1959, publicity proclaimed, "Unique as it is as a new concept in family entertainment, Disneyland can claim as well the 'most complete' title, too—offering unusual services that make a visit to the Magic Kingdom still more convenient." Strollers and wheelchairs were available for rental, so every member of the family could come along. The Disneyland Baby Station provided a place for parents to feed babies and change diapers. Originally sponsored by an infant cereal company, the Pablum Baby Station offered a place for parents to warm up formula and change diapers, "those 'little things' that make Disneyland the 'happy place' for infants, too." In

Barbara and Jackie Rugh dancing with the Indians at Frontierland in Disneyland, 1958. (Author's collection.)

1962, hostess Ethel Penfield boasted that "as many as 150 babies are guests in the Baby Station on an average day." Some days they served double that number of children. Over 250 lost children were found each week in the summer season. "Even though a child is lost, his stay at the Department can be a pleasant affair. While there, he is given comic books, balloons, and something to eat if he's hungry. He can also talk to many of his 'peers' who are there for the same reason." The Disneyland Hotel ran a babysitting service for the "vacationing family," with "experienced reliable ladies available to care for and entertain the youngsters while Mom and Dad go out on their own to shop or visit." Food services catered to adult and child appetites, with hot dogs, hamburgers, and ice cream and later, more sophisticated menus for adult tastes. In the first six months, Disneyland sold 467,730 hot dogs and 558,324 ice cream bars.[43] Disneyland appealed to families because it was clean and offered wholesome family entertainment.

A visit to Disneyland was not cheap, but there were ways to be thrifty. When Disneyland opened, visitor fees were $1 for adults and 50 cents for children. On top of that, each visitor paid from 10 to 25 cents per attraction. To control the crush of visitors for the most popular attractions, Disneyland rated attractions from A to C, with C the most in demand. They invented the ABC attractions eight-ticket book for the price of $2.50 for adults and $1.50 for children. In 1956 Disneyland added the D ticket and in 1959 the famous E ticket for the most popular attractions. Families could purchase Disneyland ticket books for family groups, which contained tickets of varying values for the different rides. In 1965 the Big 10 Book was priced at $4 for adults, $3.50 for those aged twelve to seventeen, and $3 for children under twelve. In addition to the ticket books, each visitor paid a general admission fee, again scaled by age, from $2 for adults to 60 cents for young children.[44]

Lines were long, especially at midsummer, but while they were waiting, Disney provided diversions. In 1961 Disney characters began roaming the grounds in costume, signing autographs and posing for pictures. A visitor wrote in 1966, "Your Disneyland hosts understand that fun is a grim undertaking on a hot smoggy day and so they provide a free entertainment to make the waiting tolerable. A sheriff engages a black-garbed gunfighter in a showdown once each hour. Mountaineers descend the Matterhorn in bounding leaps. Dixieland combos appear to raise the spirits of those waiting for fun. . . . There is much to divert you while you wait for your fun."[45]

The Trevor family posed with the children's grandparents in front of Sleeping Beauty's Castle at Disneyland about 1956. (Courtesy Shades of L.A. Archives, Los Angeles Public Library.)

Disneyland made it easy for families to remember their visit by stocking its stores and souvenir stands with merchandise for every budget and for every age. Taking pictures also created a lasting souvenir of the visit, and family groups often posed in front of Sleeping Beauty's Castle to make a memory. The Eastman Kodak Center on Main Street offered free information on "the best way to use a camera in the Magic Kingdom" and marked spots to take pictures in Disneyland with "picture spot" signs on posts. The company offered tips like "Get close-ups of the family with a recognizable Disneyland landmark in the background." It advised people to "ask a nearby visitor to take a photo of your group." The camera should always be at the ready, "since many of the most delightful and treasured pictures will be quick, candid shots and snaps of the surprises on many Disneyland attractions."[46]

From the start, Disneyland promoted the park as a place for families. The hosts of the live broadcast of opening day in 1955—Art Linkletter, Ronald Reagan, and Robert Cummings—were all accompanied by their families. *Vacationland,* Disneyland's free magazine for visitors to Southern California sites, made a point of featuring families in its pages. In 1959 a full-page spread featured snapshots of families from across the nation having fun in the park. The Chizzicks from Denver whirled in a Mad Tea Party teacup, the Fishers from Fullerton with their grandmother from Florida enjoyed the Alice in Wonderland ride, and Mr. and Mrs. John Maas and their three children from Utah crossed the moat in front of Sleeping Beauty's Castle. Also on the page was a photo of Dick Powell and June Allyson with their family on the Casey Jr. train, its "fun-filled train ride only part of a happy family time in Disneyland." Celebrities who brought their families to Disneyland were part of Disneyland's public relations effort to attract family visitors. Almost every U.S. president and many foreign leaders visited Disneyland, and they brought the children—or in the case of President Eisenhower, his granddaughter, Mary Jean.[47]

The celebrities may have gotten the royal treatment, but ordinary visitors were also enthusiastic about their visit to Disneyland. Postcards from Disneyland distill visitor impressions into a few superlatives: unbelievable, magnificent, fantastic. Ida and Glenn wrote home to Detroit in July 1957: "Hello Folks: We saw Disneyland yesterday—It is almost unbelievable!!" Wes wrote a Sleeping Beauty postcard to "Mom" in May 1958: "Certainly is a fantastic place, . . . enjoyed it very much." A decade later, Disneyland was an adventure that lasted until well after dark. "Linda" wrote a postcard home to Mom in Colorado Springs about how to manage Disneyland with children. "Hi Mom, I was sitting under the dryer, my hair really stayed in good, but decided to get it done today while the children nap. Been to Disneyland this morning, will go back about 4:00 P.M. & stay until 10:00 or so & all day tomorrow. Just *magnificent,* the kids are having a ball." The children were delighted with the wonders of Disneyland, and Linda wrote in the margins: "Everything they see, they say got to tell Grandma when they get home."[48] Mothers like Linda realized that to do Disneyland after dark with children, one might as well put the children down for a nap and do your hair. Still, Disneyland was "magnificent."

Not long after Disneyland opened, *Better Homes and Gardens* promoted Disneyland as a place that both children and adults could enjoy. The article, by James M. Liston, featured a two-page photo spread of families enjoying the park. "What is planned as a dutiful pilgrimage for the sake of the children turns out to be an eye-opening day of adult entertainment and education." The author was impressed by the authentic details that children would not appreciate: "Children who never saw a horse-drawn car or fire wagon are delighted. But adults are literally transported by these vehicles down nostalgic Main Street, USA, and amazed by the scrupulous attention to detail in everything from the glass jars in the apothecary's shop to the oil lamps in the Santa Fe and Disneyland railroad coaches that roll across the prairies of Frontierland."

Disneyland's lasting appeal was the way it combined past and present, the Old West of Frontierland with space-age frontiers of the future. Liston continued, "Disneyland's panorama of places in the past and future" spanned "the coonskinned, stockaded actuality of frontier life" and "the serious, scientifically accurate foretaste of space travel and atomic progress." For him, it "all add[ed] up to what made us what we are today and pointing optimistically to the future." Visitors to Disneyland consumed a cleaned-up version of the American story that created a common culture of the past and shared visions of the future.[49]

Ten years later, another family magazine, *Good Housekeeping*, published an article that displayed the distance Disneyland had come to sustain its appeal to tourists. Marion Wylie's account of her family's visit in 1966 updated the Disneyland experience for readers. The Wylie family began their day in Adventureland but spent most of the day at Tomorrowland, "where bullet-nosed blue-and-orange monorail trains swished smoothly overhead." She was surprised by the engineered attack of a giant squid on the submarine ride and noted, "it doesn't pay to relax for a moment when you're on a Disneyland ride." After lunch at the Tiki Room, her husband and sons went back to Tomorrowland, where they rode the daring Matterhorn bobsled ride and drove the miniature cars on the Autopia. Meanwhile, she returned to the Plaza Inn and sat on the restaurant terrace watching the action around her. "A band of children near me were clustered around a spaceman about seven feet tall who was demonstrating a ray gun. He wore a silver suit with a huge Plexiglas bubble helmet; the children were enchanted."[50] From pistols to ray guns, Disneyland combined the Old West and space-age inventions to thrill visitors with the idea of conquering frontiers.

Frontierland was last on the Wylie family's list, but it was still an essential part of the Disneyland experience. When the family reunited, they entered Frontierland and rode the Western Mine Train to view "the wilderness and desert regions of America that were portrayed in Disney's . . . nature films." At dusk, they boarded the Mark Twain steamboat. "Sipping non-alcoholic mint juleps, we whistled round the bends past Indian village camp fires, traders' cabins, keel boats and Indian canoes." They split up again, and "my husband and I strolled on the wharf while the boys journeyed by log raft to Tom Sawyer's Island to explore old ghost forts, tree houses and Injun Joe's cave." Disneyland was safe enough that they allowed their sons to explore on their own while they had some time together by themselves as a married couple.[51]

As the western craze gave way to the space age, families viewed the future at Tomorrowland, where futuristic rides like the submarine cruise (modeled after Disney's successful 1954 movie, *20,000 Leagues Under the Sea*) opened in 1959. The Trip to the Moon ride was designed by Dr. Wernher von Braun, who had prepared Disney's three-part televised miniseries, *Man in Space,* in 1955. Although no trip to the moon had yet taken place, publicity promised "the sights, sounds and sensations of the half-million mile journey are accurately portrayed in Tomorrowland's 'Trip to the Moon.'" Riders, imaginations influenced by contemporary air travel, entered a "circular, arena-like 'space-chamber,'" where they were "seated by an attractive 'space-age' hostess." The sense of space travel was supplied by a color television monitor on the floor that screened a view from the tail of the rocket, with another monitor on the ceiling with a view from the rocket's nose. The feelings of space travel were accentuated with sound effects: "As the ship leaves its launching pad the vibrations of blast-off are felt while the fiery discharge of the engine is seen." Clever use of video imagery helped riders in the space chamber imagine the distance they were traveling: "As the rocket pushes further and further away, the earth seems to recede," and the moon looks larger. "The rocket veers around the moon for a close look, dropping flares to enable views of the dark side." For excitement, the rocket ship "passe[d] through a hail of meteorites" before it returned to earth. Several years before satellites, and over a decade before the first moon landing, children and their parents could "Climb aboard and preview the future."[52]

By 1966 Disneyland featured nearly fifty major attractions and had attracted almost 50 million visitors. As Disneyland matured, it grappled with the racial conflicts and youth movements of the 1960s in subtle ways that spoke to a changing America but without disturbing the virtual reality within. Scholars have rightly criticized Disney for serving up a vision of America that was white; indeed, the 1890s Midwestern Main Street entrance evoked a decade in which segregation was legalized. The Jungle Cruise, with its African headhunters and the depictions of Indians as exotic "others" in Frontierland, inscribed notions of whiteness in attractions that were meant to provoke fear in the riders. A journalist wrote, "You venture into the dark heart of Adventureland by means of a Congo launch that takes you on a cruise of jungle rivers. You are warned by the guide of approaching crocodile and cannibals." Originally inspired by the movie *The African Queen,* the imaginary trip along Asia's Mekong River was a pastiche of African headhunters, Cambodian temples, and the Indian elephant god Ganesha, all of which played on visitors' fears of the unknown and an underlying racism.[53]

The irony is that in the era of Jim Crow, when black families could not be served ice cream at Howard Johnson's, African Americans and Mexican Americans were welcome as guests at Disneyland. Photographs and movies of the early years do show African Americans among the park visitors, and in the 1960s the Disney company stepped up publicity of its black visitors like baseball player Maury Wills of the Los Angeles Dodgers and Sammy Davis Jr.[54] In 1963, as racial confrontations in the South were horrifyingly violent, Disneyland diversified its cast of characters, albeit in caricature. African American "shoe shine boys Gene and Eddie" greeted guests on Main Street; the "Gonzalez Mexican Trio" serenaded guests.

Jazz music was a way to integrate people of color into the Disneyland scene by limiting them to a genre that whites had already accepted. The summer 1963 shows featured jazz artists Count Basie, Tex Beneke, and Harry James. Clara Ward's Original Gospel Singers, who first appeared in 1962, became a summertime regular. Publicity emphasized the multicultural roots of the music played by the New Orleans jazz bands on the river boat Mark Twain: "It is the driving music that has spread from African, European and American roots to pervade and change the whole history of music: Dixieland jazz." However, the commentary stressed racial stereotypes that trivialized the struggles then ongoing to gain equal civil rights: "It is a music that reflects all the drive, spirit, and happy-go-lucky optimism that is so much a part of the American heritage."[55] Disneyland was a product of its times in conveying a racialized America in its stereotypes of African Americans, but it was in the forefront of opening its gates to anyone who wanted to be amused by its imaginary world.

As the children who had come to the new Disneyland became teenagers, in 1964 the park created Disneyland After Dark to attract them with "a whole new dimension of romance and music." The Dixieland jazz bands were livened up with the addition of the "famous Firehouse Five Plus Two," or teens could hang out at the "exotic Polynesian show in the Tahitian Terrace or the rocking sounds of Kay Bell and the Spaceman at the Tomorrowland Space Bar." Graduation night parties for high school students provided a fun and safe place to celebrate a coming-of-age ritual.[56] As children grew up, Disneyland kept them coming back, without their parents, for a different kind of fun.

Western-themed amusement parks developed as part of a broader enthusiasm for cowboys and the West that began with the entertainment empire of kid television heroes. With their gun-toting, Indian-fighting cowboys and old-time Main Streets, amusement parks provided a stage for children to act out their own fantasies of the Wild West. In its first decades, Disneyland enlarged its borders of virtual reality from the Old West to futuristic exhibits, but visiting Frontierland still remained important to visitors. Through its linkage with Disney television and movie productions, Disneyland offered tourists more than the Old West. Indeed, by featuring the space-age frontier, Disneyland signaled the emergence of a new west and a new frontier.

Even though the passion for westerns cooled, the West still sought and retained its vacationing families. For years visitors to Hollywood had come to Grauman's Chinese Theatre to inspect the footprints of movie stars in the cement sidewalk, but it was not until July 4, 1964, that Universal City Studios opened its gates to studio tours. Studio brochures explained that "tours of production facilities give you an inside look at the complicated, expensive world of mass entertainment, and lucky groups will see a few stars or even watch some actual production work." In 1965, nearly half a million people took the tour on the GlamorTram, with its lovely tour guides. The brochure promised, "we're sure you will share their same enthusiasm when you and your family visit Universal." A travel article warned parents that children may be disappointed "when they find that a Munsters' house is nothing but a false front, and that the ships in McHale's Navy are really only replicas on a man-made pond," but the children seem to have had no trouble separating fantasy from reality. Although tourists were usually frustrated in their desires to see stars on the back lot, Universal found the tours to be a successful public relations machine. Over 6 million visitors came in the first five years to revel in the fantastic illusions of television studios and movie sets. Eventually Universal Studios established a theme park in Hollywood with thrill rides based on its productions, taking advantage of the formula for fun invented by the first theme parks in Southern California.[57]

Gene Autry, Walter Knott, and Walt Disney made a fortune from selling the West to children and to their parents on vacation. When they realized the western craze was fading, they spun off newer versions of the West. Western star Gene Autry invested his fortune in television and radio broadcasting, and in the pro baseball club, the Los Angeles Angels. Walter Knott funneled his profits into right-wing political organizations; he hosted a rally at Knott's Berry Farm for presidential candidate Barry Goldwater in 1964, attended by 28,000 persons who came to see John

Wayne and Ronald Reagan. He opened an exact replica of Philadelphia's Independence Hall on July 4, 1966, because "just as Ghost Town vividly reminds us of our gold rush beginnings in California, Independence Hall takes us back to the very founding of our country." The park's ghost town West was overshadowed by the thrill rides added in the 1970s, and attendance jumped 50 percent in the first year. Walt Disney exported the West by building Disney World in Florida in 1971, followed by Frontierlands in Tokyo and Paris. Disneyland's utopian urbanism inspired a new West of planned suburbs to house all the newcomers to the West.[58]

It all began with a ghost town, cowboy songs, and Davy Crockett's coonskin cap. The enthusiasm for westerns may have waned, but family vacationers still went west for adventure. In the postwar years, television westerns lured tourists to dude ranches and amusement parks that recreated the Old West they saw on television. By the 1960s Americans were finding a new West in an entertainment industry that was selling its version of America around the globe. But they did not skip a visit to Frontierland or Knott's Berry Farm, where they could find the myths of the Wild West as seen in the westerns. To see the real American wilderness, they would have to go camping in the national parks.

chapter five

Back to Nature

In July 1954 the *Ladies Home Journal* featured a story about how a fireman's family was able to afford a two-week vacation camping in Yosemite National Park in California. Dick and Geegee Williams took their two children, Dickie (age five) and Leslie (age seven) on their first vacation in six years. The story highlighted the vacation as well deserved after "six years filled with important job and financial decisions, an attack of polio, the only big fights of their marriage, and plenty of growing up." During the war, Dick served in the navy, and Geegee married him on leave in 1944. Typical of other young couples, they started their life together with little money. He built their house with his father's help; when little Leslie suffered an attack of polio, the National Foundation for Infantile Paralysis paid the bills. On his salary and with a mortgage and car payments, vacations "just don't exist, unless they're inexpensive."[1]

Camping was the perfect solution to vacationing on a tight budget for the family of the young veteran. The drive north from Los Angeles to Yosemite took all day, and when they arrived, they found a spot with a view across the river with a nearby play area for children. They had rented a trailer tent from a fellow fireman, and they had also rented a gasoline stove and a portable icebox. Geegee immediately set up house. She unpacked the four wooden boxes and "set the boxes upright to make shelves, and reorganized everything—food and eating equipment on the shelves, pots and pans on an old card table." They used the camp's picnic table for eating a simple supper, "canned pork and beans, fruit and coffee." The children were in their sleeping bags by 8 P.M., their parents by 8:30. The first night's sleep was interrupted by a bear that ate the food in a pack that they had not hung high enough; while Dick and Geegee cowered in their tent, a nearby camper scared the bear away by beating a dishpan with a wooden spoon. In the bear attack, they lost two pounds of bacon, a jar of blackberry jam, cheese, eggs, and two boxes of chocolate chip cookies.

Dick was the veteran camper, but Geegee was a complete novice. By 7:15 A.M. the next day, Dick, "who does not cook at home—had pancakes, bacon and coffee going strong." He relished the delights of camping: "M'm-m," he said. "That's camping—a great big breakfast and lots of time to lie down afterward." The family ate heartily, and Geegee washed up the breakfast dishes in water heated on the stove. Dick readied the campfire pit with fuel, put up a clothesline, swept out the tent, "and stretched out on the ground under a shady tree, his day's chores done." Both Dick and Geegee were happy with the change in their routine. "'You can't beat this for living,' he said dreamily." She liked the fact that camping was less housework. "Ideal," she said, "just wash the dishes, fold the pajamas into the sleeping bags, and close the flap on the tent." Freed from her housework at home, Geegee agreed, "it's a vacation for me all the way."[2]

Even cooking was easier while camping. Geegee learned how to broil steak over the fire and "discovered to her delight how really simple it is." Her "boldest experiment" was to wrap "individual portions of lamb stew in aluminum foil" and cook them over the coals. She regarded the results as "Absolutely delicious. You get a flavor cooking this way you just don't get at home." The park made it easy for her to do her shopping. Four general stores in the park sold fresh food, ice, and wood for campfires. Stores rented a variety of equipment for camping families, "cooking utensils, towels, tents, even a children's crib." Twice a day a truck visited the campsites carrying milk, eggs, and bread, and a mobile "laundrecar" meant she could do the laundry and ironing any day of the week. Yosemite catered to camping families like the Williams. "Pretty civilized camping," Geegee said, "but a big help when you go with children."[3]

Camping provided opportunities for family togetherness. Their days were spent visiting park highlights like Happy Isles Rapids and Vernal Falls, and the giant redwoods forty miles away where they drove through Wawona Tunnel Tree. They fished in the river and floated downstream on air mattresses. After morning activities, they lunched on peanut butter sandwiches and took short naps; later, Dick took the children for a swim or a hike. The park offered evening entertainment: campfire lectures on the plants and animals in the park, sing-alongs, and square dancing. They stayed up late to see the famous Firefall, "a mass of glowing coals, pushed over the cliff at Glacier Point each night down a thousand feet in a stream of living fire." The Williams, however, "discovered that they much preferred sitting quietly by their own evening fire." Camping in Yosemite even rekindled their romance. "Honey girl," Dick said, taking Geegee's hand, "we sure are lucky." At the end of the two weeks, they were pleased with their choice to take a camping vacation. It was inexpensive (under $200), offered a change of routine, and the family had fun together outdoors.[4]

The Williamses were typical of the families who contributed to a huge boom in family camping in the 1940s and 1950s. Camping together appealed to family vacationers for the same reasons it appealed to Dick and Geegee. It was seen as inexpensive, fun, and wholesome to be outdoors. In 1958 a family magazine proclaimed, "Camping, today, is for everyone. Your family can pack up for a weekend—or a month—in state and national parks across the land. It's an inexpensive, carefree way to have fun together." In an era of family togetherness, "camping brings the family together in the clean, wholesome outdoors." Once limited to men's hunting and fishing trips, camping became a common family vacation choice. It was an all-American family vacation with baby carriages and a station wagon, and a carload of camping equipment to make a home in the outdoors.[5]

People went back to nature because nature was made more accessible to them. States opened new campgrounds and refurbished old ones after the war to meet the needs of the waves of campers that overran their sites. New dams meant new reservoirs for family boating and fishing. About one-third of those who took vacations in 1962 visited a federal or state park; of those, three-fourths stated that "being outdoors close to nature" was the reason they visited the park. The groundswell of enthusiasm for camping surged throughout the decade; camper registration totaled 10 million in 1950 and tripled to 30 million by 1960.[6]

Those who promoted camping as a healthful vacation—easy on the budget and good for the children—might have tempered their enthusiasm if they had been one of the millions who visited the parks after the war. Caught off guard by the flood of campers, the National Park Service (NPS) undertook Mission 66, a ten-year program to improve their facilities, and the National Forest Service launched Operation Outdoors to increase the number of campsites from 41,000 to 125,000.[7] The complaint letters from Yellowstone National Park visitors reveal the reality of camping, with crowded campgrounds, stinking toilets, cafeteria lines, bear attacks, and even death. At Shenandoah National Park, African Americans discovered segregated campgrounds and park facilities, and officials in Washington battled with local park officials to enforce the ideals of democracy that were the foundation of the park's mission.

A Camping Vacation

The rise of enthusiasm for camping was linked to Americans' desire to leave the pressures of civilization behind and to relive America's pioneering past. Motoring magazines cited the advice of sociologists and psychologists to "escape from mass-induced conformity, high-strung urbanized living in the asphalt jungle, smog and noises." Escaping modern life was made easier by "increased mobility, intensified interest in family-orientated activities, shorter work week, more leisure time, more money." Camping guides argued that "a camping vacation is probably the most relaxing type of vacation" a family could take; "no schedules have to be met, no need to lay out large amounts of money for accommodations." Camping allowed families "a chance to enjoy nature to any degree wanted, from the rustic forest campsite to the seashore recreation area."[8]

Parents took their children camping to acquaint them with nature. American parents who had grown up in rural America's wide open spaces wanted their children to know the pleasures of being outdoors, away from the cul-de-sacs of suburbia or the blacktop playgrounds of the city. Immigrants wanted to explore America with their children to make them more American. Men who had camped with their buddies on fishing trips discovered that camping with the family was a way to sustain their connection to the outdoors. Children were thought to be natural campers, curious explorers who needed to take only a few precautions for their own safety. Fishing, boating, hiking, and swimming drew children away from the campsite to a more immediate experience with nature. Children "might be following the campsite's nature trails, or 'exploring' by themselves." Park rangers provided nature talks and walks to entertain and inform the children. The point was to get children closer to nature, to have a fresh view of the flora and fauna of their setting. A motoring magazine promised exciting outdoor entertainment: "Trails close to camp tempt hikers; a fresh-water stream provides an always-changing spectacle to watch; and the more fortunate of the small fry find excitement with a glimpse of a wild animal or a bird that's new to them."[9]

Camping was seen as a way to teach children responsibility for themselves and others in a safe environment. Older children were expected to help parents with campground duties. Little ones were kept nearby, "playing about the family tents; digging in the sand; or sprawled in a portable playpen, peacefully snoozing in the camp's cool shade." Parents wanted children to explore on their own and seemed to worry little about hazards beyond insect bites or losing their way. "It's true that toddlers have to be kept in sight, and older children must be warned about poison ivy, strange bugs, and cliff scaling. But, hazard for hazard, the campground is safer than the average home." Camping manuals urged parents to teach children about poison ivy, and to give them whistles to blow or advice to stay put when they got lost.[10]

Children were seen as adaptable and uncomplaining campers. Experienced campers claimed, "the switch from the home to the camp, from beds to sleeping bags or cots or the back of the station wagon is taken as an exciting adventure." Because they were small, children could sleep in smaller bags or in their homemade bedrolls. Children could wear their regular play clothes, jeans, shorts, and swimming suits with footwear of sneakers or loafers. Parents were advised to take along rain gear, a sweater for evening, and warm jackets for higher elevations. Even "feeding children in camp is not difficult, especially if you take along some of their favorite foods." Baby bottles could be heated in the car bottle warmer and they could eat their usual canned baby food, but parents were warned to take along a supply of water for formula because campground water could upset their stomachs.[11] Young children were no impediment to getting back to nature. To have a family adventure, all that was needed was a little planning and care, and the right equipment.

In a time of tight budgets for young families, the camping explosion was fueled by its affordability. A minimum of equipment was required to camp out, and camping equipment was improved to make it easier to use. Advancing technologies attracted more women to camping by making it more comfortable and less like roughing it in the woods. New types of vehicles made camping easier as well. Families slept in station wagons or bought tent trailers, and campers, trailers, and recreational vehicles allowed families to take their homes with them. Family magazines like *Better Homes and Gardens,* map companies like Rand McNally, and camping equipment manufacturers published camping guides that advised campers on every detail, from how to buy a tent to making foil-wrapped dinners in the campfire. Buying the right equipment, choosing the right place to camp, and taking the right food would mean the family could have the comforts of home in the outdoors.

Camping was supposedly as cheap as staying home. The American Automobile Association magazine, *Motorland,* asserted that "a camping vacation costs little more than staying at home, once you've got the camping equipment." Campground fees were as low as 25 cents to $1.75 a night for a family. Like the Williams family, "a family of four should be able to take a two-week camping tour for slightly over $200, including food, camp fees, auto expenses, laundry and miscellaneous." Veteran campers were especially enthusiastic about the budgetary virtues of family camping. Coleman, an outdoor equipment manufacturer, issued a promotional booklet in 1953 that interspersed advertisements with stories from experienced campers. One veteran camper claimed that "we've had more fun for less money than ever before in our lives."[12]

Campers did not need much to get started. The basic list of equipment in 1958 included "camp kitchen, portable ice chest, gasoline stove, cooking utensils, and a tent." A metal table and stools were also nice to have. In the early 1960s, that list expanded to shelter (tent or trailer, car top); sleeping gear; camp stove, lantern, icebox, cooking utensils, a camp ax or saw; and personal items including rain gear, flashlights, sporting equipment, and toys. Campers were advised to start slowly and buy pieces of gear one at a time, not to rush out and purchase a whole set of camping equipment. But trying to get by on less might mean "your first trip may be your last."[13]

As more equipment became available, camping outfits became more elaborate. The *Rand McNally Camping Guide* in 1963 provided a long list of equipment in its "Camper's Check List." The standard equipment included a tent, stove, bedding, silverware, plates, cups, frying pan, stewpots, coffeepot, can opener, knives, bottle opener, spatula, cooking forks, roasting forks, and serving spoons. A long list of items were "Camp Living Necessities": soap, detergent, paper napkins, wax paper, toilet paper, paper towels, pot cleaners, pot holders, gallon thermos jug, rain coats or umbrella, warm jackets and caps, an extra pair of shoes, mosquito repellent and medication, toilet and shaving articles, toothbrushes and toothpaste, dishcloths and towels, washcloths and bath towels, and a plastic tablecloth. It was a good idea to pack orange crates with handy items like a clothesline and clothespins, mirror, oilcloth, clock, whisk broom, hatchet or ax, wash pan, spade, folding chairs, sleeping bags, flashlight, lantern, flyswatter, bug bomb, first aid kit, coat hangers, laundry bag, sewing kit, twine, rope, pencil and paper, jackknife, tarpaulin, and, last but not least, a deck of cards.[14]

How did all this equipment get carried to the wilderness? In the family car. Families loaded their camping gear in the trunk of the family sedan or the back of the station wagon. Car manufacturers boasted, "The wagon has created a new kind of vacation—the family camping or wilderness vacation with all the comforts of home." It was large enough to carry "the entire family and all its stuff—not just clothes and fishing rods but a complete outfit for outdoor housekeeping. It is the land yacht of the highway, sleeping four." Instead of spending money on resorts, consumers were advised to buy a bigger car and spread out air mattresses for sleeping. The car's electrical system provided power for appliances like "an electric shaver, a coffee maker that also warms the baby's bottle, extra lights or a small motor blower for inflating mattresses." To expand the space, car owners could buy a "boot," a tentlike cover that projected from the rear tailgate. A popular camping guide compared the station wagon to pioneer transportation: "Today's version of a Conestoga, the station wagon, is going mighty strong."[15]

A tent was essential, and consumers could choose from finding an older tent in the attic or splurging on newer tents that were easier to set up. Older tents were made of waxed canvas without a floor, and they were supported by vertical poles and adjoining ridgepoles. They were heavy and took a strong man and several hours to erect with the help of patient assistants. The virtue of older tents was their roominess, and guidebooks recommended that they be at least ten by twelve feet for a family, with room to stand up inside. Dad's wood-framed army cot required ample space provided only in older tents. More modern tents featured a sewn-in floor and mosquito netting in the openings with outside frame supports so they were easier to set up in a hurry. Lightweight tents and camping equipment made of nylon and aluminum components were not invented until the late 1970s.[16]

Camping reduced vacation costs because families cooked their own food. Coleman's guide asserted, "By cooking your own meals out of doors . . . instead of eating in strange restaurants, you can enjoy delectable 'home-cooked' meals in the scenic 'dining room' of your choice—and save $6 to $9 per family a day doing it." Improved camp cooking equipment made camp cooking easier. The Coleman Company, which diversified from producing lanterns to manufacturing an array of outdoor equipment, tried to convince consumers that camping was easier with their equipment. The purchase of a Coleman stove meant that "Adjustable cooking heat is available at the turn of a valve. Quick snacks or full course dinners can be prepared easily by almost anyone with the help of such labor-saving equipment as a gasoline Coleman Camp Stove." Their 1953 camping manual supplied menus and recipes for outdoor cooking with their Outing Pals. Car camping meant that they could carry along the equipment and as much food as they could fit into the station wagon:

Campers preparing dinner at Mt. Rainier National Park, 1955.
(Photograph by Louie Kirk, National Park Service Photograph Collection. Courtesy NARA.)

"Just load up your Coleman Outing Pals along with your food and utensils and head for the open road."[17] With their coolers, camp stoves, portable tables, and lanterns, families were not roughing it but were living almost as comfortably as if they were at home.

Outdoor cooking required advance planning. A family campground guide advised, "Keep the menus simple" but plan for bigger appetites because "you'll see how quickly a stack of hotcakes disappears at breakfast and mound of hamburgers goes at lunch or dinner." Processed food like biscuit mixes or canned meat were perfect for camp cooking. Indeed, "canned luncheon meat, fried crisp and brown, is a good substitute for bacon." Families should plan on sandwiches or canned beans for lunch to allow more time for activities. The true camping feast was saved for the evening meal. Meat was the featured menu item: "Steak, pork chops, lamb chops or chicken can be grilled, fried, or barbecued. Pot-luck stew is another favorite." Evening meals could be quite elaborate, with corn steamed over the fire, side dishes of instant rice, or potatoes cooked in foil over the fire. In 1955 a Reynolds Aluminum television commercial advertised its booklet, "Vacation How-to," as their spokeswoman demonstrated many uses of aluminum foil—cooking, wrapping sandwiches, and waterproofing matches. Children's appetites could be quickly satisfied with chocolate milk (made from instant dry milk and chocolate syrup), peanut butter and jelly, and cookies and crackers.[18]

Camp cooking was not quite like being at home because men were more likely to cook in the outdoors. One guide noted, "Even Dad, who was hard put to boil water at home, is now becoming (much to Mom's joy) a skilled cook on family outings." A freelance photographer who traveled with his wife and two young daughters as "highway gypsies" told of his pride in his camp cooking feats: "At home Jane is the cook, but on trips I usually take over. I get a kick out of it and it's more of a vacation for her that way." He made cooking sound easy: "It's no trick at all to dish out a meal of chicken and dumplings, mashed potatoes, peas, coffee and chocolate pudding with present day foods."[19] Camp cooking for men not only allowed them to demonstrate prowess, but it also gave their wives a break from the routine.

For the most part, camping experts advised families to sustain traditional gender roles. "Junior keeps the camp clean, gets the firewood and perhaps proves to be a whiz as a packer and unpacker. Daughter sees to it that all the clothes are properly cared for and sleeping gear stays in top condition." Dad may have cooked, but women were in charge of cleaning up. Outdoors made it more pleasurable: "For Mom, dishwashing will be anything but drudgery with a mountain to look at and chipmunks for company."[20] While camping, the rest of the family was more likely to help Mom with the housekeeping while performing their usual roles.

By the 1960s, camping equipment manufacturers realized that they had to cater to women's needs to sell equipment, and they designed them to be more like home. "Many of the newest products have been planned to help her keep the camp in as good order as she keeps her home." Women who had to keep house in the outdoors wanted modern equipment to make "modern camping far more fun and more carefree." With the right equipment, "Even the most sophisticated city homemaker, used to push-button comfort, can enjoy camping." A 1961 camping guide noted, "A visitor to a public campsite might be astonished at the number of modern Dianas who can pitch their camping home with all the aplomb and skills of a Danny Boone or a Kit Carson."[21] Women were seen as intrepid frontier heroes, even goddesses in the wilderness—provided they had modern equipment.

The idea that camping was a home away from home propelled the manufacture of wheeled camping vehicles. Although trailers and "house cars" had long been available, the 1950s saw the invention of portable camper shells mounted on the back of pickup trucks, and in the 1960s, manufacturers began to sell motor homes, fully self-contained vehicles, now called RVs (recreational vehicles), about triple the cost of a travel trailer. For families, the increasing affordability of manufactured campers and trailers meant they could be, as historian Roger White suggests, "at home on the road."[22]

Because of their lower cost, travel trailers were the mainstay of the wheeled camping vehicle market. From 28,000 units in 1961, sales of travel trailers rose to 76,600 units in 1965. Travel trailer manufacturers saw their product as revolutionary; it was "America's new easy way to travel." The big selling point was that "This resort home goes with you any time . . . any place you like!" Because the trailer was lightweight, it could be pulled by a station wagon, although some owners found that they needed to buy a new car to pull the load. Because the owners did not have to worry about finding a motel or paying for lodging on the road, "It's the ideal family summer home." Trailers included the comforts of home in a small space. Priced from $800 to $2,000, they featured "kitchenettes with ice-boxes or refrigerators, porcelain sinks; built-in heating; plenty of storage space; sleeping facilities for 2 to 5." Travel trailers provided the comforts of home in the outdoors: "After a day's hiking in the woods or trolling out on the lake, there's nothing like pulling off your boots and sinking into those easy chairs in your travel trailer!" Advertisers appealed to families with scenes of dinnertime and an evening of "cards, reading, or just plain taking it easy. The children love it—there's always cold root beer in the refrigerator."[23]

Trailers or motor homes allowed families to explore, to get off the beaten path, as long as it was a passable road. Airstream advertisements declared: "Airstream puts the world at your doorstep!" An Airstream allowed its owners to "Stretch out beside a foamy beach; soak up sunshine while a playful breeze runs its fingers through your hair" or "explore pine-fringed mountains, domain of the golden trout." The trailers were homelike, with "dreamy beds, complete bathroom including toilet, tub and shower, hot and cold water, heat, bright lights and refrigeration." If a family could not afford the pricey Airstream home on wheels, they could "run away with

Trailers allowed families to camp more comfortably in the national parks. Acadia National Park, 1958. (Photograph by Richard G. Smithe. Courtesy National Park Service Historic Photograph Collection.)

home" in a tent trailer. An advertisement for Starcraft's "Great Escape Machine" featured a photo of a cozy interior where two children sat at a table reading books; a boy was asleep on the bed. Motoring magazines saw trailers as proof of the persistence of the pioneering spirit: "Today's nomad sits at the wheel of the station wagon; the prairie schooner spirit sails the highways on the wheels of a house trailer."[24] Words such as *escape* and *nomadic* assured consumers they could have home and wilderness all at once.

Family magazines featured the new campers and trailers in their pages. In 1961 Keith Brown of Villa Park, Illinois, told how he took "seven kids, the wife, and myself" in a camper to see the "entire West." They covered a lot of ground in their trailer, and no place was off limits. "Nine thousand miles in five weeks. All through Yosemite, Yellowstone, Jackson Hole, Grand Canyon—you name it. We were there." It was cheaper than staying in motels. "It cost us $300, maybe $350. Without the camper, we'd have spent $50 or $60 a day just for food and a place to stay." They had no trouble finding a place for everyone to sleep, but "we had to eat in shifts because we couldn't fit everybody at the table at once!" Brown promoted trailers as doing double duty as a fallout shelter for the family. "Since a trailer or camper is designed for extended family living, it makes a good basic unit for a home fallout shelter."[25] The cold war fears of the bomb were allayed by the purchase of the same camper that would allow them to escape civilization by going back to nature.

A more compact version of the RV, the Volkswagen Camper, was available to Americans by 1960. Its ingenious design allowed campers to "set up house wherever you like." Advertisements promised: "The great outdoors is yours for the taking, and when you're ready for a bit of indoor comfort, just go back to your own living room, bedroom, kitchen, bar (no closing time), and bathroom (no waiting!)." The camper was perfect for the family: "A VW Camper means fresh air and fun for your family whether you're planning a weekend trip, a couple of weeks vacation or a long expedition." The camper even came with a striped awning for use at the beach, and curtains to ensure privacy.[26]

Ironically, the popularity of trailers and RVs made it even more difficult to "get away from it all" because "popular campgrounds are jammed on weekends, and people trying to get away from it all are taking it all with them." To accommodate the demands for campgrounds, the American Automobile Association reported that "federal and state recreational areas are being opened up to lure campers away from some of the state and national parks that are suffering environmental damage through overuse." Private campgrounds provided a deluxe alternative to public campgrounds. Rand McNally combined its camping guidebook and travel trail guide in 1971, and it listed over 17,000 campgrounds and RV parks, including 8,000 private facilities, over 3,000 national forest campgrounds, plus national parks, state parks and forests, and city, county, and civic areas.[27] It was such a popular guide that regional editions were issued for travelers.

The 1963 Rand McNally guide pronounced that campgrounds were improving with "modern sanitary facilities, showers, stores, as well as such recreational activities as playgrounds, swimming, riding and even golf." Rand McNally employed "field representatives" to inspect campgrounds and award them ratings from 1 to 5, with 5 the best rating. National parks were rated 1 (very primitive), 2 (rugged), 3 (rustic), 4 (modern), or 5 (ultramodern)—a home away from home with all the conveniences. Commercial campgrounds advertised a variety of facilities in Rand McNally's guidebook. Landuit's Lake in Hillsdale, Illinois, was huge: "600 Electric and Water Hookups, Giant Heated Pool, Lake or River Fishing, Hot Showers—Flush Toilets, Trailer and Boat Rental, Playground, amusement rides, pee wee golf, groceries, ice, bait, dump station." The midsized Shabbona Camping Resort on ninety "Beautiful Wooded Acres" in Morris, Illinois, provided 200 sites and a store with "milk, bread, canned goods, pop & ice." Such camps provided entertainment for children such as pools and miniature golf—even a pony farm. One advertisement aimed at campers' desire for cleanliness: "The owner cleans the restrooms at Wilderness Lake."[28]

The founding of Kampgrounds of America (KOA) in 1963 revolutionized camping by creating a corporate chain that franchised campgrounds to individual owners. Like Holiday Inn, KOA offered campers a standardized camping experience. Perhaps more importantly, KOA offered a reservations system, which meant families would not face being turned away when they stopped on the highway, or have to speed down the highway to find an open site. Its advertisement promoted the features of its campgrounds: "Clean restrooms, free hot showers, laundry facilities, grocery store, and friendly hosts await you at KOA Kampgrounds from coast to coast. Rely on the Kampgrounds of America sign as you travel the highways and byways of scenic America." The franchise concept was successful in attracting both owners and customers; by 1967 KOA owned 120 campgrounds, and by 1970 KOA had more campsites than the NPS.[29]

Like Dick and Geegee Williams, Americans discovered camping was the ideal choice for the family vacation because it was an affordable way to get away from it all, even if they had to bring it all with them. Advertised as a vacation that was as cheap as staying at home, it was made possible by the family car or wheeled vehicle that had room for the whole family and all its equipment to create a temporary home in the outdoors. Improved equipment like gas stoves made camping more attractive to women, and camping offered parents an opportunity to introduce their children to the wonders of nature. Although weekends might find the family at a nearby state park or reservoir, to really get back to nature, families chose the national parks.

Burdened beyond Capacity: Yellowstone

The reopening of national parks at war's end in 1945 opened the floodgates to American tourists. Yellowstone National Park officials reported, "Immediately following VJ-Day a surge of visitors came into the park and daily travel practically doubled and continued at the greatly increased rate to the end of the travel year." With the end of gasoline rationing, "thousands of persons who had occasion to move across the country were able to make side trips to the park and enjoy the scenery, fishing and other recreation offered." All kinds of people came to the park—new veterans, war workers returning home, farm families "who converted their trucks into small houses on wheels and were moving across the country to see the beauties of the West." Almost all came in their own car, and the luckiest arrived in new cars. The surge grew in 1946 as "a deluge of visitors descended upon the park in May as soon as the roads were cleared of snow." By the end of June, "more visitors had entered the park gates than came in during the entire 1945 travel year"—close to 200,000 persons, an increase of 39 percent over the previous year and 65 percent more than had visited in 1941, the last year before the war.[30]

All over the country, parks were welcoming visitors in droves. At Shenandoah National Park in Virginia, over Labor Day "park visitors were in a holiday mood but drove carefully and were not too disappointed by the limited facilities for their convenience." On Sunday, September 2, two cars arrived every minute at South Panorama. Park officials reported, "The picnic grounds were filled to near capacity on every weekend" and "all camp sites were occupied on several occasions." Grand Canyon officials were likewise surprised by the strong 1946 season. By the end of September 1946 about 488,819 visitors had descended on the Grand Canyon, an increase of 325 percent over the previous year.[31]

The first surge of visitors turned into a flood of visitors. The total number of visits to national parks rose from 21.7 million in 1946 to 61.6 million in 1956, the year Mission 66 was announced. Under Mission 66, an ambitious program to upgrade park facilities to meet the needs of tourists, the government spent over a billion dollars. By the time Mission 66 was complete, ten years later, visitation was over 133 million. By 1970, visitation was 172 million, but in the early 1970s, it decreased, and not until 1974 did it recover. By 1976, visitation reached 216.5 million.[32]

The NPS, and the private concessioners who operated the lodging and dining facilities in the parks, struggled to provide for the explosion of visitors. In 1958 the director of NPS reported, "Campgrounds have been burdened beyond capacities, but this appropriate and beneficial experience in the parks brings enjoyment to many that could be provided in no other way." The problem of accommodating the crowds while preserving the wilderness was compounded by the fact that parks were owned by the NPS (and thus all American citizens) but operated by park concessioners—private companies with a profit motive. Historian Mark Daniel Barringer argues that concessioners were in the business of "selling nature, recreation and frontier history to Americans" to attract them to the parks. Furthermore, NPS officials were divided about how to meet visitor needs without threatening park ecologies.[33]

To understand the experience of the visitors, we can read their letters about the flagship park of the NPS: Yellowstone National Park, where park facilities were strained beyond their limits. Complaint letters from park visitors open a window into the experiences of tourists in the parks, and replies by park officials help us understand how they justified park policies. Each national park kept track of all complaints made about concessioner services and assigned them to various categories, where they were tallied. For example, in 1951 Yellowstone reported a total of fifty-one complaints about the concessioners: thirteen complaints about the "unsatisfactory condition of Accommodations," seven about the high rate for the cabins, seven about reservations not being held, two for the lack of bathing facilities, and one about the condition of the "comfort stations" (toilets). A separate tally was made of the thirty-three complaints about services provided by the government: four complained about the camping facilities, four about inadequate sanitation. The primitive condition of park roads generated eight complaints about the roads and three about road signs. One person complained that the bears were a nuisance.[34]

It is ironic that visitors who went to the national parks to "escape civilization" seemed surprised to encounter inconveniences in the wilderness. They complained about having to wait in line for meals in the cafeterias, about not finding a place to stay, about the poor quality of the primitive toilets, or about the noise of other visitors. Visitors grounded their complaints in the expectation that these were *their* parks, and that as American citizens, they were entitled to enjoy them in the way they had expected. Tourists saw themselves as consumers of park services, and they expected a return on their fees and on the investment they made in time and effort to arrive at the park. In reply, the park superintendent reminded them that they would expect a wait if they were at a city cafeteria, or a ticket if they disobeyed parking regulations in the city, and that regulations were necessary to maintain order. Park officials apologized but explained that the number of visitors had exceeded all expectations and that they simply were overwhelmed and short-staffed.[35]

Visitors complained loudly about the park's rustic sanitation facilities. In 1949 a woman from Detroit, Michigan, wrote of her trip to Yellowstone that "I had to use public toilets while traveling through and never in any part of this great country have I seen such unsanitary conditions. They were not only outmoded but they were a mess." She thought the park should hire a matron to keep the toilets clean. "People travel thousands of miles to see this natural beauty and then lose all of the enjoyment when exposed to such antiquated plumbing." A nurse saw the toilets as a threat to the health and safety of visitors. "It is truly nature in all its majestic beauty and is so wonderful a spot for relaxation etc.—but—the sanitary facilities are of the worst. . . . At home we fight for sanitation to keep down epidemics of polio, typhoid, etc. and then see such breeding places—is our effort all in vain?" She expected the parks to furnish flush toilets. Even modern toilet facilities were no match for the number of visitors, according to one male visitor: "Now for the flush toilets. The urinal is too high for little boys to stand and use so they proceed to void all over the toilet seats. Your men knocked themselves out trying to keep the place clean but this too was a losing battle."[36] Visitors who were only one or two generations away from the era of outhouses saw the primitive toilets as a backward step in civilization. The quantity of human waste from the crush of visitors overwhelmed the organic processes of waste decomposition in outdoor privies that were never designed to accommodate the numbers visiting the parks.

Most complaints related to accommodations. Families on a budget tended to stay in the cheaper tourist cabins, where the facilities were most primitive. Tourists complained that the cabins were small and dirty, or that they lacked essentials for camping. A woman from Garden City, New York, wrote to complain there was not enough kitchen space available in the park. She suggested that "Camp Kitchens . . . equipped with gas burners, counter space, sink and running water," be placed at various points throughout the park. Mr. and Mrs. Phillips from Pennsylvania arrived at Yellowstone late one afternoon in May 1952 at the Fishing Bridge Campground, where they rented a furnished cabin for the night. Phillips wrote, "We went to [the] cabin and found only a bed and a leaky wash basin and a battered up pitcher two towels and a piece of soap a wood stove and a pile of wood in the corner. All we had to set on was our suit cases." He returned immediately to the office to complain and waited an hour for benches to be delivered. They gave up and went to dinner. After dinner at the cafeteria, they went back to the office to complain, and the manager "spoke to my wife roughly and said to her if you don't like it we will return your money." Finally, at about 7 P.M., "a young man came with a wheel cart and brought two old benches," but Phillips complained they did not have a table to write on. He wrote, "[I] Don't believe they should rent to people this way and take their good money and return so little." Phillips thought that the public was entitled to better treatment at their national parks; he had made considerable sacrifices to visit.[37]

In reply, Superintendent Rogers explained that previous visitors had moved the furniture to another cabin, and he apologized for the scarcity of staff because the park had just opened. Rogers remarked, "beginning with Memorial Day, May 30, the travel has exceeded all expectations," and he cited the following figures: "On May 30 this year 8,480 persons visited the park and during the next several days there was an average of better than 4,500 per day. Last year there was less than an average of 3,000 persons per day covering the same period. Therefore, the available employees found it very difficult to try to meet the situation." Rogers thanked Mr. Phillips for pointing out the problems so that they could be remedied in the future and added, "We are sorry indeed to learn of this experience."[38]

Other visitors wrote to complain that they could not find accommodations in the park. A man who was turned away from the park in July 1952 wrote a complaint to suggest that park rangers "advise tourists regarding the availability of overnight accommodations when entering the park." In his reply, the superintendent admitted that "it is a serious problem for which we do not entirely have the answer." In his defense, Rogers cited the fact that on July 24, the day Waldman entered the park, 16,000 persons had entered the park. Because 8,300 could be accommodated in the hotels, lodges, and tourist cabins, and another 3,000 to 4,000 in the campgrounds, "it is apparent that not all visitors could be accommodated and this same situation exists almost daily throughout July and August."

He warned, "unless people make reservations in advance it is very difficult for some of them to obtain accommodations in view of the unprecedented travel since the war."[39]

Family travelers complained that they could not find what they expected for their children at the parks. Thomas W. Lanigan of Grand Island, Nebraska, took the trouble to write to the Secretary of the Interior: "Last summer, at Yellowstone Park, we couldn't find a stand selling hamburgers, hotdogs, ice cream, root beer, or anything else. The concessionaires make you stand in line, sometimes a half block long, to get any food, and then serve you when and what they want to serve you." Tongue in cheek (perhaps), he wrote, "Having no hotdogs or hamburgers in the United States is a grave, grave question, bordering almost on a national catastrophe." In his humorous reply, superintendent Lemuel A. Garrison assured him, "hamburgers have been on the menu, with all the trimmings, at lunch counters in the Park for many years. We have carefully held the line on price on them, knowing their blessed utility to harassed parents with tired youngsters." He admitted that they had not served hot dogs, perhaps because of "a vestigial feeling that the exotic animals were not welcome," but that in a recent experiment, their two-day supply of hot dogs at the Mammoth lunch counter was sold out by 5 P.M. on the first day. He invited Lanigan to join him at the lunch counter at his next visit: "When you return please drop in and get acquainted over a hot dog and malt.—although I'll still have a cheeseburger myself with mustard, lettuce, pickles and onion, Thank You!"[40] This good-humored reply suggests a genuine concern on the part of park officials to cater to the needs of their visitors, despite being handicapped by a lack of resources.

Overcrowding in the parks resulted not only from the crush of human visitors, but from cars and camping vehicles that filled the parking lots and caused "bear jams" on park roadways. Over 98 percent of visitors to Yellowstone in 1950 arrived by automobile. NPS historian David Louter argues that "Americans in the twentieth century would encounter parks primarily through autos; they would interpret the park landscape from a road and through the windshield." Camping vacationers experienced parks as "places of windshield wilderness." An old-timer saw the solution as banning cars in the park. D. S. Martin of Worcester, Massachusetts, wanted to go back to the good old days of horse and buggy, before Teddy Roosevelt opened the park for automobiles. "Where can you go today and not see automobiles? They are a pest. People rush thru the park, dump garbage and paper along the way. They don't appreciate the beauty there." A man from Montana asked, "Will my little daughter be unable to know this pleasure . . . because people are so crowded into restricted camping areas that we leave in disgust because it is impossible to get away from it all? Please, God, No."[41]

Even though visitors intended to escape civilization, the crowds meant that its evils followed them to the park. For example, in July 1956, six-year-old Betty Jane Laird of Orem, Utah, was fatally struck by a car, which was only one of seventy-four automobile accidents reported that month at Yellowstone. The overflow of cars in the national parks meant that park rangers became traffic cops regulating visitors who thought that they were on vacation from the rules of the road. In 1953 a man from Kansas was ticketed for violating parking regulations, and he was warned by the ranger that a second ticket would result in his being required to appear before an officer of the local court at nearby Mammoth. Wary of unwittingly committing a second offense, their vacation was spoiled. His complaint letter compared being in the park to living in a communist country. "When we finally drove out of the gate we felt we knew how the Iron Curtain people must feel when escaping from Soviet Zones." He accused the park officials of maintaining the rules of a totalitarian state, terrorizing American citizens on vacation.[42]

Superintendent Rogers, sensitive to the criticism, apologized for his ranger's "poor choice of words," but he bristled at Hemphill's allegation that the park was like the Soviet police state. He argued, "Park Rangers are quite lenient in dealing with park visitors, rather than typifying the police methods you characterize in your letter." He defended the parking regulations as reasonable for an area with a high concentration of traffic, and stated, "The experiences of the vast majority of the one and one-third million people who visit Yellowstone annually are certainly not such as to occasion the fear and doubts that you say assailed you until you left the Park, nor do we think your fears were well founded." He hoped Hemphill would return to the park: "We sincerely hope you may avail yourself of another opportunity to visit Yellowstone with your family and experience the many pleasures to be derived from a vacation spent here."[43]

As if cars were not enough of a problem, the increasing use of trailers and campers prompted complaints from visitors. As trailers and truck-mounted campers became more popular, it became clear that friction resulted from the mix of tents and trailers. A couple from Pennsylvania wrote in June 1952 to complain about the nuisance of motor-driven electric generators used by trailer owners. "The noise and fumes spoil for the majority the pleasures provided by the Park and nullify thereby the primary reason for the setting aside of the Park." They suggested the park prohibit the use of such generators in the park, or alternatively, "One might be to segregate owners of engine driven generators so that they might suffer together their own nuisance." In that way they could help visitors "enjoy the quietness and beauty of the Park."[44]

By the late 1950s, campers began to clearly favor travel trailers to tents, but without sufficient funds, parks were behind the curve on trailer facilities. In 1954 officials of the Department of the Interior began studying the possibility of adding trailer courts to the national parks. A 1962 survey showed "that camping is no longer the nearly exclusive preserve of the family under a canvas tent on the ground." Just over 50 percent used wheeled camp vehicles. "Nineteen camped in house-trailers, seven in tents erected on trailers, six in camper-coaches, six in station wagons or specially equipped buses, three in tiny sleeping trailers, and eight utilized more unusual equipment—or none at all." Use of tents in Yellowstone National Park declined 11 percent in the 1960s; in the same period, wheel-mounted equipment rose 14 percent. But despite the increase in use of trailers and campers, the Fishing Bridge Trailer Court was only 77 percent occupied. RVs dominated the other campgrounds, at 69 percent, with only 27 percent in tents.[45]

The park service carried out an exhaustive survey of its park campgrounds in 1966 and reported that campgrounds at the largest parks were over-occupied every day of the two-week study. The campgrounds accommodated huge numbers of persons. For example, Yellowstone's Grant Village had 399 campsites, but it was occupied by an average of 484 camping parties, and on the highest day, 620 camping parties! Rangers were working six days a week to cope with the overcrowding in the park in August. In response to the crowding and mechanization of camping, more visitors chose to camp in the backcountry, where there were no facilities. At Yellowstone, rangers reported in 1962 that "Back country use continued to be excellent," but the total of 962 visitors undertaking hiking-fishing trips "to the more remote areas" was a mere fraction of the visitors to the park.[46] Most visitors congregated in the busy campgrounds and cafeterias of the metropolitan areas of the parks.

Frustrated park visitors wrote complaint letters to their congressmen. It upped the ante, and park officials found themselves in the unenviable position of explaining their position to those who decided their annual budgets. Often they took advantage of the situation to argue to Congress that they needed more funds to improve the parks. In September 1951 the acting director of Yellowstone National Park replied to a complaint letter forwarded by Senator Everett M. Dirksen of Illinois: that "Unless sufficient funds are appropriated so that adequate developments can be provided, the gap between available facilities and the demands by the visitors will increase steadily.[47]

Park officials' letters blamed their problems on postwar shortages or lack of funds; after Mission 66 was launched in 1956, they promised that the problems would be solved by the ambitious park-building program. Superintendent Rogers responded to a visitor complaint about the poor state of the cabins in October 1956 with enthusiasm about the improvements undertaken as a result of the Mission 66 program. Five hundred "modern cottage rooms, all with bath and heated" were being built in the new Canyon Village area by the Yellowstone Park Company. Rogers boasted that the new rooms were "comparable to those better motels found outside the park" and were costing the Yellowstone Park Company $5 million. Dwight Pitcaithley, historian of the NPS, explained, "By 1966 the National Park Service had increased the number of parking lots fivefold; created 1,197 miles of new roads; added 575 new campgrounds and 742 new picnic areas; constructed 535 additional water systems, 521 new sewer systems, and 271 new power systems; developed 50 marinas; and constructed or rehabilitated 584 new comfort stations (the service's term for toilets)."[48]

The packaging of nature of the national parks did not mean that parks were safe places for families. Park operators feared that if nature was fenced in and roped off, made safe for visitors, tourists would not come to the parks and profits would fall. The NPS, which had conservation as one of its goals, likewise opposed making a Disneyland out of the national parks. The tensions between preservation, profit, and popularity meant that family vacationers experienced the national wilderness with all its hazards, including boiling thermal features, steep canyons, swift-moving rivers, and hungry bears.

Forest Sweet from Battle Creek, Michigan, who had taken his family in a house trailer to Yellowstone in August, wrote a letter in October 1950 that exemplifies the problems faced by family campers. Sweet suggested that they build playgrounds for the children where "you might provide children's swings, slides and climbing bars like most elementary rural schools provide." He also thought the park could be made safer for children by building handrails on the paths to Tower Falls and mudpots. And he was very tired of hearing about the dangers of bears. "We attended twenty campfire meetings and resented the harping on bears, even tho' most of the rangers tried hard to vary the story. We recognize bears for dangerous wild animals and also for perhaps the most attractive single feature of the Park." In reply, the NPS official stated that they had avoided installing playgrounds because "we believe it would attract many campers purely for the play opportunities provided for the children rather than for a visit to the parks for the enjoyment of the inherent values." As for the bears, he insisted that it was necessary to overemphasize the bear issue because it was one of the main safety problems.[49] The NPS refused to make playgrounds in the parks and install fences around every possible danger, so the safety and welfare of children was left to parents. As we shall see from the accident reports, parents were not always up to the job of protecting their own children. Ultimately, the confrontation between park visitors and the wilderness could result in death.

The parks established programs and museums to educate the tourists about the local environment and its hazards. Thousands of tourists attended the nighttime campfire programs with slides at Yellowstone every night, where they were taught about the history, plants, geology, and wildlife at the park. Crowds gathered at designated viewing platforms at spectacular park features to listen to rangers point out the features. The educational features of the parks were popular with tourists, but children paid little heed to the lectures in the museums and were more engaged out of doors on nature walks. The park established a junior nature program as early as 1947 for children aged six to fourteen years. Led by a park ranger, it met every weekday in the afternoon and "consist[ed] of special exploring trips for the youngsters and a treatment of nature lore with some work being done on nature craft." Children clustered around the rangers as they pointed out the wild grasses and other environmental features, accompanied by only a few adults. Photographs demonstrate that most attentively listened to the ranger, and one curious boy leaned down to inspect the grass himself. The nature program at Yosemite offered a weekly schedule of classes covering topics from reptiles and insects to birds and Indians, culminating in a Friday nature hike.[50]

More likely, children accompanied their parents as they took in the sights. Photographs of children in the parks demonstrate the absence of barriers between tourists and the sights. Parents held their small children, but older ones sat on the edge of the boardwalks or stood at the edge of the pools, heedless of the ranger's warnings. Tourists in cars were free to pull up alongside Yellowstone's thermal features like Beryl Springs, where a rushing stream of thermal waters coursed a few feet from the road. Children stood at the edge of hissing Roaring Mountain and played on

The Junior Nature Study group with a park ranger at Yellowstone National Park, 1948. (National Park Service Photograph Collection. Courtesy NARA.)

the banks of the Firehole River while watching Riverside Geyser erupt.[51] There was nothing to keep children from harm's way except their parent's vigilance or their own sense of self-preservation.

Children were likely to explore and wander away from their parents, distracted by sightseeing or unaware of the hazards in the park. Twelve-year-old Allis Lovel fell 130 feet into Yellowstone Canyon when "she followed what she thought was an established trail along the rim," but she took a wrong path. Luckily, she was "pulled to safety by members of the ranger force and suffered only minor bruises and scratches." The rushing rivers and falls also posed a hazard to children. In July 1955 twelve-year-old David Gaskill was swept off his feet by the current while fishing with his father in the Yellowstone; "his father was unable to reach him." The next month a seven-year-old boy fishing with his grandfather drowned in the Yellowstone River when he "slipped from the rocks into the swift current and attempts to rescue by his grandfather were unsuccessful." A

The swift-moving Firehole River and thermal features posed a danger to children in Yellowstone National Park, ca. 1955. (National Park Service Photograph Collection. Courtesy NARA.)

father and son out fishing on Lewis Lake were caught in a storm and presumed lost after weeks of searching for their bodies.[52] A simple fishing trip could quickly turn to tragedy in the park.

The thermal features that attracted visitors to Yellowstone could be perilous to children who could not read the signs and were unaware of the dangers surrounding them. In 1949 two children died in the same season, prompting the NPS to reconsider its policies. NPS director Newton B. Drury replied in detail to Senator Hubert Humphrey's inquiry prompted by a letter from a constituent who had been visiting the park. On July 14, 1949, Mr. and Mrs. Philip Kasik sent their two sons, Robert (age five) and Phil (age ten), to Hamilton's store for groceries. The boys mistakenly headed for the park cafeteria, where two employees saw them round the corner and approach hot pools east of the cafeteria building. The park official reported that the employees "heard one of the boys yelling and they immediately ran in the direction of the yelling and found that the younger boy had fallen into one of the hot pools. They pulled the boy from the pool. Apparently, he had stepped on slippery ground and had slid into the pool." The boy was given first aid while park officials found his parents, and he was taken to the hospital in Mammoth, where he died the next morning.[53]

The second victim was Karen Lee Anderson, who was four and a half years old at the time of her death on September 13, 1949. Mr. and Mrs. Theodore Anderson, Karen, and a younger brother had parked near the Emerald Pool in the Upper Geyser Basin "to sightsee and take pictures." The report continues:

> Apparently, the family did not stay on the board walks which are provided for safe travel over geyser formations. The son called to his mother, saying that he was going to try to find the Emerald Pool. Karen Lee turned away from a point near her mother and walked toward her brother, apparently with the intention of following him. She had only progressed about twenty-five feet when her mother saw that she was walking toward one of the hot pools in the area. Mrs. Anderson called to Karen Lee to attempt to warn her, but the girl walked straight into the pool.

The pool was only a few feet wide and two feet deep, but its sudden vertical drop trapped little Karen Lee in two feet of "violently" boiling water. Unable to lift her daughter out of the pool, Mrs. Anderson "called her husband and he removed the girl from the pool as quickly as possible." The doctor and nurse on duty "wrapped the girl's body in Vaseline soaked gauze and administered a hypodermic to lessen the pain." Karen Lee suffered third-degree burns over 90 percent of her body, and despite being given emergency treatment and rushed by patrol car to the nearest hospital at Livingston, she died just over three hours after the accident.[54]

With two deaths in close succession, and a higher than usual number of injuries occurring in the thermal pools, park officials admitted that "it may be necessary to restrict somewhat the freedom that people now enjoy in seeing the geyser basins." But as Drury told Humphrey, "With limited funds, it is quite impossible to fence or otherwise guard all of the potentially dangerous places in the park, and there may be some question as to the desirability of doing so." Indeed, it "may not be practicable to protect all of the dangerous areas in the park." Furthermore, they were "reluctant" to fence off the dangerous pools because "it is desirable that people be permitted to enjoy the parks fully, with a minimum of restrictions."[55] Park officials adamantly maintained that if they had the resources to protect all visitors from the hazards of the park, the park would no longer give visitors the sense that they were in the wilderness.

Despite signs instructing parents to watch their children, the accidents demonstrate that parents were unable or unwilling to control the actions of their children. In contrast, accidents involving adults resulted from what a former ranger called "foolhardiness or negligence." Examination of the personal injury reports for summer 1955 reveals patterns of careless behavior of park visitors that resulted in a visit to the park nurse. Through these reports, we get a gruesome picture of what people did all day in the park. In two separate incidents, visitors stepped backward into hot pools while attempting to take pictures. Both were severely burned on the ankles and lower legs. A man accidentally caught a fishhook in his lower right eyelid while he was casting on the Yellowstone River. A woman trying to roll a log in her campground fell and broke her left wrist. A six-year-old boy suffered cuts and a broken nose when he was thrown against the windshield as his father hit the car in front of him when it suddenly stopped at Artemesia Geyser.[56] Except for stepping backward into the hot pools and mud pots, the accidents were not unlike accidents people would have suffered at home or on an outing. But the possible consequences were more serious in the remote park—and likely to interrupt a vacation.

Teenagers seemed especially prone to accidents. A fourteen-year-old boy walking with his pocketknife open stumbled over a log and fell against a tree, "forcing the knife to make a cut along the right side of his nose." Another fourteen-year-old boy was chipping wood with an ax, and it made a deep two-inch laceration in his shin; he required six stitches. A girl the same age was playing with her brother in the cabin when she fell across the hot stove, resulting in two burns on her neck. A campground table tipped over on a twelve-year-old girl, leaving her with a swollen knee. A thirteen-year-old girl from Los Angeles was cut on the right forearm by the metal sunshade of a parked car as she walked through the parking lot near Old Faithful Cafeteria. As a seventeen-year-old girl was walking along the beach of Squaw Lake, the ground gave way, and she fell into a hot pool; both legs were burned to the knees.[57] The number of mishaps suffered by teenagers suggests that their urge to be independent (and in the case of the boys, to perform manly tasks with sharp tools) was made more dangerous in an outdoor environment.

The biggest draw of Yellowstone National Park was its bears, and they posed one of the greatest dangers to tourists. Tourists insisted not only on seeing the bears but also on feeding them and posing for pictures next to them. And although visitors wanted to go back to nature, they imposed their own views of a benevolent nature on a place that was more dangerous than they could have imagined. Some may have been genuinely ignorant of the hazards bears posed to the safety of them and their children. Camping manuals downplayed the danger of bears in camp, saying they would cause "little trouble" if "food has been stowed correctly and campers avoid irritating the animals." It cautioned campers, "Remember, these are wild animals," but it did not specify the dangers of an encounter with bears. Children's books portrayed the bears as lovable cubs "who play all day" and "sleep so peacefully the whole night through."[58]

Despite park policies, visitors continued to feed the bears, and in the 1950s bear injuries and damages spiraled out of control. From 40 incidents during 1952, reported bear injuries rose to 70 in 1955, and 109 in 1956. In 1956 park officials analyzed the figures and reported, "18 victims were feeding bears which bit them and in an equal number of cases nearby people were feeding the bears. Thirty of the visitors who were bitten knowingly approached bears or permitted bears to come too close to them." The bears were also endangered by the visitors. Park officials responded by removing dangerous bears and destroying eight bears. "Four additional bears were killed by traffic, one was destroyed because it had a tin can lodged in its throat." Park officials destroyed approximately forty bears yearly in the latter half of the 1950s.[59]

Park officials reasoned that the injuries resulted from visitors disobeying park rules or knowingly placing themselves in a dangerous situation. Despite warnings to keep their food away from bears, "Food probably tempted the bears in 81, or 67% of the incidents." Since campers usually carried in their own food, the problem seemed insurmountable. A man from Alabama wrote in 1966 about the difficulty of keeping food away from the bears. He and his wife and three children had stayed in their Apache camper-trailer for a few days in the Fishing Bridge campground, where "the bears were allowed to invade our campsite at their pleasure and much to our dismay." The bears were ruthless: "They pawed and clawed our rig in broad daylight although there was no food in it, nor had there been any." Campers *with* food endured worse fates: "In the camp next to ours a bear wrested an ice-box right out of the arms of a woman carrying it. He opened it easily without unlatching it and feasted on its contents." Frightened by the incident, they decided to pack up and leave. "After witnessing this, you can be sure that we lost all heart for preparing our breakfast or for staying in that park for another moment." His suggestion was to "put stout electric fences around each campground to keep bears out, and to keep people out of bears." The fact that this man claimed the bear invaded *his* space in Yellowstone suggests that campers had little understanding of the park as a home to wildlife. He saw his claims to the park's nature as superior to those of the bear, who lived there year round.[60]

Park visitors came to Yellowstone to see bears, and bear stories made family vacations to Yellowstone memorable. Forty years after his family's tussle with a bear in Yellowstone, Dan Malaney recalled how a bear surprised the family at a picnic breakfast in 1963. The four children hurriedly ran for the station wagon, and after tossing the sizzling frying pan onto the floor, Mom began snapping photos of the bear's attack on their ice chest. When his father failed to frighten away the bear by throwing rocks, he jumped in the car and drove toward the bear, honking the horn. They recovered the ice chest, but it "was empty and so badly damaged that Dad reluctantly threw it in the next trash bin."[61]

Property damage by bears may have been funny, but personal injury was more serious. In July 1955 Edna Hagerty of Sunland, California, was awakened when a bear crashed into her tent, resulting in a four-inch wound on her shoulder and neck. Accident reports reveal an astonishing number of injuries inflicted on children by bears as a result of parental carelessness. They seem to have lost all sense of judgment when given the chance to see a bear. Most injuries occurred, oddly enough, while the children were still in the family car. Because air-conditioning was not available in cars, tourists drove through the park in the hot summer months with their windows down. In two separate incidents, bears reached into car windows and clawed or scratched children sitting by the rear window. A three-year-old girl was bitten on the wrist when she put her hand out the window when her parents stopped the car to watch a tourist feed a bear. One can only imagine the skepticism of the nurse who treated a three-year-old boy bitten by a bear, teeth marks visible on his hand. His parents protested that they were not feeding the bears, but that before they realized what was happening, a bear had climbed into the backseat to take a bite of the cookie that the boy was eating! When the Hendrickson family car stopped to observe a bear, six-year-old Nancy reached out to "pet" it and suffered a deep bite that required five stitches. Accustomed to cartoon bears like Yogi the Bear or the firefighting Smokey the Bear, neither parents nor children were prepared for the savagery of the bears in the park.[62]

Injury was more likely if park visitors got out of their cars to observe the wild animals. When the Brittendalls stopped in September 1956 to

Bears boldly approached cars on Yellowstone's roads, 1958. (Photographer Jack E. Boucher. Courtesy National Park Service Historic Photograph Collection.)

watch a group of people take pictures of a coyote, four-year-old Gale Lee got out of the car with her parents to take a closer look. The coyote was going from person to person, begging for food, and when it came to her, she became frightened. When she turned and ran, the coyote nipped her in the behind, resulting in three small puncture wounds "on the child's posterior." When a woman from Georgia got out of the family car to feed a bear, the bear bit her three-year-old son on the neck. And despite park literature that prohibited feeding bears and verbal warnings from rangers, a visitor from Sacramento was feeding cookies to a bear when it bit her on the right wrist.[63]

The number of injuries began to slowly decline after the institution of a new bear management plan in the 1960s, including removing dangerous bears and fining visitors. In 1962 the superintendent reported that "13 cases of bear feeding have been brought before the U.S. Commissioner to date, with a total of $110 in fines." Finally, only by slapping stiff fines on visitors who were caught feeding bears were park officials able to reduce the incidence of violence.[64]

In 1962 the director of the NPS reported, "Today, Americans are crowding the highways and visiting the parks and recreational areas of the country as never before in history. Yearly visits to the national parks have leaped from 22 million only 15 years ago to more than 80 million last year." That same year the park service welcomed its one billionth visitor with public hoopla. In light of the complaints by park visitors, one has to consider the irony of the 1963 report's statement that the park system "affords Americans opportunities to enjoy great scenic and inspirational areas of their country in a natural, unspoiled condition and the rare quality of the primitive wilderness that was America before it was touched by civilization."[65] Yellowstone, with its parking lots, cafeterias, lodges, and trailer parks, was hardly untouched by civilization. However, it was as close as many families in America would get to what was regarded as wilderness, and it was wilderness at a price they could afford. Best of all, they could get there in the family car or camper, even if it could not protect them from the bears they had come all that way to see.

Contrary to Democratic Principles: Shenandoah

In an era of Jim Crow, black travel guides advertised the national parks as suitable travel destinations because they were not allowed to practice racial discrimination. In 1958 the *Green Book* contained a four-page spread on the national parks, which had a "non-discriminatory policy . . . regardless of the policies of City or State where they are located." Despite these claims, certain national parks complied with local custom and did discriminate against African Americans. Although the NPS's policy prohibited racial discrimination, evidence suggests that parks located in the South practiced a covert segregation well into the 1950s. Faced with the pressure of local custom (or legal Jim Crow in some parts of the South), local park officials circumvented NPS policy by providing separate facilities for blacks and whites in both accommodations and dining services. Because of NPS policy not to discriminate and an increasing number of complaints about discrimination, parks created a situation of plausible deniability by obscuring their discriminatory practices from observers.[66] Overcrowding at Shenandoah put pressure on the racially segregated facilities that had been put in place when the park was built in the late 1930s and tested NPS goals of democratic service to all its visitors.

From its inception, Shenandoah National Park practiced Jim Crow by allowing the Virginia Skyline Company to build separate facilities for blacks and whites. In 1939 it was decided that three campgrounds (Skyland, Dickey Ridge, and Big Meadows) were built "for Whites only," and

"Lewis Mountain would be provided with facilities for Colored only." Locally based park concessioners who feared losing their white customers went to great lengths to sustain Jim Crow and to hide it from NPS top brass. For example, the park maintained segregated toilets but did not provide signs to that effect. In response to an inquiry from the national director's office promoted by a complaint that came to the solicitor's office, in 1939 Shenandoah National Park superintendent J. R. Lassiter wrote, "I wish to advise that we do not have any signs on any of our comfort stations indicating that colored men and women are to use identical facilities. In all cases we have separate toilet facilities for colored men and colored women, usually with the entrances adjacent to or on the same end of the building as those for white men and women, respectively." And in response to allegations that black campgrounds were not equal but were inferior to campgrounds reserved for whites, Lassiter claimed, "Despite the fact that the views were not as pleasing from Lewis Mountain," the facilities were "all identical—that is, standard comfort stations, standard fireplaces, standard tables, standard walkways, standard drinking fountains, and hard-surfaced driveways and parking areas." He explained that it did not make sense to make Lewis Mountain as large as the white campgrounds because "it is not felt that facilities of equal size should be provided for a group which constitutes less than one percent of our total visitors."[67]

Associate director Demaray of the NPS worked with Shenandoah superintendent J. R. Lassiter to bring the park in line with NPS policy. In 1939, when large construction projects were underway, he informed Lassiter that the solicitor's office was preparing a memo to the secretary of the Department of the Interior "urging him to break down the segregation of Negroes and whites in Shenandoah National Park." The secretary "indicated that the Park Service must insist upon early provision for Negro accommodations equal to facilities for white persons." Demaray suggested that Lassiter "urge the operators to immediately provide some facilities for Negroes so that [the] charge cannot be made that we are not furnishing at least the same type and character of facilities that are provided for whites."[68]

Park operators balked when NPS officials asked whether blacks could be served in a corner of the dining rooms at Panorama and Swift Run Gap, replying that "the southern people would not stand for it, that he had hired all white help." Although blacks had long been served at lunch counters or in the dining room for the "help," they were not allowed in the public dining rooms. The NPS settled on the solution of temporarily

The lunch counter at Shenandoah National Park was open to all customers, but its dining room remained segregated. Lunch Room at Panorama, 1940. (Courtesy National Park Service Historic Photograph Collection.)

serving them in the corners of an adjacent alcove until the park operators could construct "small structures for Negroes adjacent to the present dining rooms."[69] The stopgap solutions allowed a pattern of segregation to persist.

A complaint from a cranky camper exposed the discriminatory practices in Shenandoah after the war. In July 1947, when and Mr. and Mrs. Otis Murray overstayed the thirty-day limit in Big Meadows campground at Shenandoah National Park in Virginia, park superintendent Edward D. Freeland told them he could only accommodate them at Lewis Mountain, seven miles south. Mrs. Murray wrote to Senator Harry F. Byrd to ask him to intervene, and in his letter to Freeland, he stated, "She does not want to move to Lewis Mountain, which she understands is a colored camp." Freeland replied that "Lewis Mountain is open and used by all visitors to the Park," and added that it "contains all the convenient facilities found at Big Meadows, except a laundry and shower building." He grounded his policy in a statement about accessibility of the parks to all: "Use of the areas must be arranged for the greatest use and enjoyment by the greatest number of people with exclusive use privileges granted to none. Only in this manner can we carry out our obligations to the people of the Nation." Freeland refused to grant Mrs. Murray the privilege of whiteness to which she was accustomed, on the grounds that the parks were open to all.[70]

When Freeland would not relent, Mrs. Murray wrote to Hillary A. Tolson, acting director of the NPS. Of the superintendent's offer to move them to Lewis Mountain, she wrote, "Mr. Freeland was reared in another part of the country and did not hold the same views as we do. But Ranger Gibbs was born in Virginia and he well knew that he was insulting me in a legal way. I am all white." She explained her refusal to move not in terms of her own racist attitudes, but in terms of not disturbing the inhabitants of Lewis Mountain. "But that camp was built for the Negroes and it is not right to take away from them any pleasure they get out of it. And a high-respectable negro will not mix with any white trash who would move in with them." She concluded by accusing the NPS of covering up the fact of de facto segregation in Shenandoah. "At Big Meadows, the Lodge caters only to whites, and I would just like to see one colored guest get in there." Tolson refused her request and supported Freeland's position that to "favor one park visitor over another would be contrary to democratic principles of government" and "would permit a relatively few persons to preempt these great properties which are owned by all of the citizens of the United States."[71] His defense of a park that was explicitly segregated by race—a park that would not serve whites and blacks in the same dining rooms, or allow them to use the same toilets, or to camp on the same grounds—is ironic at best.

Despite some pressure from the NPS, Shenandoah continued its policy of segregated facilities after the end of the war. African Americans complained about being refused service in the dining rooms, not being allowed to rent horses, or being moved to Lewis Mountain upon their arrival.[72] When two black students at Catholic University who accompanied a group of white nuns complained about not being served in the dining room, the NPS conducted a formal investigation in July 1950. Park planner Arthur F. Perkins exonerated the park officials in his four-page report, but hints of discriminatory practices suggest that few blacks tried to break the invisible color line at Shenandoah. Most blacks came on weekends, roughly 2 percent of total visitors. The African American groups who chartered buses tended to eat at the picnic areas or lunch counters, where they ate along with white visitors. At the Panorama dining rooms, "It is quite likely that colored diners may be led to tables in the archways or side room unless they specifically request some other table." When he inquired further about the practice, "I was assured that such requests would be honored and that if colored patrons are in the alcoves and side room, white patrons do use these rooms at the same time." His investigation of the customary white lodging yielded a similar finding "that no colored persons have asked for cottages or rooms specifically at Skyland nor have any colored persons requested reservations." He explained that Lewis Mountain was no longer segregated but that "whether because of that beginning or because of the fact that it has a colored staff and has developed a reputation among colored people over the years, it appears that a number of the colored visitors specifically request directions to Lewis Mountain and make reservations at Lewis Mountain when they desire cottages." He observed white diners at the lodge and the manager confirmed that "a good portion of his cabin rentals are also to white people." Its origins as a segregated park shaped patterns of park use that sustained Jim Crow in a region where segregation persisted in public accommodations.[73]

Although there is scant evidence that whites were aware of the problems faced by blacks, a particularly virulent letter from a white park patron indicates the resistance of some whites to racial integration in the parks. A "Mother & Voter" wrote to the NPS commissioner in 1956 to complain that the cabins in Yosemite should be segregated because "after nigers leave the same tent is rented to whites which *smell,* nigers smell penetrates through all the bedings pillos and mattresses, nothing has *been* done about." She believed that rather than using the restrooms, blacks defecated around the cabins and campsites, causing the areas to stink. Furthermore, she thought that their use of Yosemite was just one more step in the breaking down of white privilege. "It is your duty and obligation to see that this disqualified black horrible race stays on its place. . . . We demand segregation and restrictions on the line. We don't want them for what they are and how they are. We demand justice quickly before we face helplessness."[74] Because the author supplied no address, no reply was written, but the letter survives as a measure of the vituperative extremes of white racism that park officials had to contend with as they hosted millions of Americans in the parks that claimed to be open to all in a democratic country.

At the national parks, people of all classes and races mixed in ways that they did not at home in a segregated America. Although those with greater means could afford to stay in the lodges and eat in the dining rooms while working-class families camped out of their cars and heated canned beans over a fire, visitors mixed on the trails and in the cafeterias and on the roadsides. Few African Americans could afford to travel to—or chose to travel to—remote national parks like Yellowstone, and relatively few found their way to the accessible Shenandoah, but when they did, they discovered that the parks were not as democratic as they claimed to be.

On July 4, 1970, a counterculture group of long-haired hippies rioted in Stoneman Meadow in Yosemite National Park, a confrontation between generations. The riot between the young people and the "establishment" marked the end of an era of family camping in the park. In part as a result of the oil crisis, visitation dropped in the early 1970s, and park rangers were more occupied with law enforcement than making visitors feel welcome in their parks.[75]

In the postwar era, camping seemed to be the perfect family vacation for penny-wise parents who loaded up their station wagons with coolers and tents and went camping with their children. Visitors to the national parks demanded the comfort and safety of civilization that put distance between them and the natural wonders, resulting in a mediated experience of nature. Campers who could afford to escape the crowded campgrounds retreated to the privacy of their recreational vehicles or trailers. The camping boom grew into a mass movement that resulted in overcrowding, making getting back to nature more and more difficult.

In its democratic policy of access to the American public, the national parks that had offered access to the wilderness for war veterans and their children had become so crowded that the only way to escape civilization was to set off on foot. Backpacking offered the hiker freedom to "wander as far as his legs can carry him, away from hotels, roads, campgrounds, commerce and other people. . . . he has the satisfaction of knowing he is in a place that is seen only by those who have the energy and love of wilderness to come on their own feet." The Sierra Club and the Wilderness Society promoted wilderness preservation, and manufacturers developed lightweight camping equipment that could fit in a backpack, not the back of the station wagon. The children who slept in the back of the station wagon in the 1950s claimed the wilderness as their own, rejecting the car-oriented consumerism of their parents who took them to the parks in the first place. They left cars behind and shouldered backpacks full of lightweight camping gear and walked into the backcountry in search of not nature, but wilderness.[76]

Despite the overcrowding, getting back to nature in the parks helped raise a consciousness of the environment that would lay the foundation for movements to set aside federal lands as wilderness, to implement regulations to reduce industrial air and water pollution, and later to reduce the consumption of energy. Camping offered Americans with children a closer experience with the natural environment through recreation. Being in the woods fostered an expanded appreciation for the environment that motivated many to political action.[77] The child campers of the postwar era were among those who turned out en masse for Earth Day, 20 million persons who had somehow come by an environmental sensibility, maybe in a tent by a river in Yosemite Valley on a family vacation.

chapter six

Summer in the Country

More than fifty years later, Carol Crawford Ryan still remembered the car trips from Iowa City to Gilman's fishing resort in Minnesota in the 1930s. Her father worked in the post office at Iowa City, so they planned ahead for the two weeks he could take off. Her mother cooked "lots of food," and she and her brother Dean "really looked forward to this epic journey every year." Their Chevrolet did not have air-conditioning, so they left at 4:00 A.M. to avoid the heat. They always stopped at Cannon Falls to eat a picnic lunch of fried chicken and potato salad at one of the picnic tables along the highway. As they passed Lake Mille Lacs, they noticed Ojibwe Indians in their birchbark wigwams, who were selling woven baskets and maple sugar candy. They drove north through Crosby and saw the old iron mines before arriving at Mitchell Lake in the early evening.[1]

At the end of the dirt road was Gilman's Resort, a cluster of small cabins on the shore. The Gilmans greeted them with keys and ice, and they settled into a cabin. They usually stayed in the same old log cabin her parents had first stayed in on the north bank of the creek "because it was by itself." There was no electricity until after World War II, so "our days and nights were dictated by light." During their two-week stay, her father and brother fished while her mother read books on the screened porch. Carol roamed the woods and creeks when she was not swimming or boating. She remembers those summer weeks as "a very freeing kind of experience for me. . . . I was kind of a proper little girl, but here I could do almost anything I liked to do."[2] In her lake summers Carol found a sense of freedom, but she also found an anchor of stability in an ocean of change. The familiar sound of the wind in the pines and the sight of glistening sun on the lake drew her family back to the lake country each year, the same place every summer.

Like Carol, many Americans vacationed in rural resorts, usually at the same place every summer. The postwar nation was changing from largely rural to largely urban, but the countryside was still close enough to the cities to be within a day's drive from where most people lived. Families who wanted to fish or swim in the warm summer lakes, who drove north for the cooler air, found recreation in rural America. Resorts were family owned and depended on the labor of family members, including children, who were taught that guests were part of the family. Because they depended on family labor, resorts were affordable for almost any middle-class family's budget.

Class was not a barrier to summer resort vacations, but race and religion were. Resort owners restricted the kind of clientele they served, so excluded Jews and African Americans founded their own resorts. Their communities helped them cope with the upheavals of racial violence and insidious anti-Semitism of the postwar years, and when discrimination lessened, the communities dispersed. A history of African American resorts and the Jewish resort community in the Catskills of New York provides a fresh look at the effect of discrimination in the everyday life of parents and children. African American and Jewish families who summered in the country created vibrant communities where shared cultural traditions made them feel at home away from home. Whether along the shore of Minnesota's many lakes or in the Catskill Mountains of New York, families found respite in rural resorts during their summer vacations.

Changes in the American family affected both resort owners and guests, signaling changes in family vacationing that altered the cultural ritual of the family vacation. The individualism of the sexual revolution and youth rebellion of the 1960s challenged parental authority and constituted a critique of consumer society. The women's liberation movement and the civil rights movement challenged hierarchies of gender and race that had sustained a racialized and patriarchal family ideal. As a part of this process, the middle-class family vacation took new shapes. The era of the family car trip was superseded by a greater variety of family vacations that better fit the diversity of American families. The history of resort vacationing opens a window into the remaking of the postwar American family vacation, and the family.

Up at the Lake: Resorts in Minnesota

Minnesota's summer resorts dated from the late nineteenth century, when the railroads laid tracks to the lakes. In the early twentieth century, Minnesotans formed outing clubs and associations to buy small lots of land on which to construct cottages. Local businessmen built rustic log resorts in the Brainerd Lakes and Gull Lakes areas in the 1920s, and because of their wealthy clientele, early resorts were able to survive the Depression. The end of World War II invigorated the resort industry, and resorts expanded to attract guests from all over the Midwest. Iowa farmers, Oklahoma City matrons, and Chicago businessmen escaped the summer heat at Minnesota's family resorts. The remote country resorts were within a day's transportation by rail from major Midwestern cities, and blacks usually rode the train. White middle-class families loaded the car, packed a picnic lunch, and drove north to Minnesota to fish and splash and relax away from the summer heat.[3]

The state of Minnesota was no different from other states promoting postwar tourism as a strategy of economic development in a period when farming and agricultural processing industries lost their prominence. In the decades after the war, the best way to attract tourists was to focus on families, as in the 1959 state publicity guide that beckoned tourists: "This year treat yourself and your family to a relaxing, wholesome vacation in Minnesota—and enjoy the treasures of nature's own vacationland." A vacation in Minnesota was a healthful escape from workaday life. "Let your work-worn nerves relax and faded appetites be rejuvenated as you play and sleep in Minnesota's invigorating, cool, fresh air."[4] The theme of attracting families to "Minnesota's Water Wonderland" was central to their campaign as the "family vacation state" featured in nationwide magazines.[5]

The prime target for summer vacationers was Minnesota's Arrowhead region, bordered by Lake Superior on the east and studded with lakes for fishing and boating. Well north of the Twin Cities, the air was cooler in the summertime, and after the region's old-growth forests had been removed, the frigid winters scared off all but the most hardy residents. The Minnesota Arrowhead Association (MAA), a trade group of resort owners in nineteen counties, commissioned an extensive survey in 1958 and reported, "The vacation travel industry is one of the top revenue producers in northern Minnesota," bringing in an estimated $32 million. Most travelers were city residents, and family travel dominated (one-third of the travelers were children). Visitors were usually from the Midwest, but less than a third came from Minnesota, with 20 percent from Illinois, 18 percent from Iowa, and about 5 percent each from Indiana, Missouri, and Nebraska. Most were repeat visitors, and they most commonly stayed one or two weeks. The study ranked the top three reasons persons traveled in northern Minnesota: rest and relaxation, fishing (over 80 percent bought a fishing license), and sightseeing.[6]

The goal of the MAA was to modernize the family-owned resorts in order to attract more tourists. Because most resorts were small and operated on a "low-profit basis," they needed capital to upgrade the primitive cabins and recreational facilities. The picture of the situation was sobering: "The great majority of cabins are of simple construction. They are largely frame cabins with a room heater, electric lights, refrigerator, bath facilities in only a third of them, inside toilet facilities in only about half of them, hot water in only a third of them and no water at all in another third." Because resorts were open only three months a year, it was hard to justify the expense of upgrading the facilities. The resorts depended largely on the labor of family members, and they catered to the family trade by keeping accommodations affordable. Housekeeping cabins (no meals provided) cost around $35 a week, but it cost more to stay at one of the forty-three resorts offering the American plan of three meals a day.[7]

A rich collection of oral histories of Minnesota's resort owners allows us to reconstruct the history of Gilman's, the small fishing resort Carol Crawford Ryan visited, and Ruttger's resorts, a group of five resorts that catered to the higher end of the family vacation market. We also gain a glimpse into the history of two black resorts in Minnesota, Northern Lights and Flagg's resort. No matter the size, the resorts were run by families for families, but their size and resources determined how long they could last in an increasingly competitive summer resort market.

Edward and Kay Gilman came from Chicago to Minnesota after World War II because Ed loved to fish, and he knew Minnesota from fishing trips. In 1946 they became the third owners of one of three resorts on Mitchell Lake. The resort consisted of seven cabins on forty acres, including twelve acres underwater. Their guests came from Iowa, Nebraska, and Chicago, and a few came from Missouri, Kansas, and the Dakotas. The season began when fishing season opened in May and lasted until Labor Day; then groups of fishermen came in the fall, and hunters came during deer season in October. Some Midwestern farmers would come in the spring and others in August after harvest. The Gilmans recalled, "They weren't wealthy, but they loved to fish and loved to eat fish." A guest remembers it as "very much a working class resort." A mix of people stayed at Gilman's: farmers from Iowa or Indiana or Illinois, and

The cabins at Minnesota's small resorts were primitive but affordable. Cabin No. 7 at Gilman's resort, 1950s. (Courtesy of Minnesota Historical Society.)

government workers like her father. Guests from the Twin Cities would come for a weekend, but out-of-state guests usually stayed a week or two, and some for the whole summer.[8]

The Gilmans belonged to a resort association that distributed their brochures at sports shows in the Midwest, but word of mouth was the best advertisement. Customers were loyal; over the years, three generations of families stayed at the resort. The Gilman's housekeeping cabins were quite affordable, only $25 a week (including a boat), but conditions were rustic in the years before they had electricity. Instead of refrigerators, cabins were equipped with iceboxes, and Ed hauled ice every day of the year. In spring a crew came to cut the ice from the frozen lake and store it between layers of sawdust in the icehouse. It made a handy place to keep freshly caught fish. By the 1950s the cabins had running water, and most were equipped with electricity. The kitchens were simple: a sink, refrigerator, cupboard, and gas stove. The cabins were heated by wood-burning stoves until one cabin burned down; they replaced the stoves with heaters. The cabins did not have televisions, but the Gilmans kept some extra radios to lend to guests.[9]

Gilman's was a family resort for people, mostly men, who wanted to fish from dawn to dusk. For the Gilmans, a normal summer day would start with a guest arriving at the backdoor to get minnows before breakfast. In the evening Ed would take guests out in his boat to show them the best spots for fishing the next morning. "There were live boxes out in front of every dock, in front of every cabin and you kept what you caught in there. Ed Gilman would come out and weigh the fish and everyone would exclaim over the big catches. People would come to see what you'd brought back, but then you'd eat it." People did not go out to eat. "They ate here, and they ate fish, and almost entirely fish, all week, the fish that they caught."[10]

Children were free to play and swim along the shallow lakeshore or in a nearby creek with the other children. The Gilmans took the older children out water-skiing on the big motor boat, "and we had a fly [canvas roof] for the little ones to go in the creek swimming. So it was a nice place for families with little children too." When Ryan was little, the family would start fishing early in the morning and stay all day with a picnic lunch. She "was made to sit in the bottom of the boat" with toys, but "by the end of the day, I was really awfully tired of that." At the age of six, she was rowing on the creek by herself in a wooden canoe. Her parents put the boat on a long rope, and she could row as far as the length of the rope would let her and come back. It made her feel "enormously grown up." She played with other children at the resort and with the Gilman's son, Donny.

Children were allowed from the age of nine or ten to go up Crooked Creek by themselves. They picked wild strawberries on the shore of the lake, collected wildflowers, and "looked for birds." While she played, her mother "spent most of her time up here reading" in the screen porch at the cabin. As Carol grew older, she learned to run a motorboat in a time when "there weren't a lot of sports open to young women and this was something, I could run a motor boat myself. And I was a very good swimmer by that point and I could row well, and I could do that, and I felt very competent doing all those things." Piloting the boat gave her a sense

Cathy Gilman with fish at Gilman's resort, 1950s. (Courtesy Minnesota Historical Society.)

of freedom, an escape from the restrictions of proper gender behavior in Iowa City.[11]

Gilman's was out in the country on a dirt road until 1978. So they stocked fishing licenses, soda pop, groceries, and mosquito repellent so guests did not have to drive back to town. On a rainy day the vacationers would go to Brainerd, where there were restaurants and stores, or the women would go shopping for antiques while the men played bingo at the town sports club. In the evening, guests mingled at parties, picnics, and potlucks or sang along with the player piano at the Gilman's house.[12]

Because the resort was so small, Ed and Kay and their children did most of the work themselves. In the winters Ed brought in extra income driving a school bus and doing carpentry and logging. Kay laundered and

Children playing in a canoe at Gilman's resort, 1950s. (Courtesy Minnesota Historical Society.)

starched the curtains and cleaned the cabins. She remembered, "the winters were sort of a time to write letters and be more with the children, with the family." In the spring they painted the wooden flat-bottom boats and readied the cabins for visitors. In the summer Ed would "cut grass and haul wood, haul ice to the cabins, haul garbage." Kay was busy with the six children. She recalled, "I just about had to wash clothes every day: diapers, linens, and, of course, the children helped, too." It was a family resort sustained by family labor. Kay recalled that because they could not afford to hire help, "you have to be a jack-of-all-trades. You have to be a carpenter, a plumber, and a good housekeeper to run a resort." She felt her job was to "make the people feel at home." The Gilman children had the job of helping entertain the children of the guests. Kay recalled that when they complained, she placated them by telling them: "It's our bread and butter. Just a few more days. Be nice to them and the days will go by fast."[13]

Gilman's clientele demanded more amenities in the prosperous postwar years. At first they brought everything with them, but as salaries rose, "they would spend more because it was their vacation." The Gilmans increased the rates and began to charge extra for boat rental. Ed remembered that over the years the women became more demanding. "The fellows would come up and the roof could leak and the boat could leak, but if they could catch fish they were happy. But the women began to want more and it was getting harder to keep up and keep everybody happy." He saw it as an upsetting of the proper gender roles: "I always say they began to get the upper hand, and they were chronically unhappy." The children wanted more attractions too, and many went to Paul Bunyan Land, a local amusement park, or to the large towns a bit further away.[14]

As customers became more demanding, the Gilmans were less able to run the resort. By the 1970s Kay had arthritis in her legs, and the family could not keep up with the increase in taxes and insurance and compete with the larger resorts. They could never afford enough liability insurance because about 25 to 35 percent of their income went to taxes and insurance alone. She lamented, "We were way under-insured. We couldn't keep up." They sold in 1976, when the weekly rates were $90. But they did not regret their years at the resort because, as Ed said, "It's a good way to raise a family." It provided them a livelihood and "it was a good education for [the children] because they made friends and they enjoyed the summers." Kay enjoyed "the association with the people," most of whom were "lovely," and Ed enjoyed the fishing.[15]

During Carol Crawford Ryan's childhood, her parents came to Gilman's every year because her father preferred it for summer vacations. "My father, especially enjoyed this place, and I think he liked coming back to the same place year after year, it was comfortable for him. And he liked the fishing." Her mother, on the other hand, "became a little restive. She had taught geography and she had wanted to travel more than we had." So after the war, "the rest of us sort of grudgingly [did] take trips to her places. . . . But we'd always end up coming back" to Gilman's.[16] In the Crawford family, vacation goals conflicted. The father was happy to just fish, but the mother thought travel should be educational, that the children should see more of America. But when they did summer in the country, they chose to fish and swim and read and drink soda pop in the coolness of Minnesota's lake resorts.

The Ruttger's resort empire was built with capital from German immigrants Joe and Josephine Ruttger. Their resort was established in 1898 as a place for fishermen to stay, and Josephine's good cooking kept them coming back. Over the years Joe and Josephine helped each of their sons get a start in the resort business, resulting in five Ruttger's resorts by the 1930s. The flagship was Ruttger's Bay Lake Lodge in Deerwood, Minnesota—triple-A rated and recommended by Duncan Hines. It advertised itself as "The Family Resort of Minnesota [with] facilities for every member of the family," noting that "this is indeed an ideal vacation spot for the entire family."[17]

Ruttger's brochures claimed that in forty years of business, they had discovered "the essential services and comforts for better vacations." Those essentials included "the best beds in clean, cozy cabins" and "delicious meals with home-grown vegetables, pasteurized milk, home-made ice cream, sherbets, and ices." They offered an array of recreational facilities, including a private golf course, sandy beach, tennis court, stables, playground, and "excellent fishing." The brochure boasted they had "the best bass fishing" in the state, but one could also catch walleyed pike, great northern pike, black bass, or crappies on the daily stringer. Those who did not want to fish could take advantage of "scores of other attractions: beautiful scenery for home movie fans, concrete tennis court, saddle horses, sailboat, large speed boat, surf boards, water toboggans, aquaplaning, trap-shooting, ping-pong, croquet, quoits, campfire roasts, auction and contract parties, shuffle board courts, roller skating." While their parents were busy golfing or fishing, children were fully supervised on the playground, or they could ride horses selected for their gentle qualities.

The resort's "Restful Accommodations" were designed to fit into the north-woods landscape but provide the amenities travelers demanded. Ruttger's facilities were a cut above the typical Minnesota resort:

> Every one of our rustic-built, lakeshore cabins have cobblestone fireplaces or stoves, private tub baths, water flush toilets, hot and cold running water, screened and curtained sleeping porches, and nestled among cool, shady trees where cool lake breezes blow. All have electric lights, pure running drinking water, best inner-coil beds, rustic tables, easy chairs, dressers and other essentials. Most of our rooms have private baths, large, light and airy with the same equipment as the cabins.

In the 1940s all of this was available for $5 to $7 a day. Jack Ruttger remembered how happy the guests were to get there: "Some people would arrive by cars, even in the forties, with no air conditioning, and geez, they'd be just all beaten up. They'd sit there like they'd found heaven, even with the mosquitoes and all."[18]

Slightly less luxurious was Ruttger's Pine Beach Lodge on Gull Lake, "created for the man and his family who desire a vacation largely filled with golf and enjoys play on an excellent course." Resorts offered healthful recreation, from fishing to tennis, sailing to ping-pong. There children would enjoy "bathing" on their sloping sandy beach equipped with a diving raft and floats, or parents could leave children with "our reliable playground supervisor." At Pine Beach, two children's hostesses would take the children at lunch- and dinnertimes. They fed the children a half hour before the dining room opened, "and the kids loved it, too, because they would get through and get out, and they could go out and go back swimming again."[19]

Their cabins were purposely rustic but "modern." Guest cabins featured "a cozy, cobble-stone fireplace, private bathroom with toilet, lavatory, tub, hot and cold water, electric lights, and very comfortable single or double inner-spring beds." To protect from swarms of mosquitoes, "All porches and openings are screened." The resort offered a half rate for children under ten. At Pine Beach, cabins were twelve feet wide and fourteen feet long (one bedroom) to twenty-six feet (two bedrooms) and longer for three-bedroom cabins. Because the Ruttgers wanted people to come to the lodge and get acquainted with other guests so they would come back the next year, the cabins did not have sitting areas except the spacious porches. As Ruttger grandchildren took over each resort, they modernized the cabin bathrooms, replacing bathtubs with showers and installing new draperies and carpets, but they kept the log furniture and old multipaned windows and shutters to keep the authentic rustic feel.[20]

The Ruttger's Shady Point Resort at Whitefish Lake was purchased by thc family in 1935, a few years before the Rural Electric Administration brought electricity and the Works Progress Administration built a road to the site. Under the supervision of Bill and Carol Ross Ruttger, Shady Point offered a genteel resort in the wilderness. Their daughter Theresa remembered, "There were white starched tablecloths, and waitresses in the uniforms with the little hats and everything, and . . . five-course meals, in the midst of all this brush and bramble and everything else." The guests arrived at the railroad stations with their "maids and trunks" for the summer, and men shuttled back and forth. Maids stayed in the girls' dormitories with the staff, not with the families. Later, as car travel became more common, guests arrived after a long car ride "in those big old station wagons that were loaded with kids and luggage."[21]

Shady Point's lodge contained an extensive library, and tables were set up for continual card games, slapjack in the day, hearts in the evening. On rainy days, people would sit in the big wingback chairs by the fireplace. The resort had a recreation room with ping-pong tables and a place to play bingo at night. The outdoor deck was used in the summer for children's activities. The dining room at Shady Point held over one hundred persons, who ate at long pine tables covered by two layers of white linen tablecloths. The chairs were handmade hickory and wicker, and the large windows lining the dining room looked out on the lake. A huge Victorian grand piano graced the corner, available to any guest who wanted to play a tune.[22]

All the Ruttger's resorts were famous for their food, because "Fine food is essential to complete any vacation. You will not be disappointed at Ruttgers." Ruttger's resorts featured the American plan with full meal service at set hours. Bay Lake hired its own pastry chef, and the cooks rose early to set the cinnamon rolls to rise while making egg coffee for the fishermen. Guests could order just about anything for breakfast, from eggs and bacon to French toast, and lunch featured a hot dish, potatoes, and meat. Because all Ruttger's resorts were family resorts, they did not serve liquor, so guests made cocktails in their cabins. At Pine Beach, employees rolled an ice cart along the sidewalk in front of the cabins selling ice and drink mixes. Dinner was a formal affair; men put on coat and tie and women wore cocktail dresses. At Shady Point the resort staged a "Coketail" hour for the teenagers on Sunday evenings.[23]

Because the family ran the resort, the Ruttger children worked too. From their youngest years, their job was to play with the guests' children and make sure they were "having a good time." The "play lady" ran a program from nine until noon and one until five, as well as an evening program during the formal dinner hour. As Theresa Ruttger grew older, she was given simple tasks like bundling the sheets on changeover day (Sunday), raking leaves, and painting the rowboats in the off season. By the time she was in her early teens, she was assigned to wash dishes, help the maids, or run errands into town in the morning. In the afternoon, she drove the boat and taught the teenage guests how to water-ski. She might fit in a tennis game with a guest. Summer evenings were spent washing the dishes and kitchen floor, then watching a movie or playing cards until late, when "everybody was just kind of sitting around, like in a family living room." There was no air-conditioning and no television. Guests would play old-fashioned games like bingo or cards, and eat popcorn and watch movies together.[24]

The Ruttger children saw themselves and their guests as part of one big happy family. Theresa remembered that if bad weather was coming in, they would warn the guests by ringing a loud bell and running a danger flag up on the flagpole. She felt "personally responsible" for the guests because "this week they were part of your family, and so you needed to take care of them." Randy Ruttger, who took over a Ruttger's resort right out of college, recalled, "My earliest memories are that the resort was just like home. I just assumed that this was part of my life and would spend my days going back and forth between home and the resort and just hanging out at the resort and playing with the kids that were staying at the resort." It was homelike because "many of the people came year after year, and in some instances came here for several generations." He knew which families would be there which week and where they were from. All the young people mixed in summer social activities—the Ruttgers, the guests, and the locals. "As we got older, into our teenage years, lots of teenage romances and things like that occurred between the local kids that lived around here and the employees of the resort and the guests at the resort."[25]

The mixing among the young people resulted in boisterous activity in the lake towns at night that alarmed some in the community. The "wild weekends" at Bar Harbor attracted the attention of the Minneapolis newspaper, which reported that the problem began in the early 1950s, when "the momentum was gathering and the jammed joint began to bounce." Parents did not know their children were out, and the kids were "just out for a whee. Fine kids when by themselves, but let a gang spirit explode and eyes were blackened, teeth knocked out, knuckles bloodied." A month later the local paper reported, "For years area boat owners, summer residents, and business people have suggested that Bar Harbor do something about the steadily growing 'kids' problem." The paper claimed it was common knowledge that "the young dancers of the past *lost all restraint* when in the Bar Harbor Area." To save their business, in June 1960 the Bar Harbor Night Club announced it was becoming a supper club, open only to those over the age of twenty-one. Their decision meant that "The high spirited teenage dancing crowd must be refused admittance at the Harbor."[26] Teenage guests at the resorts, who wanted more excitement than popcorn and card games, became mixed up in the late night scene at the bars a short drive from the sequestered family resorts.

Not only were the teenagers becoming a problem, but the family share of the clientele declined in the 1960s. Ruttger's owners recalled that when more women started working, families could not stay at the lake all summer, and gradually the one- and two-week visits were cut down to long weekends. Some of the resorts shifted to the European plan of charging for meals because guests wanted more flexibility during their shorter stays. Because women worked, "there were a lot of families that didn't really care for the children's programs, because it was the only time they had to be with their kids, so we were going to more babysitter-type services." As stays became shorter, fewer people came from the larger Midwestern region and more from the Twin Cities. When airfares became cheaper, the doctors and lawyers started taking their families to Europe rather than pay for a week at a resort.[27]

The owners of Ruttger's Shady Point chose to close the resort in 1978 rather than change with the times. Bill and Carol Ruttger got tired of the work and of never being able to take a summer vacation themselves. Their daughter remembered, "My parents were chained to the place. They never went out to dinner, they never did anything." On top of having no time of their own, they were plagued by the high costs of liability insurance and the multiple tax forms they had to fill out as small business owners. Instead of taking on debt to improve the resort, they sold off their land in parcels as lake home sites in 1978. Theresa was devastated by the news that her parents were shutting down the resort. "It was horrible, it was just awful, because this was what life was, and this was what you loved and where all your friends were, and your whole being was this place." As a senior in high school, she went to work at nearby Madden's resort, working the front desk and learning the operation. Her parents stayed in their home on the lake, and her father died at age fifty-four, just six years after he retired.[28]

In a sense, the smaller resorts had outlived their usefulness. Because they were capital poor, they were no longer able to compete with the larger resorts that could afford to borrow money to offer the latest amenities. Nor could resort owners cope with the increasing amount of paperwork and government regulations that necessitated expensive liability insurance. And unless the second and third generations were committed to the same exhausting summer life, the aging owners saw no choice but to sell the resort. Second-generation Jack Ruttger saw it as part of the larger changes in industry that were "squeezing out the little person." He thought that "it was sad to see the little gas station fade, sad to see the little corner grocery store fade. And now the same thing is happening to the resort industry." As the number of resorts declined while the number of beds rose, his children left the state for hospitality industry training so they could take over from the older generation. According to Jack, "if you don't grow, you're out of it."[29] But to grow involved going into debt and becoming so big that the guests were no longer seen as part of the family.

One of the attractions of the Ruttger's resorts was vacationing with the right people—the best people of the proper class. Their advertising brochures provided a box headlined, "Ask a Ruttger Guest" with a list of the Midwest's major cities and the name of a family from each. And at the bottom of the brochure, in all caps, it stated, "CLIENTELE CAREFULLY RESTRICTED." Certainly that meant they excluded black customers, but it also meant that Jews were not welcome to stay at their resorts.[30] The resorts of the excluded form an important part of the history of family vacationing because they offered African American parents and children a place safe from the hostility of discrimination on vacation.

African Americans founded their own resort communities in states with large black populations. In the back of each *Negro Traveler's Green Book* was the vacation guide, a nine-page list of resorts in various states to which the traveler could write directly. Idlewild, Michigan, Oak Bluffs, Masachusetts (near Martha's Vineyard), and Atlantic City and Belmar, New Jersey, were favorite vacation resorts built by and for African Americans. In the early 1960s, it was still almost impossible to find a cabin or cottage in the Midwest that was not segregated by race.[31]

Two resorts in Minnesota catered to black customers. In 1926 the Lyght family founded the Northern Lights Resort on Caribou Lake, and it was patronized by black professionals from the Twin Cities, Chicago, and Iowa. Flagg's resort was established by William Flagg, a thirty-year-old Chicago policeman who came north to fish. The first time he and his wife saw it in 1950, the five cabins were surrounded by weeds, but "we fell in love with this place." In 1961 they sold their house in Chicago and spent every summer on the lake until William's retirement in 1968, when they moved to the resort. It was the only black-owned resort in the area in 1961. They found African American clients among his colleagues in the Chicago police department, and they advertised in the Minneapolis papers—the *Spokesman* (an African American–owned paper) and the *Tribune.* They also received referrals from other nearby resorts.[32]

The Flaggs worked hard to upgrade the old fishing cabins. Installing indoor plumbing was crucial because "The women simply would not go to the outside toilets." The housekeeping cabins originally had a little two-burner stove and an icebox. They put in modern kitchens and baths, and they replaced linoleum with carpet. William rewired the cottages, converting the switch from a pull chain in the middle of the ceiling to wall switches. The secret to the Flaggs' success was gradual improvement, fixing up one cabin at a time and paying off the place with outside wage work rather than taking on debt. Later they built a lodge that became a draw for family reunions, and Flagg's expanded to 192 acres of land. Because of the high cost of liability insurance, as time went by, they eliminated boats and gave up plans for a diving dock and water skis.[33]

Most customers were families who brought their own food, and people came to fish. Although once everyone had fished, Flagg noted, "Now it's mostly among the men and the children, mostly the boys." In the early days, men and women were together more, but in later years, men and women chose different activities at the resort: "Of course, the wives, if they stay for a week, they like to go in and look at TV or mingle among themselves. But the men will go out and fish." Originally 99 percent of his clientele was black, and the change to a mostly white clientele was so gradual that he claimed he could not recall when it happened.[34] It was never a notable resort, but Flagg's offered African Americans from Chicago and the Twin Cities a respite in the wilderness. It provided a place to fish and to visit as it gradually changed from an all-black resort to one where anyone would come, as long as they wanted to fish.

In the Mountains: The Catskills

Like African Americans, in response to the prejudice against them, Jews developed their own resorts, primarily in Sullivan and Greene Counties in the Catskills region of New York State. The history of discrimination against Jews in private clubs dates to the 1880s and was common by the 1920s in the better hotels and resorts. From the end of the nineteenth century until the decline of anti-Semitism in the two decades after World War II, the Catskills resorts provided Jewish families with their own vibrant community. Sociologist Phil Brown, who grew up working in the Catskills, argues, "These New York Jews created a whole resortland shaped by their urban culture. They imported their music, humor, vaudeville revue style, culinary customs, language, and worldviews."[35] Reminiscences of the Catskills have a nearly timeless quality that makes it difficult now to chart the changes in the resort community, but the sources do allow us a view of the community at the height of its vitality.

A range of accommodations, from the humble bungalow colonies to the fancy hotels like Grossinger's, meant that Jews of every class could vacation in the cool mountain air of the Catskills. Brown has counted over 900 hotels in the region, and he estimates that every summer, more than a million people vacationed in the Catskills. In 1957 the completion of an expressway brought the area within a ninety-minute drive of New York City. The growth of the resort area occurred as Jews were dealing with the painful memories of the Holocaust and as they were forming vacation habits that sustained their cultural traditions while demonstrating their growing affluence.[36]

The bungalow resorts originated as a strategy by Jewish farmers to bring in income by building summer rental properties. They cut down pine and hemlock trees to build one- and two-room bungalows, which were painted white with green trim and were clustered around a central green or court. The earliest bungalow colonies featured a shared kitchen, called a *kuchalein,* but by the 1940s each bungalow had its own kitchen and bath in addition to the bedrooms. Bungalows did not have a living room but featured a porch, often screened. Immigrant Jews drove or took the train from New York City to the small villages and towns that reminded them of the European shtetls they had left behind. Women and children stayed all summer, and men commuted each weekend to be with the family. Although bungalows were cheaper than hotels, even some who could afford hotels preferred the colonies for their flexibility with meals and their sense of community.[37]

The end of World War II brought the golden years to the Catskills, when demand was so high that one owner claimed, "You could rent anything!" Summer was the only time to escape from living with the in-laws during a housing shortage. In the 1950s bungalow owners updated the kitchens, tiled the bathrooms, and installed more electrical outlets to attract guests. Bungalows that rented for $250 a summer before the war rose in price to more than $450 by 1946, still a bargain for a summer in the country. The colonies were family operations, run with little capital and dependent on the labor of all members of the family.[38]

Each bungalow colony formed a community, a world unto itself. During the week the resorts were a matriarchal society; in the daytime the women did their household chores and visited as the children played. They passed the time shopping or throwing birthday parties for the children. After putting the children to bed they played cards or mah-jongg, or they took turns going to the movies together. Irwin Richman, whose family owned a bungalow colony, remembers his childhood days as pastoral. He and his friends swam in the nearby Neversink River's swimming hole next to a hotel that had trucked in sand to make a beach. When children tired of taunting the hotel lifeguard who tried to run them off, they fished in the river with strainers and nets, and collected frogs and tadpoles. They sailed their wind-up toy boats or boats they had made from scraps of lumber. When they were not at the river, they climbed through the barbed wire fence to explore the neighbor's farm and follow "Indian paths" in the woods. At the colony, they shot baskets in the hoop nailed to the tree, played badminton and volleyball, or shot water pistols and cap guns. The children entertained themselves by making paper airplanes and handkerchief parachutes. On a rainy day, they played cards or looked at ViewMaster reels. As they grew older, they walked to the soda fountain in town where they could get a shake and play pinball, or they went to the movies. Because the countryside was considered safer than the city, the children were free to be out after dark.[39]

When the men arrived late Friday evening, the colonies became more festive. The women had spent the afternoon doing their hair and preparing food for the weekend. On Saturdays men played baseball in the colony leagues. By the 1960s, most bungalow owners had installed swimming pools, and handball courts were common. Saturday nights were the highlight, with a cookout where they grilled hot dogs and roasted marshmallows, drank soda, and played musical chairs. They might put on a homegrown variety show or host a traveling entertainer. Saturday night was for entertainment and sex. Richman recalled, "After the kids were put to bed, the adults would sing, tell risqué jokes, and generally horse around."[40] By then the older teenagers had left for the hotels, where they sneaked into the nightly shows.

Like the bungalow colonies, the fanciest hotel in the Catskills started on a farm. Selig and Malke Grossinger left New York's East Side in 1914 to open a seven-room boarding house in Liberty, New York, on a few acres of farmland. Known as "Waldorf in the Catskills," by 1964 the resort covered over 1,000 acres and hosted 70,000 guests annually, grossing $7.5 million. Their daughter Jennie (who married her cousin, Harry Grossinger) presided over the resort's expansion in the post–World War II years. A legend arose around her persona, complete with the story of her beginnings as a factory girl who rose to prominence as a career woman, friend to Hollywood celebrities, and benefactor to Jewish causes. She served as matchmaker to singer Eddie Fisher and actress Debbie Reynolds, who were married at the resort in 1955. Its guests included the rich and famous of the day: Milton Berle, Danny Kaye, Moss Hart, Jerry Lewis, Irving Berlin, and Eleanor Roosevelt. The Catskills welcomed African Americans long before other resorts opened their doors to them and featured the visits of prizefighters and baseball star Jackie Robinson. Jennie's hospitality made people feel a part of the family even when the resort was serving over a thousand guests a week.[41]

The resort's founders established a resort for Jewish guests that served food prepared in accordance with the strict dietary laws of orthodox Jews and observed the weekly Sabbath from sundown Friday. They attracted the cream of Jewish families, who came not only for the summer but also the Jewish holidays of Passover, Rosh Hashanah, and Yom Kippur. The high-end travel magazine, *Holiday,* published a nine-page spread on the resort in August 1949. If the bungalows were for the upwardly mobile immigrants, going to Grossinger's meant that you had arrived. But after the war, "a new clientele was also beginning to come to Grossinger's—assimilated young suburban couples who had abandoned the strict Orthodoxy of their parents." To change with the times, Grossinger's gave up observing a strict Sabbath; to avoid violating Talmudic law prohibiting work on the Sabbath, on each Friday at sundown, the main house was legally transferred to the hotel's gentile stage designer. The agreement of convenience allowed them to stage a variety show both weekend nights and keep their customers from leaving the resort for movies in town. Although they continued to hold Friday-night services and later built a synagogue, the changes attracted guests who did not hold to the strict religious observances of their parents' generation.[42]

However, Grossinger's continued to keep kosher, with two completely separate kitchens that served traditional Jewish food in elaborate menus three times a day. Dinner was a formal event, seating 1,600 at 250 tables, served by young people waiting tables to earn money for college. A 1947 menu featured prime rib, roast lamb, chicken paprika, stuffed veal breast, and the standard chicken soup with matzo balls. The pastry chef presented an array of tempting pies, cakes, cookies, and ice cream for dessert. Guests savored the familiar traditional dishes made with fresh chickens, eggs, and produce from local farmers out in the country.[43]

Grossinger's expanded in the decade after the war by building an airport, an Olympic pool, tennis courts, a golf course, and an indoor pool. The resort's entertainment was presided over by the *toomler,* the man who made sure guests had a good time. From after-breakfast games of Simon Says to the nightly floor show, the *toomler* told jokes, ribbed the guests, and matched up the awkward bachelor with the shy single girl. Afternoon entertainment included tours of the kitchen, free group dance lessons, handball, baseball, golf. Jennie Grossinger arranged to have lectures by newspaper columnists and statesmen, as well as an occasional psychologist. Women attended makeup classes while men watched boxing greats sparring as they trained at Grossinger's. The extensive grounds allowed guests to go on walks or fishing, or spend their days at the pool swimming, playing cards, or just lounging in the sun.[44]

Nightly entertainment at Borscht Belt resorts like Grossinger's featured big-name singing stars and comedians who poked fun at Jewish culture. After dinner men played pinochle and women mah-jongg or canasta while waiting for the ten o'clock show. In the early days, the staff presented Monday's show, and on weekday nights, guests could enjoy a Broadway touring show or a variety show at the playhouse. The week's highlight was the Saturday night show featuring stars like Red Buttons, Roberta Peters, Jackie Mason, Vic Damone, Joan Rivers, Peter Nero, Tony Bennett, Gordon MacRae, Diahann Carroll, and Alan King. Teenagers congregated in their own lounge and listened to their own bands.[45]

Grossinger's provided separate activities for the children of guests so the parents could relax at the resort. Tania Grossinger, whose mother was the social director, recalled that day camp was "like a little resort in itself." About sixty children attended, anywhere from four to thirteen years of age. Mixed among the children of the guests were the children of the staff. They played organized sports like basketball, volleyball, badminton, ping-pong, archery, and croquet; they visited the nature house; and they made objects in arts and crafts. The day camp even had its own swimming pool, and the children also swam in the lake, fished, or hiked to the waterfall. Grossinger's had its own children's dining room with Disney characters painted on the wall, so guests who preferred to eat later could do so without their children, who had been fed already. After dinner children gathered around a campfire, went on a scavenger hunt, treasure hunt, or enjoyed a "Cowboy and Indian night."[46]

Of course, children of the owners had less time to play because they were required to help run the hotel. Children were not too young to work, and they would take on small tasks like readying laundry, selling concessions, or cleaning the pool. At adolescence they were strong enough to work in the dining room as busboys or sort and deliver the mail. They were taught that guests were almost like family. But because parents worked such long hours, children lamented that they rarely saw their parents during resort season, and they even had to give up their rooms when the hotel was overbooked.[47]

The naughty humor of the Borscht Belt was based in part on the reality of increased opportunities for sexual dalliance. Like at the bungalows, women at the hotels experienced a sense of freedom on vacation because their husbands were working in the city and were at the resort only on weekends. Those whose children attended day camp were free to participate in the resort's many activities and to socialize with other women, forming friendships that kept them coming back year after year. Borscht Belt comedians made sexual affairs legendary in their jokes, and although there is ample evidence of sexual relations among the coming-of-age staff members, reliable evidence of sexual activity has proved elusive. Indeed, Brown maintains that there was no more sex at the Catskills than at other resort areas, and he suspects the reputation of rampant sex in the Catskills was exaggerated by the bawdy comedy routines. But even if the affairs

Children being awarded swim trophies at Grossinger's resort, 1959.
(Courtesy of the Archives of the YIVO Institute for Jewish Research, New York.)

were no more than flirtations between the married women and the young staff members, they represented a relaxing of the rules that made vacations a respite from daily life.[48]

There is no doubt that the Catskills resorts served as a marriage market, and one estimate suggests that over 10,000 persons met their spouses at Grossinger's. *The Goldbergs,* a New York–area television show written by Gertrude Berg, who grew up in the Catskills, featured the foibles of the Goldberg family during their yearly stay at the fictional Pincus Pines. In a 1954 episode, daughter Rosalie found it difficult to keep the attentions of a young doctor because the mothers of the other eligible young women were interfering. Her mother, Molly, arranged for members of the band to dance with the girls, thus allowing Rosalie to continue her romance alone with her marriage prospect. Upon departure, Mr. Goldberg complained about the expense as he handed out tips to the various staff members. Their daughter, who had met a nice young doctor, summed it all up: "We did have a wonderful time!"[49]

A children's costume party at Grossinger's resort, 1954.
(Courtesy of the Archives of the YIVO Institute for Jewish Research, New York.)

The Catskills resorts began to lose clientele in the late 1950s and by the 1960s were experiencing a notable decline. The defection of Jews from the Catskills was partly because they were being welcomed elsewhere. A study of resorts by the Anti-Defamation League in 1957 found that about one-quarter of those surveyed had explicit policies restricting guests. Travel agencies used the "flower code" to signal the status of their guests so that they could be directed to lodging that would accept them: oleander was a gentile, hibiscus was a Jew, and poinciana meant the customer was Asian. But especially in Florida, anti-Semitism was declining. A study of Florida hotels found that 55 percent discriminated in 1953, 18 percent in 1957, and only 12 percent in 1960.[50]

Laws prohibiting discrimination were passed in an effort to open resorts to all paying customers. National Jewish organizations served as watchdogs and took legal action to challenge discrimination in public accommodations. In 1953 the American Jewish Committee filed a complaint with the New York State Commission Against Discrimination regarding the Westkill Tavern Club in Greene County, New York. The club advertised that it catered to "a strictly selected clientele in a Christian community." The commission ordered them to cease collecting that type of information and to admit all applicants.[51]

High-end resorts were among those that continued to discriminate. They justified their policies by claiming that because their resorts were family oriented, their guests expected management to be selective in admitting lodgers. For example, the Camelback Inn in Phoenix, Arizona, demanded detailed information from its prospective guests with suspicious last names to establish that they were not Jewish because "our guests demand that we cater only to those who can be entirely a part of their tastes and interests." When the National Association of Attorneys General moved their 1954 convention from the Camelback Inn to West Virginia to protest the well-documented discrimination against Jews, it was the beginning of the end of discrimination at such highly visible resorts, which realized that they would lose money to hotels that did not discriminate.[52]

In the 1960s the use of the bungalows began to decline as the children grew up and older people dominated the clientele. At the same time, costs rose to $1,200 for a two-bedroom bungalow for the summer, and more for day camp. The second generation did not return with their children because "the mountains simply were too Jewish, too immigrant-oriented, for the younger, upward-bound Jews." Children did not want the same kind of vacation their parents and grandparents had wanted in the Catskills, where being Jewish meant eating gefilte fish or kreplach while listening to Milton Berle crack jokes about his mother-in-law. Instead, as airfares became lower, they went to ancestral homelands of Europe or Israel. When families moved out of the cities to the suburbs, they had access to swimming pools, and as residential air-conditioning became affordable, they no longer sought the cool air of the mountains. Now the bungalow colonies have been taken over by orthodox Hasidic Jews, so it remains a place where Jewish culture and traditions can still flourish.[53]

Grossinger's closed in 1986, its buildings were auctioned off, and its nightclub imploded. The cream of Jewish society had long since stopped going to the Catskills on vacation; indeed, the downturn began in the 1960s as New York Jews began to vacation in Miami, which became known as "the southern Borscht Belt." Elderly Jews became winter snowbirds, and many stayed; by 1960 Jews comprised 15 percent of Miami's population. The other new center of Jewish population was Los Angeles, where a thriving Jewish community spread from Boyle Heights to the city's western suburbs, and delicatessens like Canter's served up cheese blintzes or corned beef sandwiches to former New Yorkers.[54]

Ironically, the increasingly pluralistic American society, where differences of religion and race became more accepted, dealt a death blow to the resorts for Jews and blacks. The decline in anti-Semitism and the increasing acceptance of interfaith marriages meant it was no longer as important to keep kosher, or to find the right match for one's daughter at Grossinger's. African Americans who summered at Flagg's were no longer denied public accommodations, and the resorts ceased to be a distinctive summer community that served as a refuge from discrimination. In Minnesota, as customers demanded more amenities, owners required capital beyond the reach of the mom-and-pop fishing resorts. Quaint resorts became run down and closed when their rusticity was no longer charming. Working women could not take the whole summer off, so families took shorter, more frequent vacations. Larger Minnesota resorts adopted a corporate-driven marketing scheme to fill their cabins and pay the insurance bill. Ruttger's added indoor pools and more golf courses, and they cultivated convention business to fill in the holes left by families. Some Americans built their own vacation homes in the countryside, and as suburbs expanded urban sprawl, the countryside began to disappear.[55]

Too Much Togetherness

But local adaptations could not stem the tides of change for American families. An episode of the family television show *The Wonder Years* captures the essence of why family vacations evolved. The show was set in the summer of 1971 at Lake Winahatchee, where Jack and Norma Arnold rented cabins "to get away from the aggravations of modern life." Fifteen-year-old Kevin complained, "All this family togetherness was more than any adolescent soul could take." His older brother dropped him at the drive-in movie theater, where Kevin was immediately smitten with a girl he saw in the back of a pickup truck. She had long blonde hair and smoked. "No matter how hard I tried, I couldn't get that girl off my mind." He left his best friend, Paul, behind as he and the girl took off in her brother's truck to the lake. They chatted while reclining on the hood of the pickup, and he fell in love: "Even though I just met this woman I felt like I had known her my whole life." She pulled out a cigarette for him to light, and instead he kissed her.

Kevin's romance ruptured the relationships with his family, especially with his father, who said he arranged this vacation because he wanted "the whole family to be together." One evening at dinner Jack ordered

Kevin to stay with the family, but Kevin stormed out the door to spend his last night with his summer love. "That night huddled in that cab, we left the whole world behind. I had to be with Kara, I had to hold her, I could not bring myself to tell her I was leaving." She guided his hand to her breast as they kissed, and he yearned to stay, but he realized he could not. He faced the truth that he could fall in love but he was not yet grown up: "I was fifteen. I slept under a roof my father owned in a bed my father bought." While on vacation with his family he caught a glimpse of his future, and he realized that "Nothing was mine . . . except my heart, and my fears, and my growing knowledge that not every road was going to lead home anymore."[56]

Seventeen-year-old "Baby" Hausman felt similarly trapped by her family in the film *Dirty Dancing,* set in 1963 at a Grossinger's-like resort in the Catskills. The naive young heroine, on vacation with her father (a doctor), mother, and homely sister, was not interested in the resort's staid rituals of dressing for dinner, and she struck up a friendship with the staff. In their hangouts, she discovered open expressions of sexuality, symbolized by their "dirty dancing," and soon she was drawn into an erotic relationship with the working-class dance instructor. Her commitment to social justice intertwined with her own sexual awakening when she became involved in the plight of a dancer with a botched abortion.[57]

The erotic tensions of family resorts, long veiled by custom and supervised by parents, surfaced and burst as the waves of the sexual revolution washed over the summer resorts. Whether it was the first kiss or the first experience of sex, teen sexual behavior threatened the habit of the family vacation. Teens who watched California beach movies longed for the same romances they saw on screen or read about in the newly popular young adult novels. Summer romances gave teens a taste of a wider world beyond the bounds of the family, beyond the boundaries of authority and behavior within which they had grown up. Such experiences were the first steps leading adolescents away from the family to a wider world where they would be on their own.[58]

The sexual revolution affected not only teens but also their parents. Vacations could be a "Danger Time for Marriage," wrote Ernest Havemann in the *Ladies' Home Journal* in 1968. Drawing on interviews with psychologists, he declared: "The evidence is overwhelming that vacations are booby-trapped with marital danger." Experts advised parents to put a higher priority on their own needs, such as "Vacation-time sex. Many couples fail to plan for it; they commit themselves to sleeping in the same tent, camper or motel room with the children." The experts suggested "planning at least an occasional night alone with the children in a motel room of their own—a room that is at least one door removed."

The dream of taking the whole family on vacation was going sour because togetherness was not an altogether good thing. One expert identified automobile travel as a problem because "togetherness offers no privacy." And "the couple who travel are sitting on top of each other most of the time, and this is bound to produce tensions."

Tensions arose from the work of the vacation and from trying to adhere to gender roles that were no longer comfortable. In the women's magazines, men received most of the blame because "On the typical American vacation the man may drive, but the woman does the work." However, at this distance, it is clear that togetherness could be combustible, no matter how hard one tried. In the defense of men, one expert observed, "It's not unusual for a man to work hard all day Friday before his vacation, rush home, pack the gear, sleep a couple of hours, set off with the family at daybreak, drive 400 or 500 miles and then hurry to set up camp before night falls. And it's no wonder that this man and his wife are soon screaming at each other." Experts argued that the fatigue, stress, and work of the typical family road trip put too much pressure on even a healthy marriage. To top it all off, "by the time they have reached their teens, most children hate the idea of a family vacation; they think it's a hopeless drag." Teen rebellion was the last straw; if the family vacation was such a drag, why go?[59]

The optimistic view of family vacations in the early postwar years was giving way to the idea that separate vacations were acceptable and even desirable. The ideal of family togetherness was wearing out, and the self-sacrificing habits of their parents did not suit the newer families formed in the 1960s. No longer could everyone's needs be met by traveling together. Women, who were increasingly holding down a job while running a household, were no longer willing to put up with the work of the traditional family vacation. Men wanted a break from work, and they were not eager to drive all day long and then set up a tent at sunset or lug suitcases in and out of motel rooms. Children were growing into teenagers who cared more about their friends than family, and they were not keen on sitting in the backseat and playing travel games while watching for exit signs on the freeways. Instead of the long summer road trip in the car, American parents took romantic getaways and more frequent, shorter trips with the children. As Americans adapted to change, they realized that they could go on vacation without having to take the whole family.

Epilogue

The modern American family vacation began to disappear as the baby boomers grew up. When the children of the greatest generation became adolescents, they began to chafe at the constraints of parental authority and took their own path forward. For some that path led to Woodstock in August 1969, a counterculture rockfest set in a farmer's field in the Catskills near the Jewish resorts where they had spent summer vacations. For other baby boomers who rebelled in the 1960s, that path took them to antiwar marches near the steps to the Lincoln Memorial, where they had posed for pictures as children. Others may have been in Yosemite's Stoneman Meadow in 1970 throwing bottles at park rangers to defend their rights to use the park as they chose, to "find themselves" by smoking pot or lacing flowers in their hair.[1]

But most baby boomers were probably like me, following a conservative and timeworn path to adulthood by having children and taking them on summer vacations. We raised our three sons in Chicago, and except for one trip to Disney World courtesy of airline frequent flyer points, we usually piled into the car and drove west to see the grandparents. As our sons grew, that car morphed from a used Buick to a shiny new Japanese compact to a spacious minivan, full of snacks and games to entertain the children. We packed our own breakfasts and lunches, and everyone remembers eating sandwiches at a playground near Albuquerque watching the lizards slither across the blacktop. Just like in the old days, someone always got carsick.

It's not that the family vacation went away, but it did cease to be recognized as a mass phenomenon. The family vacation declined in importance in the 1970s as the travel advertising focused on niche marketing, with slogans like "Virginia is for lovers." The family ideal of the 1950s was eclipsed by the culture of cool, where Peter Fonda's *Easy Rider* (1969) road trip movie was hip, and the family road trip was definitely not. Family togetherness was no longer fashionable, and couples getaways featured excitement and sex. The sexual revolution challenged the ideal of the traditional American family, and the travel industry capitalized on the new sexual mores with Club Med resorts that catered to the singles crowd.[2]

In the aftermath of the terrorist attack on September 11, 2001, Americans retreated again to the security of the family. They changed travel habits as a result of fears of terrorism: air travel plummeted, and international travel fell off drastically. They drove instead of taking an airplane, took more regional trips, and relied on the old standbys, camping and traveling to patriotic destinations. When Americans were surveyed about their travel plans, they said "that the war and the state of the economy had made them more interested in taking an auto or R.V. vacation." Market research firms and travel agencies noticed that "as a natural consequence of the turmoil in the world, the uncertainty, people turned for comfort to family." Marketers rediscovered the potential of the family market. Extended families met at Disney World for Magical Gatherings, part of the "togethering" trend in travel. Even Club Med, the "original singles resort, went family friendly" and now offers programs for babies and children at an array of resorts around the world. Americans appeared to be reliving their parents' and grandparents' fears of a global threat and repeating their strategy of retreating to domestic space.[3]

If the reliance on family to calm our fears is the same, family vacations are not. The most notable change is that vacations have become shorter and more frequent. Families struggle to find enough time to make vacations extend beyond a long weekend, as workers feel tied to their jobs—and when on vacation, tied to their BlackBerries or laptops. One solution is to take the family along on business trips; 62 percent of business travelers "add a leisure component to their trip, among those two-thirds bring a family member or friend with them." But compared to Europeans, Americans take far fewer vacations, and business analysts fear worker burnout.[4]

To meet the needs of today's families, the family vacation is being reinvented, but on the foundation of vacations of the past. Vacations are seen less as an escape and more as a way to bring the family together and for families to spend more time with children. This is especially true of vacations scheduled around joint custody agreements of those who have divorced and remarried, which often require elaborate advance planning. Holiday Inn celebrated its fiftieth birthday in 2005, its staying power due to its innovations of "kids stay free" and imposing standards of cleanliness and service a cut above mom-and-pop motels. But newer hotels are more likely to contain an indoor pool, or even a water park to induce families to lengthen their stay. Resort hotels offer day camps for children of all ages, as well as reduced rates on a separate room for the kids. Old motels are being fixed up as architectural gems, and baby boomers are rediscovering their affordable style.[5]

The West still offers adventures to families who ride horses at dude ranches or backpack in the national parks. Disneyland also turned fifty in 2005 in a worldwide celebration. It had particular meaning to the baby boomers, like travel writer Tom Wharton, who recalled that in the early 1960s, "a trip to Southern California and Disneyland was a family pilgrimage as important as any visit to a church shrine." He included Disneyland on his honeymoon itinerary, took his children there, and now takes his grandchildren. But after standing in long lines and buying overpriced souvenirs, he worries that the magic of Disney "has been exploited by a big, greedy corporation that has perverted the original values Walt Disney tried to convey into a cynical money-making machine." A three-day, two-night trip for a family of four is pushing $1,000, without transportation.[6] Yet Disney Parks and Disney Cruises still peddle family togetherness as they push the frontiers of fantasy amusement, for a price.

Camping, which became more popular during the post-9/11 economic downturn, has become a serious adventure pursuit with the introduction of lightweight gear, but most families still depend on car camping. Some national parks dealt with congestion by banning cars and relying on propane-powered shuttle buses, and national park attendance is trending downward. There are fewer children in the parks; some blame it on children's overscheduled summers of lessons and sports camps, while others blame the distraction of video games. To attract customers, park concessions are sprucing up the menus with local ingredients like bison and elk, and building green kitchens. The campgrounds of America are aging; the average age of a KOA camper is fifty-seven, and 50 percent of active campers are in the baby boom generation. Still, 37 percent of KOA campers camp with children under eighteen years of age, maybe grandchildren.[7]

Baby boomers are taking their children back to old-fashioned resorts where days are spent swimming, fishing, and taking walks in the woods. Parents still like the opportunity to enjoy separate activities, but have togetherness when they want it. The family cruise has reinvented the resort in packages now made affordable for the middle class. Children aboard the Disney Magic enjoy eating the chocolate chip cookies and drinking chocolate milk, interacting with the Disney costume characters, and swimming in the pool. They even provide places for teenagers to hang out and shorter shore stays.[8]

Technological innovations have reinvented the way families plan and take vacations. Surfing the Internet for deals and making online reservations has replaced writing letters to obtain information. The Internet facilitates niche marketing, and one can sign up for e-mail notices of special travel deals just for families. During the trip, instead of showing snapshots, travelers share their experiences by posting them to a travel blog. Instead of traveling with a bag full of toys, cars are equipped with fancy audio systems and DVD players that fold down from the ceiling to keep the kids entertained.[9] But some things may have gotten lost in the transition. Teenagers sequester themselves from family togetherness with their iPods and video games. There is not much chance for the family singing of the olden days, and the cows have long disappeared from most of the landscape.

As families change, so do family vacations. Only 24 percent of all U.S. households today are "married with children," and only 30 percent of those who vacationed with a family member fit the mold of the traditional nuclear family. The biggest niche in the family travel market is multigenerational travel, more popular among Hispanics and African Americans. Another overlooked market niche is single parents, who may be more pressed financially but think that it is important to sacrifice in other areas to afford a vacation with children. The nontraditional gay and lesbian family with children also seeks "safe, fun, affordable vacations," especially as some gay-oriented getaway destinations prefer the freer-spending gay men to lesbians with children. Whether one is a traditional family, a single-parent family, or a gay family, going on vacation together is a declaration that you are indeed an American family.[10]

The family vacation is newly popular as the children of baby boomers discover the pleasures (and perils) of traveling with children. The Generation Xers are more likely to fly to their destinations, and their Herculean attempts to keep children occupied while confined in a narrow airplane seat make one long for the good old days when children roamed around the family car. At least then they only disturbed their parents and siblings, not a plane full of irritable passengers. When they do travel in the car, it is easier with the gadgets like a DVD player, and it requires less planning because there are fast food restaurants at every freeway exit. They are intrepid in taking their children along and discover that their old singles haunts of Las Vegas, Miami, and Los Angeles make fine family-friendly vacation spots if trips are carefully planned.[11]

The older baby boomers have long gone gray, but they have not given up the family vacation. They take their children and grandchildren on cruises, or buy RVs and drive around the country sightseeing and visiting. Some write accounts of their attempt to recreate the cross-country trips of their youth, and despite their mishaps (or maybe because of them) discover a renewed affection for their children and parents. When travel writer W. D. Wetherell realized that his teenagers were too busy with summer jobs, music, and sports camps for the regular summer vacation trip, he was wistful for the happy memories of the past: "Of all the rewards travel has brought me, nothing has ever matched the joy I've found in seeing new places through the eyes of my children." His essay prompted letters from readers who had experienced the same transition but who now enjoy trips with their grandchildren, or the sister they once fought with in the backseat. But as one warned, "be prepared for a few changes. The toothless, fidgety kids in the backseat become the confident drivers, map-readers, translators and photographers. That, too, is a wonderful journey!"[12] Family vacations are life journeys, and baby boomers are again finding themselves in the backseat.

Notes

Introduction

1. *National Lampoon's Vacation,* http://www.imdb.com/title/tt0085995/business (accessed 8 August 2007); http://www.imdb.com/title/tt0085995/ (accessed 3 August 2007); Variety Staff, "*National Lampoon's Vacation,*" *Variety Review Database,* 1 January 1983; 1 January 1989, http://www.proquest.com.erl.lib.byu.edu/ (accessed 3 August 2007).

2. *Morey Amsterdam Show,* DuMont Television Network, 1949/04/28, T85:0933, LA105610, Museum of Television and Radio, Los Angeles.

3. *The Bob and Ray Show,* NBC, 1952/04/08, Bob Elliott and Ray Goulding, T81:0454 LA103070, Museum of Television and Radio, Los Angeles.

4. Frederic F. Van de Water, *The Family Flivvers to Frisco* (New York: D. Appleton and Company, 1927), 98, 240; Edward D. Dunn, *Double-Crossing America by Motor: Routes and Ranches of the West* (New York: G. P. Putnam's Sons, 1933), 59.

5. "The President's Vacation Trip," 17–23 November 1946, at President Truman's Travel Logs, Truman Presidential Museum and Library, http://www.trumanlibrary.org/calendar/travel_log/index.htm (accessed 16 July 2007).

6. Gallup Poll [computer file], *Public Opinion, 1935–1997* (Wilmington, Del.: Scholarly Resources, 2000), 1954: 1256; Outdoor Recreation Resources Review Commission, *National Recreation Survey* (Washington, D.C., 1962), 63; Thomas Frank, *The Conquest of Cool: Business Culture, Counterculture, and the Rise of Hip Consumerism* (Chicago: University of Chicago Press, 1997).

7. Elaine Tyler May, *Homeward Bound: American Families in the Cold War Era* (New York: Basic Books, 1988); Wendy Kozol, Life*'s America: Family and Nation in Postwar Photojournalism* (Philadelphia: Temple University Press, 1991); Lynn Spigel, *Make Room for TV: Television and the Family Ideal in Postwar America* (Chicago: University of Chicago Press, 1992).

8. Lizabeth Cohen, *A Consumers' Republic: The Politics of Mass Consumption in Postwar America* (New York: Knopf, 2003), 7; Andrew Hurley, *Diners, Bowling Alleys and Trailer Parks: Chasing the American Dream in the Postwar Consumer Culture* (New York: Basic Books, 2001), 277–78. For consuming the vacation, see Hal K. Rothman, *Devil's Bargains: Tourism in the Twentieth Century American West* (Lawrence: University Press of Kansas, 1998); Richard Butsch, ed., *For Fun and Profit: The Transformation of Leisure into Consumption* (Philadelphia: Temple University Press, 1990). The linkage between consumerism and national security can be found in David Farber, *The Age of Great Dreams: America in the 1960s* (New York: Hill & Wang, 1994), 15–16; and Karal Ann Marling, *As Seen on TV: The Visual Culture of Everyday Life in the 1950s* (Cambridge, Mass.: Harvard University Press, 1994), 274–79.

9. Dean MacCannell, *The Tourist: A New Theory of the Leisure Class* (1976; reprint, Berkeley: University of California Press, 1999); Chris Rojek, *Capitalism and Leisure*

Theory (London: Tavistock, 1985); Nelson H. Graburn, "The Anthropology of Tourism," *Annals of Tourism Research* 10 (1983): 9–33. A useful anthology is Shelley Baranowski and Ellen Furlough, eds., *Being Elsewhere: Tourism, Consumer Culture, and Identity in Modern Europe and North America* (Ann Arbor: University of Michigan Press, 2001).

10. Cindy S. Aron, *Working at Play: A History of Vacations in the United States* (New York: Oxford, 1999); Warren James Belasco, *Americans on the Road: From Autocamp to Motel, 1910–1945* (Baltimore: Johns Hopkins University Press, 1979); Marguerite S. Shaffer, *See America First: Tourism and National Identity, 1880–1940* (Washington, D.C.: Smithsonian, 2001). For the variability of citizenship, see Linda K. Kerber, "The Meanings of Citizenship," *Journal of American History* 84 (December 1997): 833–54.

11. For a protest against popular imagery, see Stephanie Coontz, *The Way We Never Were: American Families and the Nostalgia Trap* (New York: Basic Books, 1992); Joanne Meyerowitz, *Not June Cleaver: Women and Gender in Postwar America, 1945–1960* (Philadelphia: Temple University Press, 1994). For more diverse portraits of American families, see Becky M. Nicolaides, *My Blue Heaven: Life and Politics in the Working-Class Suburbs of Los Angeles, 1920–1965* (Chicago: University of Chicago Press, 2002); Jessica Weiss, *To Have and To Hold: Marriage, the Baby Boom and Social Change* (Chicago: University of Chicago Press, 2000); and Andrew Wiese, *Places of Their Own: African American Suburbanization in the Twentieth Century* (Chicago: University of Chicago Press, 2004). For the movement of the worker into the middle class, see Meg Jacobs, *Pocketbook Politics: Economic Citizenship in Twentieth-Century America* (Princeton: Princeton University Press, 2005), 249–50.

12. The family remains an important category of analysis in public policy; see, for example, "The Fragile Families and Child Wellbeing Study," available at http://www.fragilefamilies.princeton.edu/ (accessed 15 August 2007). The field of family history has not adapted well to the cultural turn, and certain of its inquiries have been appropriated by the history of women, gender, and childhood. Nevertheless, I argue that it is important to study the family as a social institution, if only because the notion of family retains its saliency in public dialogue. See Nara Milanich, "Whither Family History: A Road Map from Latin America," *American Historical Review* 112 (April 2007): 439–58; Susan Sessions Rugh, *Our Common Country: Family Farming, Culture, and Community in the Nineteenth-Century Midwest* (Bloomington: Indiana University Press, 2001).

13. David Farber, ed., *The Sixties: From Memory to History* (Chapel Hill: University of North Carolina Press, 1994); Farber, *The Age of Great Dreams*; Maurice Isserman and Michael Kazin, *America Divided: The Civil War of the 1960s*, 2nd ed. (New York: Oxford University Press, 2004). Recent studies suggest the persistence of local cultures; for example, see Matthew D. Lassiter, *The Silent Majority: Suburban Politics in the Sunbelt South* (Princeton, NJ: Princeton University Press, 2006); Kevin M. Kruse, *White Flight: Atlanta and the Making of Modern Conservatism* (Princeton, NJ: Princeton University Press, 2005).

14. The number of studies that rely on the concept of memory are too numerous to be listed here. For an overview, see David Thelen, *Memory and American History*

(Bloomington: University of Indiana Press, 1990). For the limits of memory studies, see Alan Confino, "Collective Memory and Cultural History: Problems of Method," *American Historical Review* 102 (December 1997): 1386–403.

15. Calvin Trillin, *Travels with Alice* (New York: Farrar, Straus and Giroux, 1989), 1–2.

16. Ibid., 4, 6, 12.

17. Lucia Maria Perillo, *The Oldest Map with the Name America: New and Selected Poems* (New York: Random House, 1999), 41–42.

18. Soozie Tyrell, "White Lines," *White Lines* (Treasure Records), released 8 April 2003, available at http://www.soozietyrell.com/html/press.htm (accessed 8 August 2007).

19. Suzaan Boetger, *Earthworks: Art and the Landscape of the Sixties* (Berkeley: University of California Press, 2002), 200–205; Eugenie Tsai, "Robert Smithson: Plotting a Line from Passaic, New Jersey, to Amarillo, Texas," in *Robert Smithson*, ed. Eugenie Tsai and Cornelia Butler (Berkeley: University of California Press, 2004), 11–31.

20. Heribert Frhr. V. Feilitzsch, "Karl May: The 'Wild West' as Seen in Germany," *Journal of Popular Culture* 27, no. 3 (winter 1993): 173–89.

21. Interview with Nancy Heller, 27 December 2006, New York City.

22. Steven Mintz and Susan Kellogg, *Domestic Revolutions: A Social History of American Family Life* (New York: Free Press, 1988).

23. For the meanings of vacation, see the introduction to Baranowski and Furlough, *Being Elsewhere*, 4–5. For example, even countercultural groups identify themselves as part of a "family" such as the Grateful Dead and their followers, the Deadheads, or the 1960s hippie subculture in San Francisco; see George Lipsitz, "Who'll Stop the Rain? Youth Culture, Rock 'n' Roll, and Social Crises," in Farber, *Sixties*, 216.

24. U.S. Census Bureau, *Historical Statistics of the United States*, Part 2, Series Q (Washington, D.C., 1975), 717.

25. Gallup Poll 1946: 554–55.

26. Outdoor Recreation Resources Review Commission, *National Recreation Survey*, 40, 45, 63.

27. Shaffer, *See America First*, 6.

28. For the idea of different Americas, I am indebted to Greil Marcus, *The Old, Weird America: The World of Bob Dylan's Basement Tapes* (New York: Henry Holt, 1997).

1. Selling the Family Vacation

1. "America Takes a Trip," *Business Week*, 26 July 1947, 22; "Biggest Year for Resorts," *Business Week*, 10 June 1950, 90; "Biggest Season Yet: 55 Million Americans on the Move," *Business Week*, 18 June 1952, 150–52.

2. Cindy S. Aron, *Working at Play: A History of Vacations in the United States* (New York: Oxford University Press, 1999).

3. U.S. Department of Labor, Bureau of Labor Statistics, *Collective Bargaining Provisions, Vacations: Holidays and Week-End Work*, Bulletin 908-2 (Washington, 1948), 1–2.

4. "Paid Vacations on Increase throughout Industry," *Management Review*, November 1949, 621; "Vacations and Holidays: 1956," *Management Record*, August 1956, 276–79;

"Vacation Trends and Policies," *American Business Magazine,* Survey of the Month, April 1956, n.p.; George Soule, "The Economics of Leisure," *Annals of the American Academy of Political and Social Science* 313 (September 1957): 16–24.

5. Tom Lewis, *Divided Highways: Building the Interstate Highways, Transforming American Life* (New York: Viking, 1997), 121–23.

6. Edward D. Fales Jr., "More Super-Roads Coming!" *Better Homes and Gardens,* January 1956, 68.

7. Ibid., 132.

8. James J. Flink, "Three Stages of Automobile Consciousness," *American Quarterly* 24, no. 4 (October 1972): 451–73; U.S. Census Bureau, *Historical Statistics of the United States,* Part 2, Series Q (Washington, D.C., 1975), 717; Ford Company Advertisements, Box 28, Ford, 1949, F, Series I (cars), Accession 19, Benson Ford Research Center (hereafter BFRC), the Henry Ford Museum, Greenfield Village, Dearborn, Michigan. For an overview of the car in American life, see James J. Flink, *The Automobile Age* (Cambridge, Mass.: MIT Press, 1988).

9. American Automobile Association, *Post-War Travel Trends,* survey by the American Automobile Association [n.d.], 5, California State Automobile Association Archives, San Francisco; Ford, 1946, G-S, Ford, 1946, S-Z, Box 27, Ford Company Advertisements, Series I, Accession 19, BFRC.

10. Ford, 1946, S-Z, Box 27, Series I, Accession 19, BFRC.

11. Ford, 1946, S-Z, Box 27, and Ford, 1947, F, Box 28, Series I, Accession 19, BFRC.

12. Virginia Scharff, *Taking the Wheel: Women and the Coming of the Motor Age* (New York: Free Press, 1991); Ford, 1947, F (5 of 6), Box 28, and Ford, 1949, W, Box 30, Series I, Accession 19, BFRC.

13. American Automobile Association, *Americans on the Highway* (Washington, D.C.: AAA, 1952) 6; Harry Sharp and Paul Mott, "Consumer Decisions in the Metropolitan Family," *Journal of Marketing* 21, no. 2 (October 1956): 149–56; Ford, 1948, F-Z, Box 28; Ford, 1954, T, Box 31; Ford, 1957, P-T, Box 32, Series I, Accession 19, BFRC.

14. Ron Kowalke, ed., *Standard Catalog of Ford, 1903–1998,* 2nd ed. (Iola, Wisc.: Krause Publications, 1998), 91, 93, 94, 96, 98, 101, 104, 107, 110, 113, 116–17.

15. Ford, 1954, T, Box 31; Ford, 1957, F, Box 32; Ford, 1964, Box 33, all Series I, Accession 19, BFRC; Folder 3, Box 405, N. W. Ayer Advertising Records, Archives Center, National Museum of American History, Washington, D.C.

16. Ford, 1956, T; Ford, 1957, A-E; Ford, 1958, Q-Z, all in Box 32, BFRC; *Life,* 19 July 1954, 41.

17. *Sunset,* July 1962, 44.

18. Autos, Mercury, 1959, Box 65, Acc. 19, BFRC.

19. Folder 2, Box 400, Ayer Advertising Records.

20. Autos, Mercury, 1959, Box 65, Acc. 19, BFRC.

21. Edward D. Fales Jr., "Travel Tricks," *Better Homes and Gardens,* July 1956, 62; "Seat Belts," *Motorland,* 1959, 18–19; "Gadgets for Folks on the Go," *Better Homes and Gardens,* 1956, 128; "Motorist, Save Your Child," *Motorland,* 1977, 24–25; U.S. National Highway Traffic Safety Administration, *Federal Motor Vehicle Safety Standards and Regulations*

(Washington, D.C., 1999); Charles Jesse Kahane, *An Evaluation of Child Passenger Safety: The Effectiveness and Benefits of Safety Seats* (Washington, D.C., 1986).

22. Carol Lane, *Traveling by Car: A Family Planning Guide to Better Vacations* (New York: Simon and Schuster, 1954), vii; Sharp and Mott, "Consumer Decisions." See also *Have Fun on Your Tour with Texaco* (Chicago: Rand McNally & Co., 1958), Rand McNally Collection, Newberry Library, Chicago, Illinois. Carol Lane was the pseudonym of Caroline Iverson Ackerman. She learned to pilot a plane and became aviation editor for *Life* magazine during the war, served as Shell's travel director from 1947 to 1950, and was the writer of a nationally syndicated travel column. After marrying in 1949 and raising a family, she became a professor of journalism in the Boston area; see Collection Description, Caroline Iverson Ackerman Papers, Schlesinger Library, Radcliffe Institute, Harvard University; Sally Knapp, *New Wings for Women* (New York: Thomas Y. Crowell Co., 1946), 100–116.

23. Lane, *Traveling,* 4, 6.

24. Ibid., 6–8.

25. Ibid., 6–10.

26. Ibid., 20–24.

27. Ibid., 26.

28. Ibid., 29–30.

29. Ibid., 27–28.

30. Ibid., 32–34, 36–37.

31. Ibid., 43.

32. Ibid., 47, 51.

33. Ibid., 53; Apple self-cooling water bag, Hirsch-Weiss Canvas Products Co., Portland, Oregon [ca. 1948], ID 88.354.1, and Automobile Air Conditioner, window mounted [1930s–1940s], ID 82.63.1, Henry Ford Museum, Greenfield Village, Dearborn, Michigan (hereafter HFMGV); Fales, "Travel Tricks," 62; Advertisement, Frigikar Corporation, *Motorland,* July–August 1964, 33.

34. Lane, *Traveling,* 53–54.

35. Ibid., 59, 62–63.

36. Ibid., 72–74; "Games to Make the Miles Go!" *Better Homes and Gardens,* July 1962, 87.

37. Lane, *Traveling,* 79; Fales, "Travel Tricks"; "Baby Hammock," *Travel,* October 1961, 61. For approaches to child rearing, see Julia Grant, *Raising Baby by the Book: The Education of American Mothers* (New Haven: Yale University Press, 1998), especially chap. 7.

38. Jiri and Goody Herrmann, "Taking the Baby on Automobile Trips," *Motorland,* 1952, 9–12; Child's car seat, Object ID 89.48.2, HFMGV.

39. Lane, *Traveling,* 65; "Dee's Half Pint, the Portable Urinal for Small Boys," 89.268.1, HFMGV; New Products, *Motorland,* 1961, 14–15; "Gadgets for Folks on the Go," 128; *Parents Magazine and Better Homemaking,* 1975, 74.

40. Wayne R. Riser, "Vacationing? Take Your Dog, Too," *Better Homes and Gardens,* June 1958, 126, 128.

41. Gordon K. Clifton, *Golden Book of Automobile Stamps* (Toronto: Musson Book Company, 1952), 44–47, Coloring Books, 1894–1971, BFRC.

42. Frances W. Keene, *Travel Fun Book for Boys and Girls* (Pelham, N.Y., 1954), Coloring Books 1894–1971, Box 1, BFRC.

43. Keene, *Travel Fun Book,* 27–28.

44. Ibid., 25, 29–30.

45. Ibid., 27–28.

46. Ibid., 41–66, 73, 100–105.

47. Joyce Sozen, ed., *Travel Fun for Kids* (New York: Maco Publishing, 1966, 1967), Cotsen E20, 13668, Princeton University Library, Princeton, New Jersey.

48. *Traffic Safety Bingo* (Chicago: Regal, ca. 1960), Cotsen Toys 13666; *Zit-Zango: The Travel Game* (Davenport, Iowa: Jay and Jay Co., 1964), Cotsen Toys 13669; *Family Travel Game of State License Plates* (Tucson, Arizona: Dumas Products, after 1960), Cotsen Toys 13667; all Cotsen toys at Princeton University Library; *Traffic Sign Bingo* (New York: Norbert Specialty Corp., 1960–70), 90.13.4, HFMGV, and *Auto Bingo Card* (Chicago: Regal Mfg. Co., patented 1943), 89.115.1, HFMGV.

49. Karal Ann Marling, *The Colossus of Roads: Myth and Symbol along the American Highway* (Minneapolis: University of Minnesota Press, 1984, 1994); Catherine Gudis, *Buyways: Billboards, Automobiles, and the American Landscape* (New York: Routledge, 2004), 147–50.

50. Bill Bryson, *I'm a Stranger Here Myself: Notes on Returning to America after Twenty Years Away* (New York: Broadway Books, 1999), 135–36.

51. Ibid., 44–45.

52. Lane, *Traveling,* 6, 9, 76–78.

53. John A. Jakle and Keith A. Sculle, *Fast Food: Roadside Restaurants in the Automobile Age* (Baltimore: Johns Hopkins University Press, 1999), 50–51, 75–76.

54. John F. Love, *McDonald's: Behind the Arches* (New York: Bantam Books, 1986), 51–54; Jakle and Sculle, *Fast Food,* chap. 6, quotation from 151; Max Boas and Steve Chain, *Big Mac: The Unauthorized Story of McDonald's* (New York: E. P. Dutton and Co., Inc., 1976), 24–27.

55. John A. Jakle, Keith A. Sculle, and Jefferson S. Rogers, *The Motel in America* (Baltimore: Johns Hopkins University Press, 1996), 18–20, 56; Warren James Belasco, *Americans on the Road: From Autocamp to Motel, 1910–1945* (Baltimore: Johns Hopkins University Press, 1979).

56. American Automobile Association, *Post-War Travel Trends,* 11; James V. Malone, "Motels—A Big Opportunity for Builders," *American Builder,* February 1950, 116; "Highway Hotels and Restaurants," *Architectural Record* 114 (July 1953): 158–77.

57. "Motels Become Big Business," *Business Week,* 13 September 1952, 184.

58. Ibid., 184; "Highway Hotels," 158; Jakle et al., *Motel,* 337–38.

59. "Highway Hotels," 158; Fales, "Travel Tricks," 62.

60. Ray Vicker, "How to Travel by Motel," *Better Homes and Gardens,* July 1953, 160; "Motels Become Big Business," 188; "Hotel Pools Continue to be Popular," *Hotel Monthly* 70 (April 1962): 18.

61. "What's the Industry Situation Today?" *Hotel/Motor Hotel Monthly,* October 1962, 18; "Motel and Hotel: The Gap Narrows," *Business Week,* 11 June 1955, 102–10; "Hotels that Look Like Motels," *Business Week,* 14 March 1953, 62.

62. Kemmons Wilson, *The Holiday Inn Story* (New York: Newcomen Society in North America, 1968), 16–18, 21; Jakle et al., *Motel,* 266.

63. Wilson, *Holiday Inn,* 9; "Motels—A Big Opportunity for Builders," *American Builder,* February 1950, 116; Jakle et al., *Motel,* 263.

64. Wilson, *Holiday Inn,* 16–18, 21; Jakle et al., *Motel,* 273–76; "Special Report: On Franchise Motor Hotels," *Hotel Monthly,* July 1961, 34.

65. Peg Bracken, "Taking a Family Vacation," *Saturday Evening Post,* 13 June 1959, 25.

66. Benjamin Spock, "Can Parents and Children Share Vacation Fun?" *Ladies' Home Journal,* June 1961, 20–24; Diana Charlton Van Deusen, "Vacation for Two," *Life,* July 1960, 28.

2. Pilgrimage

1. Ralph Gray, "Vacation Tour through Lincoln Land," *National Geographic Magazine* 101 (1952): 141–84.

2. John F. Sears, *Sacred Places: American Tourist Attractions in the Nineteenth Century* (New York: Oxford University Press, 1989); John Jakle, *The Tourist: Travel in Twentieth-Century North America* (Lincoln: University of Nebraska Press, 1985), chap. 14; Marguerite S. Shaffer, *See America First: Tourism and National Identity, 1880–1940* (Washington, D.C.: Smithsonian, 2001).

3. Michael Kammen, *Mystic Chords of Memory: The Transformation of Tradition in American Culture* (New York: Knopf, 1991), 533, 539–40, 551–52. For the distinction between history and heritage, see also David Lowenthal, *Possessed by the Past: The Heritage Crusade and the Spoils of History* (New York: Free Press, 1996); John Bodnar, *Remaking America: Public Memory, Commemoration, and Patriotism in the Twentieth Century* (Princeton: Princeton University Press, 1992); Wilbur Zelinsky, *Nation into State: The Shifting Symbolic Foundations of American Nationalism* (Chapel Hill: University of North Carolina Press, 1988). The idea that civic sites were sacred is discussed in Edward T. Linenthal, *Sacred Ground: Americans and Their Battlefields* (Urbana: University of Illinois Press, 1991); David Chidester and Edward T. Linenthal, eds., *American Sacred Space* (Bloomington: Indiana University Press, 1995). For the idea of authenticity, see Dean MacCannell, *The Tourist: A New Theory of the Leisure Class* (1976; reprint, Berkeley: University of California Press, 1999), 14–15. For national identity, see Benedict Anderson, *Imagined Communities: Reflections on the Origin and Spread of Nationalism,* rev. ed. (New York: Verso, 1991), 6–7.

4. Thomas S. Bremer, *Blessed with Tourists: The Borderlands of Religion and Tourism in San Antonio* (Chapel Hill: University of North Carolina, 2004), 3–6; Scott A. Sandage, "A Marble House Divided: The Lincoln Memorial, the Civil Rights Movement and the Politics of Memory, 1939–1963," *Journal of American History* 80 (June 1993): 135–67; Linda K. Kerber, "The Meanings of Citizenship," *Journal of American History* 84 (December 1997): 833–54.

5. Susan Scholten, *The Geographical Imagination in America, 1880–1950* (Chicago: University of Chicago Press, 2001), 176, n. 10; Catherine A. Lutz and Jane L. Collins,

Reading National Geographic (Chicago: University of Chicago Press, 1993), 37–38; James R. Akerman, "American Promotional Road Mapping in the Twentieth Century," *Cartography and Geographic Information Science* 29 (July 2002): 175–91.

6. Douglas A. Yorke Jr., John Margolies, and Eric Baker, *Hitting the Road: The Art of the American Road Map* (San Francisco: Chronicle Books, 1996), 40–44, 106.

7. James R. Akerman, "Blazing a Well-Worn Path: Cartographic Commercialism, Highways Promotion, and Automobile Tourism in the United States, 1880–1930," *Cartographica* 30 (1993): 10–19.

8. Rand McNally's *Cosmopolitan Atlas* (1949) looked cleaner and allowed for more detail because the company shifted from wax production to offset lithography (Scholten, *Geographical Imagination,* 229–33); Akerman, "Blazing."

9. Yorke et al., *Hitting the Road,* 36, 41, 58, 74–75; Akerman, "American Promotional Road Mapping," 185; *Life,* 7 June 1963, R4; *Life,* 1 June 1959, 17. For Touraides and Trip-Tiks (AAA), see James R. Akerman, "Private Journeys on Public Maps: A Look at Inscribed Road Maps," *Cartographic Perspectives* 33 (winter 2000): 27–47.

10. For changes in maps, see J. S. Keates, *Understanding Maps,* 2nd ed. (Essex, England: Longman, 1996), 266. For the U.S. Geological Survey as source, see Yorke et al., *Hitting the Road,* 21. For the relationship between mapmakers and states, see Folder "Rand McNally Co. (Maps)—Misc. Corres.," Box 26, State Department of Publicity and Industrial Development, Series 1138, Utah State Archives and Records Service, Salt Lake City, Utah.

11. Yorke et al., *Hitting the Road,* 102–3, 114, 116; Colorado, Wyoming (Texaco, 1977); *Wyoming Highway Map* (State Highway Department, 1949), Rand McNally Collection, Newberry Library, Chicago (hereafter RMC).

12. Yorke et al., *Hitting the Road,* 117–19; *How Important Are Free Road Maps to Your Customers and Service Station Operators?* (Rand McNally, ca. 1972–73); RMC 1950–74, 4A Stacks.

13. Elmer Jenkins, ed., *Guide to America* (Washington, D.C.: Public Affairs Press, 1947–48). For histories of the American Automobile Association, see Bellamy Partridge, *Fill 'er Up! The Story of Fifty Years of Motoring* (New York: McGraw-Hill, 1952); J. Allen Davis, *The Friend to All Motorists: The Story of the Automobile Club of Southern California through 65 Years, 1900–1965* (Los Angeles: Automobile Club of Southern California, 1967); Richard R. Mathison, *Three Cars in Every Garage: A Motorist's History of the Automobile and the Automobile Club in Southern California* (Garden City, N.Y.: Doubleday & Co., 1968); and Kathy Talley-Jones, Letitia Burns O'Connor, and Dana Levy, *The Road Ahead: The Automobile Club of Southern California, 1900–2000* (Los Angeles: Automobile Club of Southern California, 2000).

14. Susan Sessions Rugh, "Branding Utah: Industrial Tourism in the Postwar American West," *Western Historical Quarterly* 37 (Winter 2006): 445–72; Akerman, "American Promotional Road Mapping," 186–87.

15. Akerman, "American Promotional Road Mapping," 184; Yorke et al., *Hitting the Road,* 100; *Washington D.C. Street Map,* Cities Service (1964), RMC.

16. *Chicago Highway Map* (Standard Oil Co., 1952), *Missouri Tourguide Map* (Gulf Oil, 1954), Gulf Oil Company, Box 1950–1957, RMC.

17. *Delaware, Maryland, Virginia, West Virginia Tourguide Map* (Gulf Oil, 1949); *Idaho, Utah* (Texaco, 1942), RMC. See also Susan V. Spellman, "All the Comforts of Home: The Domestication of the Service Station Industry, 1920–1940," *Journal of Popular Culture* 37, no. 3 (2004): 463–77; Shelly M. Park, "From Sanitation to Liberation: The Modern and Postmodern Marketing of Menstrual Products," *Journal of Popular Culture* 30 (1996): 149–68; see also Sharra V. Vostral, "Masking Menstruation: The Emergence of Menstrual Hygiene Products in the United States," in *Menstruation: A Cultural History*, ed. Andrew Shail and Gillian Howie (New York: Palgrave Macmillan, 2005), 243–58.

18. *Rand McNally Vacation Guide* (1953), 5, 14, 22; *Rand McNally Vacation Guide* (ca. 1955); *Rand McNally Vacation Guide* (ca. 1958); *Rand McNally Vacation Guide* (ca. 1963); Richard Dunlop, *Rand McNally Vacation Guide* (1966), RMC.

19. *Rand McNally Vacation Guide* (1953); *Texaco Travel Atlas, by Rand McNally: U.S., Canada, Mexico* (1970), RMC. Rand McNally organized the atlas into regional sections, each identified by a symbol and preceded by a description of regional character. For example, the Midwest was represented by stalks of corn and a cow under the Gateway Arch, the Liberty Bell symbolized the Northeast, palm trees and a rocket symbolized the South, a surfer stood for the Pacific Coast, and fish and pineapple were used for the New Frontier region of Alaska and Hawaii.

20. *State Farm Road Atlas: U.S., Mexico, Canada* (Rand McNally, 1960), RMC.

21. Akerman, "American Promotional Road Mapping," 184; *Metropolitan Atlanta Tourguide Map* (Gulf Oil, 1955); *Metropolitan Atlanta Tourguide Map* (Gulf Oil, 1966); *Rand McNally Vacation Guide* (1984), 15, RMC.

22. *Rand McNally Road Atlas, U.S., Canada, Mexico* (1957); *Long Beach and Metropolitan Los Angeles* (Texaco, 1956); *Rand McNally Texaco Travel Atlas: U.S., Canada, Mexico* (1970), 44, RMC.

23. *Life*, 8 June 1959, 88.

24. *Souvenir Map and Folder of the Civil War Centennial*, 1961, Map Collection, Harold B. Lee Library, Brigham Young University, Provo, Utah.

25. *Rand McNally Road Atlas* (1975); *Official Transportation Map, 1975–76, Massachusetts*, RMC.

26. *Region 1: Maine, New Hampshire, New York, Vermont, Maritime Provinces, Ontario, Quebec: Heritage Roads, McDonald's* (1974), Rand McNally 4A, McDonald's.

27. *Texaco Travel Atlas* (1970), 34; advertisement, *Better Homes and Gardens*, June 1959, 113.

28. Pennsylvania Department of Commerce, *Pennsylvania Pictorial and Historical Map* (1947), RMC.

29. *Texaco Travel Atlas* (1970), 97, RMC. Alex Haley, *Roots* (New York: Doubleday, 1976); Charles Hobson and Chris Tomassini, "Television," in *Encyclopedia of African-American Culture and History*, ed. Colin Palmer, 2nd ed. (Detroit: Macmillan Reference USA, 2006), 5:2168–79, in Thomson Gale, *Gale Virtual Reference Library*.

30. Bremer, *Blessed*, 3–6.

31. Gray, "Vacation Tour," 143.

32. Ibid., 144, 157.

33. Ibid., 158–59.

34. Ibid., 164; State of Illinois, Division of Parks and Memorials, *The Home of Abraham Lincoln,* Springfield, Illinois, Trav Vert 4104.S5 1957; and Department of Conservation, State of Illinois, *The Lincoln Tomb,* Trav Vert 4104.S5 196–, both Newberry Library.

35. Interview with Ann Whiting Orton, 19 July 2006, Salt Lake City, Utah.

36. Interview, Orton; Cornhusker State painted tin coaster; Empire State Building Observatory, *The Empire State* (ca. 1954), USA; Uberman Novelty Co., *Natural Color Picto-Chrome Pocket GuideBook, Washington, D.C.* (Washington, D.C., 195–), all in the author's collection.

37. *Texaco Travel Atlas* (1970), 78. The idea of Washington as a pilgrimage site for tourists has roots in the early twentieth century; see Carl Abbott, *Political Terrain: Washington, D.C., from Tidewater Town to Global Metropolis* (Chapel Hill: University of North Carolina Press, 1999), 115–19.

38. *Life,* 26 April 1948, 115.

39. Lewis J. Nesterman, *Washington Handy Guide* (Washington, D.C., ca. 1942), Stacks 3, Aisle 31, RMC.

40. D.C. Transit System, *Sightseeing in Washington D.C. and Vicinity,* Washington, D.C., Travel Vertical File 3850 1964m, Newberry Library.

41. Bodnar, *Remaking America,* 194–96; National Park Service, *Annual Report of the Commissioner,* 1962, 114, Box 71; *Annual Report,* 1963, 120, Box 74, both Appendix 7a, Administrative Files, National Park Service Collection, RG 79, NARA.

42. *Annual Report of the Director, National Park Service to the Secretary of the Interior,* 1958, 315; *Annual Report,* 1959, 363–64; *Annual Report,* 1960, 303; *Annual Report of the Commissioner, National Park Service, to the Secretary of the Interior,* 1961, 384, Box 71; *Annual Report, National Capital Region, for the Fiscal Year 1964,* 18, Box 71; "Highlight Briefing Statement, Central National Parks, 1965," 2–3, A2623 WASO, Part 4, Box 106, all Appendix 7a, Administrative Files, RG 79, NPS.

43. *Esso Washington, DC, and Vicinity Pictorial Guide,* G3850 1949.G4; Rand McNally, *1945 State Farm Road Atlas, United States, Canada, Mexico,* 112; *Rand McNally Special Road Atlas* (1952), 116; *Washington, DC, Map and Visitor's Guide, Esso* 3850 1963.G4; Cities Service, *Washington D.C. Street Map,* 3850 1964.G6; CITGO, *Washington DC* G3850 1972.G6, all RMC.

44. Marjorie Holmes, "This Is Your Year for Washington," *Better Homes and Gardens,* May 1955, 68.

45. Ibid., 155; Lonnelle Aikman, "U.S. Capitol, Citadel to Democracy," *National Geographic Magazine* 102, no. 2 (1952): 143–92. In 1947, over 8,000 persons a day visited the Capitol; Albert W. Atwood, "Washington, Home of the Nation's Great," *National Geographic Magazine* 91, no. 6 (June 1947): 699–738. William Graves, "Washington, the City Freedom Built," *National Geographic Magazine* 126 (December 1964): 735–81, states that more than a million visitors come to the city in the summer months (741), and that 8 million had visited President John F. Kennedy's grave since his burial in November 1963 (771). For the attack in Congress, see Clayton Knowles, "Five Congressmen Shot in House by 3 Puerto Rican Nationalists: Bullets Spray from Gallery; Capitol in Uproar,"

New York Times, 2 March 1954, available at http://www.proquest.com/ (accessed 11 January 2007).

46. Holmes, "This Is Your Year."

47. Corwin Family Photograph Collection, copy in possession of author; interview with Andrea Corwin Weitzman, 6 August 2007. For a history of the Zero Milestone erected in 1919, see http://www.fhwa.dot.gov/infrastructure/zero.htm (accessed 29 May 2007).

48. "May 13, 1956," 2–4, Box 1, June Calendar Collection, 89-M55, Schlesinger Library, Radcliffe Institute, Harvard University, Cambridge, Massachusetts.

49. National Park Service, "U.S.M.C. War Memorial," http://www.nps.gov/archive/gwmp/usmc.htm (accessed 5 November 2007).

50. Calendar, 6–7, 3.

51. When a Bronx man solicited information from the Washington, D.C., Greater National Capital Committee for a place to stay, he received letters from three separate tourist homes, all marked "White Clientele Only." In his letter to the NAACP, he identified himself as white and Jewish; he wrote a six-page letter of moral outrage and proposed solutions to the problem of segregation in the nation's capital. See Richard A. Harrow to NAACP, 29 March 1960 (NAACP III A Box 111).

3. Vacation without Humiliation

1. U.S. Senate, *Hearings before the Committee on Commerce,* 88th Congress, First Session on S. 1732, Title II, Part 1, Serial 26 (Washington, D.C., 1963), 656–57. See Charles W. and Barbara Whalen, *The Longest Debate: A Legislative History of the Civil Rights Act of 1964* (Washington, D.C.: Seven Locks Press, 1985); Jack Greenberg, *Crusaders in the Courts: How a Dedicated Band of Lawyers Fought for the Civil Rights Revolution* (New York: Basic Books, 1994).

2. U.S. Senate, *Hearings,* 257–58; "Discrimination in Hotels: Cause for Crisis?" *Hotel Monthly* 70 (May 1962): 28.

3. Martin Luther King Jr., "Letter from a Birmingham Jail," in *I Have a Dream: Writings and Speeches that Changed the World,* ed. James Melvin Washington (San Francisco: HarperCollins, 1986, 1992), 88. For the importance of car ownership to avoiding discrimination, see Kathleen Franz, "The Open Road: Automobility and Racial Uplift in the Inter-War Years," in *Technology and the African-American Experience: Needs and Opportunities for Study,* ed. Bruce Sinclair (Cambridge, Mass.: MIT Press, 2004), 131–53; Cotton Seiler, "'So That We as a Race Might Have Something Authentic to Travel By': African American Automobility and Cold-War Liberalism," *American Quarterly* 58 (December 2006): 1091–117. Auto travel during Jim Crow is recalled in William H. Chafe, Raymond Gavins, Robert Korstad, et al., *Remembering Jim Crow: African Americans Tell about Life in the Segregated South* (New York: The New Press, 2001), 130–31, 293–96.

4. The concept of citizen consumers is laid out in Lizabeth Cohen, *A Consumers' Republic: The Politics of Mass Consumption in Postwar America* (New York: Knopf, 2003). For the aspect of fear, see John Williams, *This Is My Country, Too* (New York: New American Library, 1966); Maya Angelou, *The Heart of a Woman* (New York: Bantam Books, 1981),

23–28. For historical studies of travel segregation before the postwar period, see Mark S. Foster, "In the Face of 'Jim Crow': Prosperous Blacks and Vacations, Travel and Outdoor Leisure, 1890–1945," *Journal of Negro History* 84, no. 2 (1999): 130–49; Emma Lou Thornbrough, "Breaking Racial Barriers to Public Accommodations in Indiana, 1935 to 1963," *Indiana Magazine of History* 83 (December 1987): 419–61. Marguerite S. Shaffer, *See America First: Tourism and National Identity, 1880–1940* (Washington, D.C.: Smithsonian Institution, 2001), does not examine the black experience; and Cindy S. Aron, *Working at Play: A History of Vacations in the United States* (New York: Oxford University Press, 1999), discusses African American tourists only briefly, probably because the scope of both books does not include postwar America. For color blindness, see Grace Elizabeth Hale, *Making Whiteness: The Culture of Segregation in the South, 1890–1940* (New York: Pantheon Books, 1998), 281. For the changing meanings of race in this period, see Gary Gerstle, *American Crucible: Race and Nation in the Twentieth Century* (Princeton: Princeton University Press, 2001).

5. U.S. Senate, *Hearings,* 657. For the black middle class, see Robert E. Weems, *Desegregating the Dollar: African-American Consumerism in the Twentieth Century* (New York: New York University Press, 1998); Bart Landry, *The New Black Middle Class* (Berkeley: University of California Press, 1987); Andrew Wiese, *Places of Their Own: African American Suburbanization in the Twentieth Century* (Chicago: University of Chicago Press, 2004). For contemporary awareness of black consumer spending, see "14 Million Negro Customers," *Management Review,* June 1947, 336–38; "Negro Market Highlights in Three Cities: Weekly Earnings of Negro Families, 1945," *Sales Management* 58 (20 May 1947): 20.

6. John Easterling, Denver, to NAACP, New York City, July 15, 1962, Box 110, Part III, Series A, Papers of the NAACP, Manuscript Division, Library of Congress, Washington, D.C. (hereafter NAACP).

7. For the history of the NAACP, consult Manfred Berg, *The Ticket to Freedom: The NAACP and the Struggle for Black Political Integration* (Gainesville: University Press of Florida, 2005); Gilbert Jonas, *Freedom's Sword: The NAACP and the Struggle against Racism in America* (New York: Routledge, 2005). The strength of the membership can be found in Berg, "Black Civil Rights and Liberal Anticommunism: The NAACP in the Early Cold War," *Journal of American History* 94 (June 2007): 75–96.

8. Vance H. Marchbanks, Tuskegee Institute, Alabama, 17 June 1941, to Union Oil Co. of California, NAACP II B 62.

9. James Smith, Bridgeport, Connecticut, 16 July 1962, to Ella L. Anderson, NAACP III A 110.

10. John A. Jakle, *The Gas Station in America* (Baltimore: Johns Hopkins University Press, 1994); Annie Hayes, 30 January 1948, to NAACP; Franklin H. Williams to Annie Hayes, 4 February 1948, NAACP II B 63.

11. W. N. Farlie to John A. Morsell, 22 October 1962, NAACP III A, Box 110; F. A. Watts to H. Boyd Hall, 28 September 1948, and H. Boyd Hall to Roy Wilkins, 29 September 1948, NAACP II B 185. By distributing their products through a franchisee, oil companies could avoid claims of liability on the grounds that they had not directly entered into a contract with their customers; see Sally H. Clarke, "Unmanageable Risks: *McPherson*

v. Buick and the Emergence of a Mass Consumer Market," *Law and History Review* 23 (spring 2005): 1–52. I thank Barbara Y. Welke for making this parallel known to me.

12. Jewell L. Gresham to Warren Drew, 5 January 1960, NAACP III A 110. Gresham, a graduate of Tuskegee Institute, earned a master's degree in English drama and a doctorate in education at Columbia University, and taught at Nassau Community College, New York University, Hofstra University, and Vassar College. She was active in the civil rights movement, and she later wrote to counter the negative images of the black family in the media by coediting a special issue of the *Nation,* "Scapegoating the Black Family," in 1989. See Connie Aitcheson, "Author and Literary Executrix, Jewell Handy Gresham Nemiroff, Passes at 82," *New York Amsterdam News,* 18–24 August 2005, accessed via *ProQuest Newsstand;* Jewell Handy Gresham and Margaret B. Wilkerson, "The Burden of History," *Nation,* 24/31 July 1989, 115–22.

13. Bessye Brown to NAACP, 10 September 1945; "Memorandum to Mr. Williams from Gloria Samuels," 17 August 1948; and Mildred W. Farrar to the NAACP Office, 25 September 1947, all NAACP II B 61; L. H. Holman to J. O. Young, 3 November 1961, NAACP III A 110.

14. James Monroe to Gloster Current, 29 October 1949, NAACP II B 185; Linwood G. Koger Jr. to Constance Baker Motley, 5 October 1962, NAACP III A 109.

15. Bessye Brown to NAACP, 10 September 1945, NAACP II B 61.

16. Shirley H. Day to NAACP, 5 June 1947, NAACP II B 61.

17. The *Green Book* had several names during its publication. See *The Negro Motorist Green Book* (New York: Victor H. Green & Co., 1949), 1; *The Negro Travelers' Green Book* (New York: Victor H. Green & Co., 1956), 3, 5–6.

18. *Green Book* (1956), 9–12, 29, 31, 38–41, 43, 55–56, 63, 44; *Green Book* (1953) featured Louisville, 24–29. I have not been able to locate any "Jewish travel guides" before 1947, so the reference is unclear to me.

19. The final publication date is a matter of speculation; the Library of Congress owns only the 1952–1955 editions. For its debut, see W. H. Butler to Bobbie Branche, 9 December 1948, NAACP II A 598.

20. Travelguide, Inc., *Travelguide* (New York, 1952).

21. Jack Greenberg to Jawn A. Sandifer, 17 August 1950, NAACP II B 184.

22. Admiral Tours advertised in *Travelguide* (1954), 121; King Travel in *Travelguide* (1955), 73; and Travelguide operated its own club (*Travelguide,* 1954, 120). Edwin B. Henderson, "Mexican Vacation," *Afro Magazine* section, 26 April 1955, E. B. Henderson Papers, Box 44, Manuscript Department, Moorland-Spingarn Research Center, Howard University, Washington, D.C.

23. *The Amos and Andy Show,* CBS, 1953, Museum of Television and Radio, Los Angeles, California, T76:0035, 170129; Walter White to Parker Collins, 15 June 1953, NAACP II A 598. See Donald Bogle, *African Americans on Network Television* (New York: Farrar, Straus and Giroux, 2001), 27–41.

24. George Lipsitz, *Time Passages: Collective Memory and American Popular Culture* (Minneapolis: University of Minnesota Press, 1990), 63–67.

25. U.S. Senate, *Hearings,* 584–95.

26. U.S. Senate, *Hearings,* 609–11; Martha Hodes, *Black Women, White Men: Illicit Sex in the Nineteenth-Century South* (New Haven: Yale University Press, 1997).

27. U.S. Senate, *Hearings,* 609–11. For a history of racial segregation in public pools, see Jeff Wiltse, *Contested Waters: A Social History of Swimming Pools in America* (Chapel Hill: University of North Carolina, 2007).

28. "Discrimination in Hotels," 28. Swimming pools and beaches were a flashpoint in the struggle to desegregate places of leisure; see Victoria W. Wolcott, "Recreation and Race in the Postwar City: Buffalo's 1956 Crystal Beach Riot," *Journal of American History* 93 (June 2006): 63–90.

29. Henry Lee Moon to Mr. Andrew F. Jackson, 23 March 1953, NAACP II A 598.

30. Nationwide Hotel Association, *NHA Directory and Guide to Travel* (1959), Schomberg Center for Research in Black Culture, New York City, New York; *The Travelers' Green Book* (New York: Victor H. Green & Co., 1961), 4.

31. *Travelers' Green Book* (1963), 2–4, 100.

32. Thurgood Marshall to Theodore Diamond, 22 September 1948, and George L.-P. Weaver to Carl Rachlin, 21 September 1948, NAACP II B Box 62; "Memorandum to Mr. Jones from Marian Wynn Perry," 26 September 1947, NAACP II B 61; Roy Wilkins to John C. Warner, 9 February 1956; John A. Morsell to Henry A. Stone Jr., 16 October 1956, NAACP III A 109; Ken Peterson to Roy Wilkins, 15 February 1957, NAACP III A 109. For the local context of the actions in New York, see Martha Biondi, *To Stand and Fight: The Struggle for Civil Rights in Postwar New York City* (Cambridge, Mass.: Harvard University Press, 2003).

33. Thurgood Marshall to Howard Johnson's Restaurants, 7 February 1947; E. Durgin, Howard D. Johnson Co. to Mr. Thurgood Marshall, 8 April 1947; L. Leroy Jordan, Elizabeth, New York, to Mr. Weinberg, Weinberger & Ullman, New York, 26 June 1947; Andrew Weinberger to J. Leroy Jordan, 30 June 1947; and J. Leroy Jordan to Thurgood Marshall, 8 October 1947, with notice of trial, NAACP II B 64.

34. James Clair Taylor to Legal Department, NAACP, 22 August 1947, NAACP II B 64.

35. F. Weldon Younger, St. Louis, to "To Whom It May Concern," 9 September 1960, NAACP II A 110.

36. James Farmer to Roy Wilkins, 20 June 1962; "A Call for Volunteers for Freedom Highways"; "56 Southern Howard Johnsons Open Since CORE Announces Freedom Highways"; and Roy Wilkins to James Farmer, 27 June 1962, all NAACP III A 110.

37. "Discrimination in Hotels," 28–32.

38. NAACP, *NAACP 53rd Annual Convention Resolutions, July 2–July 8, 1962,* Atlanta, Georgia, and "53rd Annual Convention NAACP Digest," 8, NAACP III A 14; Kevin M. Kruse, *White Flight: Atlanta and the Making of Modern Conservatism* (Princeton: Princeton University Press, 2005), 207–10.

39. Press release, 20 August 1962, New York State Conference NAACP; Eugene T. Reed to Hilton Hotels, Inc., 22 August 1962; Memorandum to Mr. Maria Marcus from Robert L. Carter, 31 August 1962; "Human Rights Commission against Hilton Corporation," 10 September 1962; Frank G. Wangeman to Nelson A. Rockefeller, 10 September 1962; Robert J. Caverly to George Fowler, 1 November 1962, all NAACP III A 14. The

New York NAACP requested a national ban on Hilton patronage in "Report on the Hilton Hotel Situation," 13 November 1962, NAACP III A 14.

40. Clyde J. Harris to Kivie Kaplan, 26 November 1962; Moreton Rolleston Jr. to "Dear Customer," 19 June 1962; "Atlanta's Hilton Inn Now Accepting Negro Guests," 25 May 1963; Millicent Smith to Roy Wilkins, 1 May 1963, all NAACP III A 109.

41. U.S. Senate, *Hearings,* 659.

42. Kennedy's call for democracy at home resulted in part from the embarrassment of African diplomats being refused service along Maryland's Route 40 nearby; see Mary L. Dudziak, *Cold War Civil Rights: Race and the Image of American Democracy* (Princeton: Princeton University Press, 2000), 167–69, 179–80.

43. Robert A. Caro, *The Years of Lyndon Johnson: Master of the Senate* (New York: Vintage Books, 2003), 888–90.

44. U.S. House of Representatives, *Hearings before Subcommittee No. 5 of the Committee on the Judiciary, House of Representatives, 88th Congress,* First Session, Serial No. 4, Part III (Washington, D.C., 1963), 624, 628.

45. Ibid., 691–95.

46. Kruse, *White Flight,* 219–24.

4. Western Adventure

1. Lynn Spigel, *Make Room for TV: Television and the Family Ideal in Postwar America* (Chicago: University of Chicago Press, 1992), 1; Richard Slotkin, *Gunfighter Nation: The Myth of the Frontier in Twentieth-Century America* (New York: Atheneum, 1992), 6; Jane Tompkins, *West of Everything: The Inner Life of Westerns* (New York: Oxford University Press, 1992), 4–7; Ralph Brauer with Donna Brauer, *The Horse, the Gun and the Piece of Property: Changing Images of the TV Western* (Bowling Green, Ohio: Bowling Green University Popular Press, 1975).

2. J. Fred MacDonald, *Who Shot the Sheriff? The Rise and Fall of the Television Western* (New York: Praeger, 1987), 17; Neal Gabler, *Walt Disney: The Triumph of the American Imagination* (New York: Knopf, 2006), 515.

3. Outdoor Recreation Resources Review Commission, *National Recreation Survey* (Washington, D.C., 1962), 46; Gallup Poll [computer file], *Public Opinion, 1935–1997* (Wilmington, Delaware, 2000), 1953: 1166 and 1963: 1821; "Motor Travel Trends Tabulated," *Motorland,* August 1945, 14–15; see also Kent Ruth, *How to Enjoy Your Western Vacations* (Norman: University of Oklahoma Press, 1956). For studies of travel to the twentieth-century West, see the still useful Earl Pomeroy, *In Search of the Golden West: The Tourist in Western America* (New York: Knopf, 1957); Hal K. Rothman, *Devil's Bargains: Tourism in the Twentieth Century American West* (Lawrence: University Press of Kansas, 1998); Marguerite S. Shaffer, *See America First: Tourism and National Identity, 1880–1940* (Washington, D.C.: Smithsonian Institution Press, 2001); David M. Wrobel and Patrick T. Long, *Seeing and Being Seen: Tourism in the American West* (Lawrence: University Press of Kansas, 2001).

4. Scholarly analysis of the mythology of the frontier West is widespread, but notable books include Patricia Nelson Limerick, *The Legacy of Conquest: The Unbroken Past of*

the American West (New York: Norton, 1987); William Cronon, George Miles, and Jay Gitlin, *Under an Open Sky: Rethinking America's Western Past* (New York: Norton, 1992). David M. Wrobel, *Promised Lands: Promotion, Memory, and the Creation of the American West* (Lawrence: University Press of Kansas, 2002), argues that the frontier myth powered promotion of the West long after its settlement period. The most succinct source on the uses of western myth in the twentieth century is Robert G. Athearn, *The Mythic West* (Lawrence: University Press of Kansas, 1986), but see also the more recent Michael L. Johnson, *Hunger for the Wild: America's Obsession with the Untamed West* (Lawrence: University Press of Kansas, 2007).

5. Scholarly treatment of western stars includes J. Fred MacDonald, Richard W. Etulain, and Glenda Riley, *The Hollywood West: Lives of Film Legends Who Shaped It* (Golden, Colo.: Fulcrum Publishing, 2001); Gary A. Yoggy, *Riding the Video Range: The Rise and Fall of the Western on Television* (Jefferson, N.C.: McFarland & Company, 1995); and Edward Buscombe and Roberta E. Pearson, eds., *Back in the Saddle Again: New Essays on the Western* (London: British Film Institute Publishing, 1998).

6. Dwight Whitney, "The Inside Story of Hopalong Cassidy," *Coronet,* December 1950, 87, 92–93; "*Life* Goes on Tour with Hopalong Cassidy," *Life,* 12 September 1949, 151.

7. Whitney, "Inside Story," 89; Dan Fowler, "Public Hero No. 1, Hopalong Cassidy," *Look,* 29 August 1950, 80; "Manners and Morals: Kiddies in the Old Corral," *Time,* 27 November 1950, 18.

8. Whitney, "Inside Story," 87; *Pageant Magazine,* September 1950, 82–90; "Hopalong Cassidy and the Square Dance Holdup starring William Boyd with 'California' and 'Lucky,'" Capitol Records, 1950, Autry 99.14.1.

9. Holly George-Warren, *Public Cowboy No. 1: The Life and Times of Gene Autry* (New York: Oxford University Press, 2007), 256; Gene Autry with Mickey Herskowitz, *Back in the Saddle Again* (New York: Doubleday, 1978).

10. George-Warren, *Public Cowboy,* 276–77, 288; for the sales figures, see Gene Autry and the Twentieth-Century West: The Centennial Exhibition, 1907–2007, Autry National Center, Los Angeles, viewed 9 August 2007. For the settlements and Autry's liability, see Bill Martin to Mitchell J. Hamilburg, 5 October 1951, Folder M. A. Henry Co., New York, Box 1 T-94-45-30, Gene Autry Archives, Los Angeles, California.

11. "Golden Girl," *TV Radio Mirror* 47, no. 2 (January 1957): 38, Scrapbook, Flying "A" Productions, Autry T87-36-2764; Gail Davis, "Biography," Autry T87-36-2765.

12. Doris Schroeder, *Annie Oakley in Double Trouble* (Racine, Wisc.: Whitman Publishing Co., 1958), 10, Autry 88.202.15.; Charles Spain Verral, *Annie Oakley, Sharpshooter* (New York: Simon and Schuster, 1956), 88.188.23; drawings by Lois Liets, *Annie Oakley Roundup Coloring Book, with Lofty and Tagg* (Racine, Wisc.: Whitman Publishing Co., 1955).

13. "Golden Girl."

14. "Biography," 5; "Golden Girl"; *Casper Tribune Herald,* 17 August 1956; *Toronto Daily Star,* 1 September 1956; *Omaha World Herald,* 28 September 1956; all in Scrapbook. For her relationship with Autry, see George-Warren, *Public Cowboy,* 262.

15. Autry Commercial Inventory, 1956, T87-36-5049.

16. Shaffer, *See America First*; Alfred Runte, "Promoting the Golden West: Advertising and the Railroad," *California History* 70, no. 1 (spring 1991): 62–75; Susan Sessions Rugh, "Branding Utah: Industrial Tourism in the Postwar American West," *Western Historical Quarterly* 37 (Winter 2006): 445–72.

17. Jerome L. Rodnitzky, "Recapturing the West: The Dude Ranch in American Life," *Arizona and the West* 10 (1968): 111–26; Lawrence R. Borne, "Western Railroads and the Dude Ranching Industry," *Pacific Historian* 30 (1986): 47–59.

18. Colorado Dude and Guest Ranch Association, "Dude Data," Newberry Trav Vert 4310 1962.

19. Ibid.

20. CDGRA, "For a Real Vacation Come to a Colorado Dude Ranch This Year" (1953), Autry 96.33.4; Lawrence R. Borne, "Dude Ranching in the Rockies," *Montana: The Magazine of Western History* 39, no. 3 (1988): 14–27; Julie Tatham, *Cherry Ames: Dude Ranch Nurse* (New York: Grosset & Dunlap, 1953), Autry 96.59.1.

21. Borne, "Western Railroads," 57–58.

22. Rugh, "Branding Utah"; Robert Crossley, "Where the West Is Wild, But Not Too Woolly," *Better Homes and Gardens,* July 1951, 54; *Westways,* April 1950, 39; *Westways,* April 1953, 30; *Westways,* April 1962, 29.

23. Frontier lands had long been a part of amusement parks; see Jim Futrell, *Amusement Parks of New York* (Mechanicsburg, Pa.: Stackpole Books, 2006); and for the first of America's major amusement parks, see John F. Kasson, *Amusing the Million: Coney Island at the Turn of the Century* (New York: Hill & Wang, 1978).

24. Howard Kegley, "Ghost Town Comes to Life," *National Motorist,* August–September 1945, 4, Box 8, Maymie Richardson Krythe Scrapbook Collection, Seaver Center for Western History Research, Natural History Museum of Los Angeles County.

25. Ibid., 8; "Knott's Berry Farm—Buena Park, California," 17 [n.d.], souvenir guidebook in author's possession. For the popularity of Gold Rush travel, see Sunset Books, *Gold Rush Country: Guide to California's Mother Lode and Northern Mines* (Menlo Park, Calif.: Lane Publishing Co., 1957).

26. Admission ticket, Ghost Town & Calico Railway, Autry 2000.38.1 & 2.

27. Susan Lee Johnson, *Roaring Camp: The Social World of the California Gold Rush* (New York: Norton, 2000).

28. Cecilia Rasmussen, "Hoppyland—the Time the Good Guy Lost," *Los Angeles Times,* 30 October 1995, B3.

29. William J. Ehrheart, "The World's Most Famous Movie Ranch: The Story of Ray 'Crash' Corrigan and Corriganville," *Ventura County Historical Society Quarterly* 43, nos. 1–2 (1999): 3–39; Corriganville Ranch Souvenir Program, Autry 89.143.1.

30. Ehrheart, "World's Most Famous," 23.

31. Ibid., 23–26.

32. *Dell Comic* 1, no. 117 (March 1958), Autry 88.381.58; Ehrheart, "World's Most Famous," 27–30.

33. Karal Ann Marling, "Imagineering the Disney Theme Parks," in *Designing Disney's Theme Parks: The Architecture of Reassurance,* ed. Karal Ann Marling (New York:

Flammarion, 1997), 29–178. Also germane is Erika Doss, "Making Imagination Safe in the 1950s: Disneyland's Art and Architecture," in Marling, *Designing Disney's Theme Parks,* 179–89, but Fantasyland is beyond the scope of this study. See also the provocative essay by Michael Steiner, "Frontierland as Tomorrowland: Walt Disney and the Architectural Packaging of the Mythic West," *Montana* 48, no. 1 (1998): 2–17.

34. "The Disneyland Story," *Vacationland,* winter/spring 1965, 3, Anaheim Public Library, Anaheim, California; Gabler, *Walt Disney,* 479, 481, 496; Karal Ann Marling, *As Seen on TV: The Visual Culture of Everyday Life in the 1950s* (Cambridge, Mass.: Harvard University Press, 1994), 122–25.

35. Gabler, *Walt Disney,* 514–16; "'Sixty Million Viewers Can't Be Wrong': The Rise and Fall of the Television Western," in Buscombe and Pearson, eds., *Back in the Saddle Again,* 119–49.

36. *Disneyland: A Complete Guide,* Disneyland, Inc., 1956 (Autry 94.202–40).

37. "Disneyland's Pack Mules," "E" Ticket, fall 2005, 20–31; Leo Litwak, "A Fantasy that Paid Off," *Vacationland,* summer 1966, 11–18.

38. "Where the West Is Still Wilderness," *Vacationland,* spring 1962, 14.

39. Ibid.

40. "Spectacular," *Vacationland,* summer 1963, 3; "Disneyland's Indians, a Unique Show at the Park," *Disney News,* spring 1967, 6.

41. "Frontier Gunfighters Are Even More Rugged Off the Screen," *Disney News,* spring 1967, 7; *Vacationland,* fall 1958.

42. *Disneyland: A Complete Guide,* Disneyland, Inc., 1956 (Autry 94.202–40).

43. "Services at Disneyland," *Vacationland,* spring 1959, 20; "Disneyland's Nomadic Children," *Disney News,* winter 1969–1970, 8; *Vacationland,* fall 1962, 13; *Disneyland: A Complete Guide,* Disneyland, Inc., 1956 (Autry 94.202–40).

44. Gabler, *Walt Disney,* 537; *Vacationland,* winter/spring 1965, 3.

45. Gabler, *Walt Disney,* 564; Litwak, "A Fantasy that Paid Off," 18.

46. "Shopping along Main Street," *Vacationland,* fall 1958, 13; "A Shutterbug's Paradise," *Vacationland,* fall 1964, 10.

47. *Walt Disney Treasures, Disneyland USA* (DVD) (1962); "Fun for Everyone," *Vacationland,* spring 1959, 1; "Heads of State Just Can't Wait!" *Vacationland,* spring 1961, 14–15; "Dateline Disneyland," *Vacationland,* summer 1962, 19.

48. Disneyland postcard, To Mr. and Mrs. F. Denning, 9228 Sorrento, Detroit 4, Michigan, 11 July 1957; Disneyland postcard, from Wes, to Mrs. John A. Miller, Roscoe, New York, May 1958; Disneyland postcard, from Linda to Mrs. Ann Rowe, 1719 W. Bijou, Colorado Springs, Colorado, 9 July 1968 postmark, all in author's possession.

49. James Liston, "The Land that Does Away with Time," *Better Homes and Gardens,* February 1956, 62; Marling, *As Seen on TV,* 119.

50. Marion Wylie, "Disneyland," *Vacationland,* fall 1966, 2–4. Reprinted from the April 1966 edition of *Good Housekeeping Magazine.*

51. Ibid.

52. "Disneyland Story," 3; "Blast Off!" *Vacationland,* Spring 1961, 13; Gabler, *Walt Disney,* 517; Marling, *As Seen on TV,* 122–23.

53. "Jungle Cruise," *Vacationland,* fall 1962, 2; Litwak, "A Fantasy that Paid Off," 15; Eric Avila, "Popular Culture in the Age of White Flight: Film Noir, Disneyland and the Cold War (Sub)Urban Imaginary," *Journal of Urban History* 31, no. 1 (November 2004): 3–22.

54. Litwak, "A Fantasy that Paid Off," 15; Gabler, *Walt Disney,* 528; "Disneyland Visitors—VIPs All," *Vacationland,* fall 1963, 21. Michael Steiner, in "Frontierland as Tomorrowland," argues that its Mexican restaurant and Aunt Jemima's kitchen displayed Disneyland's cultural diversity in the 1950s.

55. "Spectacular," *Vacationland,* summer 1963, 3; "Dixie on the River," *Vacationland,* summer 1964, 2.

56. "Disneyland after Dark," *Vacationland,* summer 1964, 11; Kirse Granat May, *Golden State, Golden Youth: The California Image in Popular Culture, 1955–1966* (Chapel Hill: University of North Carolina Press, 2002), 43.

57. William Murray, "They Told You Hollywood was Dead? Ha!" *New York Times,* 8 August 1971, *ProQuest Historical Newspapers: The New York Times* (1851–2003) (accessed 11 August 2007); "Show Biz—Southern California," *Motorland,* January/February 1966, 4–9; Universal City Studios, *Visit the World's Largest Movie Studio* (1966), Rand McNally Collection, Newberry Library, 4364.U9 1966. Southern California as a tourist destination is beyond the scope of this study; see Susan G. Davis, "Landscapes of Imagination: Tourism in Southern California," *Pacific Historical Review* 68 (May 1999): 173–92, *Spectacular Nature: Corporate Culture and the Sea World Experience* (Berkeley: University of California Press, 1997); and Clark Davis, "From Oasis to Metropolis: Southern California and the Changing Context of American Leisure," *Pacific Historical Review* 62, no. 3 (1993): 357–86.

58. Autry bought radio station KMPC in 1952, founding his Golden West Broadcasters empire, which acquired television station KTLA in 1964. With other investors he purchased the Los Angeles Angels expansion team in 1960, and in 1966 his ball club built the Anaheim Stadium; see Gene Autry and the Twentieth-Century West: The Centennial Exhibition, 1907–2007, Autry National Center, Los Angeles, viewed 9 August 2007. For Knott's Berry Farm, see *Visit Independence Hall,* LAPL Vertical File; and Lisa McGirr, *Suburban Warriors: The Origins of the New American Right* (Princeton: Princeton University Press, 2001), 98–100, 136. For Disney's influence on western urbanism, see John M. Findlay, "Far Western Cityscapes and American Culture since 1940," *Western Historical Quarterly* 22, no. 1 (February 1991): 19–43.

5. Back to Nature

1. Jan Weyl, "Time of Our Lives," *Ladies' Home Journal,* July 1954, 91–120.
2. Ibid., 119.
3. Ibid., 120.
4. Ibid.

5. Neil R. Kuehnl, "The How-To of Family Camping," *Better Homes and Gardens,* May 1958, 156; *Rand McNally Campground Guide: A Family Camping Directory* (Chicago, 1963), I.

6. Outdoor Recreation Resources Review Commission, *National Recreation Survey* (Washington, D.C.: Outdoor Recreation Resources Review Commission, 1962), 56, 57.

7. "Camping," *Motorland,* July–August 1960, 12.

8. Ibid., 14; *Rand McNally Campground Guide,* I.

9. "Camping," *Motorland,* 12.

10. Ibid.

11. Ibid.

12. Ibid.; Martha Foster Mertz, "Try These Travel Tricks for More Vacation Fun!" in Coleman Company, *More Fun Outdoors with Coleman* (Wichita, Kans., ca. 1953), 11, Benson Ford Research Center (hereafter BFRC), 99.44.3.

13. Kuehnl, "How-To"; Better Homes and Gardens, *Family Camping* (Des Moines, Iowa, 1961), 23.

14. *Rand McNally Campground Guide,* 216.

15. "The Wonderful World of Station Wagon Living," Folder 6, Box 5, Ford, Warshaw Collection of Business Americana, Archives Center, National Museum of American History, Washington, D.C.; Better Homes and Gardens, *Family Camping,* 37.

16. Doris T. Patterson, *Your Family Goes Camping* (New York: Abingdon Press, 1959), 17–25; George Stevens Wells, *Guide to Family Camping* (Harrisburg, Pa.: Stackpole Books, 1973), 46–42.

17. Coleman Company, *More Fun Outdoors,* 8, 12–13, 32.

18. Commercial broadcast in *Mister Peepers,* 1955-06-05, NBC Television, presented by Reynolds Aluminum, 4-AAI-5421, Film and Television Archive Research Center, UCLA, Los Angeles; *Rand McNally Campground Guide,* xx–xxii.

19. Coleman Company, *More Fun Outdoors,* 4–5, 8.

20. "Camping," *Motorland,* 11.

21. Better Homes and Gardens, *Family Camping,* chap. 3.

22. Roger B. White, *Home on the Road: The Motor Home in America* (Washington, D.C.: Smithsonian Institution Press, 2000), 153–54.

23. Ibid., 154; John Gartner, "How Big a Trailer?" *Westways,* April 1950, 10; *Life,* 8 June 1959, 119; *Westways,* June 1959, 42.

24. *Motorland,* March/April 1964, 30s; Rand McNally & Co., *Rand McNally Western Campground and Trailering Guide* (1970), n.p.; "Camping," *Motorland,* 14.

25. William Barry Furlong, "Travel Trailers—Today's Good Life on the Go!" *Better Homes and Gardens,* May 1962, 66.

26. Volkswagen Camper (T. C. Volkswagenwerk AG, ca. 1960), BFRC.

27. "Recreational Vehicles: The Great Turtle Syndrome," *Motorland* 1973, 54–55; *Rand McNally Campground and Trailer Park Guide* (Chicago, 1971), ii.

28. *Rand McNally Campground Guide,* vii, x, I; *Rand McNally Western Campground and Trailering Guide,* 1970.

29. *Rand McNally Campground Guide,* 149; White, *Home on the Road,* 170.

30. U.S. Department of the Interior, NPS, Annual Report, 1946 Yellowstone, 1–2, Annual Report, 1947 Yellowstone, 2; Box 1707, RG 79 National Park Service Administrative Files (1949–71), hereafter RG 79.

31. Shenandoah Superintendent's Monthly Narrative Reports, September 1945, Box 1640, RG 79; and Grand Canyon Superintendent's Monthly Narrative Reports, Box 1003, RG 79.

32. NPS Public Use Statistics Office, Decade Report, 1941–1950; 1951–1960; 1961–1970; 1971–1980; available at http://www2.nature.nps.gov/stats/ (accessed 12 November 2007). Historians of the park service rarely view the growth from the perspective of the park visitor, who has generally been seen as the problem to be solved; see Alfred Runte, *National Parks: The American Experience*, 3rd ed. (Lincoln: University Press of Nebraska, 1987); Dwight T. Pitcaithley, "A Dignified Exploitation: The Growth of Tourism in the National Parks," in *Seeing and Being Seen: Tourism in the American West*, ed. David M. Wrobel and Patrick T. Long (Lawrence: University Press of Kansas, 2001), 299–312. John Ise, *Our National Park Policy: A Critical History* (Baltimore: Johns Hopkins University Press, 1961), 458, compared the visitors to an infestation of insects.

33. Annual Report of the Director, National Park Service to the Secretary of the Interior, 1959, 341; Mark Daniel Barringer, *Selling Yellowstone: Capitalism and the Construction of Nature* (Lawrence: University Press of Kansas, 2002), 12, 173–74; Richard West Sellars, *Preserving Nature in the National Parks: A History* (New Haven: Yale University Press, 1997), 5.

34. Report 4a3, Annual Summary of Written Complaints Concerning Facilities and Services of the Government in Yellowstone National Park, 30 September 1951, Folder A3615, Box 382, RG 79.

35. Edmund B. Rogers to Regional Director, Region Two, 17 August 1951, Folder A3615, Box 382, RG 79.

36. Mary Cecil to Julius Krug, 14 September 1949; "An R.N.," to Gentlemen, 16 June 1952; Carl L. Eckhardt to Oscar Dick, 31 August 1961; all Folder A3615, Box 382, RG 79.

37. Drucilla C. Planson to U.S. Department of the Interior, 10 August 1956; H. G. Phillips to "The Ranger in Charge at Fishing Bridge, Yellowstone Nat'l Park, Wyoming," 5 June 1952; both Folder A3615, Box 382, RG 79.

38. Edmund B. Rogers to H. G. Phillips, 12 June 1952, Folder A3615, Box 382, RG 79.

39. Superintendent Edmund B. Rogers to Regional Director, Region Two, 18 September 1952, Folder A3615, Box 382, RG 79.

40. Thomas W. Lanigan to Fred Seaton, and Lemuel A. Garrison to Thomas W. Lanigan, 24 July 1959, Folder A3615, Box 382, RG 79.

41. American Automobile Association, "Travel Trends," May 1951, 1, Folder A88, Box 714, RG 79; David Louter, "Glaciers and Gasoline: The Making of a Windshield Wilderness," in Wrobel and Long, *Seeing and Being Seen*, 250; D. S. Martin, to the NPS, attached to Fred M. Packard to "Connie," 21 April 1955; and R. K. MacDonald to Elmer F. Bennett, 25 August 1959, both Folder A3615, Box 382, RG 79.

42. NPS Monthly Narrative Report, Yellowstone, July 1956, 8, Folder A2823, Box 320, RG 79; O. E. Hemphill to Superintendent of Rangers, 31 August 1953, Folder A3615, Box 382, RG 79.

43. Edmund B. Rogers to Orval E. Hemphill, 14 September 1953, Folder A3615, Box 382, RG 79.

44. Mr. and Mrs. Leslie C. Mackrill to the National Park Service, 29 June 1952, Folder A3615 YELL, Complaints Box 382, RG 79.

45. Annual Report of the Director, National Park Service to the Secretary of the Interior, 1959, 341; Ernest A. Welch to Department of the Interior, 14 June 1954; Thomas C. Vint to Ernest A. Welch, 23 June 1954, Folder A3615, Box 382, RG 79; Annual Report of the Director, National Park Service to the Secretary of the Interior, 1963, 81, 95–96, 98; Camping Committee of the National Park Service, Compilation of Campground Data Collected in the 1966 Camping Survey, and "A Summary Report of 17 Parks in the Campground Survey 1966," 68, Folder L3415 WASO, Box 119, RG 79.

46. Summary Report, 2; Compilation, 23–24.

47. Ronald F. Lee, Acting Director, to Senator Everett M. Dirksen, 7 September 1951, Folder A3615 YELL, Box 382, RG 79.

48. Edmund B. Rogers to E. K. Campbell, 23 October 1956, Folder A3619-B, Box 382, RG 79; Dwight T. Pitcaithley, "A Dignified Exploitation: The Growth of Tourism in the National Parks," in Wrobel and Long, *Seeing and Being Seen,* 299–312.

49. Forest H. Sweet to Mr. Drury, 10 October 1950; Paul R. Franke to Mr. Forest H. Sweet, 19 October 1950, Folder A3615, Box 382, RG 79.

50. 79-G-26H-14; 79-G-26H-34; 79-G-26H-16; 79-G-26H-28; 79-G-27C-47 and 79-G-27C-114; all Historic Photograph File, Records of the National Park Service, RG 79, and Annual Report, 1947, 11, Box 1707, RG 79.

51. 79-G-26G-30; 79-26H-25; 79-G-26E-66; 79-G-26G-68; 79-G-26G-76, Historic Photograph File RG 79.

52. Superintendent's Monthly Narrative Report, Yellowstone, July 1956, 9, 17, Folder A2823, Box 320, RG 79.

53. Newton B. Drury to Senator Hubert H. Humphrey, 17 October 1949, Folder A3615, Box 382, RG 79.

54. Drury to Humphrey, 17 October 1949; Lee H. Whittlesey, *Death in Yellowstone: Accidents and Foolhardiness in the First National Park* (Boulder, Colo.: Roberts Rinehart, 1995), 14.

55. Drury to Humphrey, 17 October 1949.

56. Whittlesey, *Death in Yellowstone,* xiii; Report of Personal Injuries for Grace Meyers, Keith Jeck, Anthony De Marco, Mary F. Kimball, and James Schmidt, Folder A762 3, Box 624 RG 79.

57. Report of Personal Injuries for Edwin Nalley, Richard Denison, Sandra Vanselow, and Lorna Kay Emfield, Folder A762 3, Box 624, RG 79.

58. Better Homes and Gardens, *Family Camping,* 115; Dr. and Mrs. N. W. Christiansen, *A Trip through Yellowstone Park: Interesting Events Portrayed in Music* (Long Island, N.Y.: Belwin, 1953), 15, in author's possession.

59. Memorandum, Superintendent of Yellowstone National Park to the National Park Service Director, 16 June 1959, Folder A26, Box 79, RG 79; Superintendent's Monthly Narrative Report, Yellowstone, August 1955, Folder A2823, Box 320, RG 79; Alice Wondrak Biel, *Do (Not) Feed the Bears: The Fitful History of Wildlife and Tourists in Yellowstone* (Lawrence: University Press of Kansas, 2006).

60. Superintendent's Monthly Narrative Report, Yellowstone, August 1955, Folder A2823, Box 320; Samuel E. McCrary to Stewart L. Udall, 22 June 1966, Complaints, Box 383, RG79.

61. Dan Malaney, "The Day Dad Fought a Bear for His Cooler," *Reminiscence,* May/June 2003, 47. I thank Jessie Embry for bringing this story to my attention.

62. Superintendent's Monthly Narrative Report, Yellowstone, June 1955, Folder A2823, Box 320, RG 79; Report of Personal Injuries for Eugene Nayes, Ann Boutte, Daughter of Robert Gloyd, Paul Brown, Nancy Hendrickson, Folder A762 3, Box 624, RG 79; Biel, *Do (Not) Feed the Bears,* 68–71.

63. Report of Personal Injuries for Gale Lee Brittendall, James Applewhite, Mrs. Robert Thomas, Folder A762 3, Box 624, RG 79.

64. Superintendent's Monthly Narrative Report, Yellowstone, August 1962, 8, Folder A2823, Box 320, RG 79; Biel, *Do (Not) Feed the Bears.*

65. Annual Report of the Director, National Park Service to the Secretary of the Interior, 1962, 111–12; Annual Report of the Director, 1963, 95.

66. *The Negro Travelers' Green Book* (New York: Victor H. Green & Co., 1958), 55. The disjuncture also officially relieved the NPS of the legal obligation to construct separate facilities; see Hillory A. Tolson to Sen. Lyndon B. Johnson, 20 April 1951, W4633 WASO, Box 2285, RG 79. However, the NPS maintained that "comparable separate facilities for members of another race is generally regarded as not discriminatory"; see J. A. Burkhart, 14 May 1951, to Dir., Big Bend National Park, Texas; Ross A. Maxwell to J. A. Burkhart, 18 May 1951; P. P. Patraw, Acting Regional Director, Region Three, to Maxwell, 23 May 1951, Folder A3615, Box 380, RG 79.

67. J. R. Lassiter to Director, 28 March 1939; Lassiter to Director, 6 April 1939; Sergeant E. Demaray to Secretary, 7 April 1939; J. R. Lassiter to Mr. Demaray, 8 February 1939; Box 1765, Central Classified Files, 1933–1949, RG 79.

68. Demaray to the Director, 11 February 1939, Box 1765, Central Classified Files, 1933–1949, RG 79.

69. "Memorandum for the Regional Director," 12 April 1939; Virginia Sky-Line Company, Inc., Memo for the files, 18 April 1939, Box 1675, RG 79.

70. Edward D. Freeland to Mrs. Otis L. Murray, 1 August 1947; Harry F. Byrd to Supt. Freeland, 15 August 1947; Edward D. Freeland to Harry F. Byrd, 19 August 1947, Box 1641, RG 79.

71. Mrs. O. L. Murray to Director, NPS, 24 August 1947; reply by Hillory A. Tolson, Box 1641, RG 79.

72. Superintendent's Monthly Narrative Report, Shenandoah, July 1947, Box 1640; Guy D. Edwards to Arthur Blumberg, 12 October 1951; W. J. Trent Jr. to Conrad Wirth, 25 September 1953, Box 396; Guy D. Edwards to J. Trent Jr., 14 October 1953, Box 380;

Acting Chief of Concession Management to Assistant Director Price, 5 February 1960, and Jackson E. Price to Regional Dir., Region One, 10 February 1960; A. M. Edwards to J. Clarence Young, 20 January 1960, A3619, Box 396, RG 79.

73. Virgil C. Heathcock to Oliver G. Taylor, 14 July 1950; Newton B. Drury to Heathcock, 3 August 1950; Oscar L. Chapman to Heathcock, 3 August 1950; Edward D. Freeland to Regional Director, 21 July 1950; Arthur F. Perkins to Regional Dir., 28 July 1950; Box 396, A3619 SHEN, RG 79. The nearby Beautiful Caverns of Luray maintained segregated toilets, complained Lillian W. Fitzhugh to Conrad L. Wirth, 31 July 1952, Box 2205, W4633 WASO, RG 79.

74. Mother & Voter to National Parks Commissioner, 14 May 1956, W4633 WASO, Box 2285, RG 79.

75. Jack Hope, "Hassles in the Park," *Natural History,* May 1971.

76. "Carrying everything he needs to survive, the backpacker is one of the freest people on earth," *Motorland*/CSAA, March 1969, 20; Sellars, *Preserving Nature,* 338 n. 5.

77. Samuel P. Hays, *Beauty, Health and Permanence: Environmental Policies in the United States, 1955–1985* (New York: Cambridge University Press, 1987), 54, 115.

6. Summer in the Country

1. Carol Crawford Ryan, Narrator, James E. Fogerty (Minnesota Resort Industry Oral History Project Collection, 1993), 1–2, OH 79.12, Minnesota Historical Society Library, St. Paul, Minnesota (hereafter MHSL).

2. Ryan, 12.

3. Paul Clifford Larsen, *A Place at the Lake* (Afton, Minn.: Afton Historical Society Press, 1998); Kathryn Koutsky and Linda Koutsky, *Minnesota Vacation Days: An Illustrated History* (St. Paul: Minnesota Historical Society Press, 2005); and Bill Holm, *Cabins of Minnesota* (St. Paul: Minnesota Historical Society Press, 2007). See also Aaron Shapiro, "'One Crop Worth Cultivating': Tourism in the Upper Great Lakes, 1910–1965," Ph.D. diss., University of Chicago, 2005.

4. Department of Business Development and Minnesota Statehood Centennial Commission, *Minnesota, 100 Years of Vacation Fun* (1958), 5, 27, 42, MHSL.

5. Division of Publicity, Department of Business Development, *Minnesota Vacations from the Land of 10,000 Lakes* (1960), F604.1 MHSL; Thomas P. Luke, "Minnesota's Water Wonderland," *Better Homes and Gardens,* July 1957, 54.

6. Minnesota Arrowhead Association, *Vacation Travel Survey, Briefs about Vacationers* (ca. 1958), Pamphlet Collection, G1-GV807, #17, MHSL; Richard O. Sielaf, *Minnesota Arrowhead Association Vacation-Travel Survey 1958* (Iron Range Resources and Rehabilitation Department, State of Minnesota, and the Minnesota Arrowhead Association, [1958]), 3, 24, 32, table 40, MHSL.

7. Sielaff, *M.A.A. Vacation-Travel Survey 1958,* 1–3, 13, 15–19. See also Bert Pfeifer, Narrator, James E. Fogerty, Interviewer (Minnesota Resort Industry Oral History Project Collection, 1999), OH 79.6, MHSL.

8. Ed and Kay Gilman, Narrators, James E. Fogerty, Interviewer (Minnesota Resort Industry Oral History Project Collection, 1999), 3, 9, OH 79.3, MHSL.

9. Gilman, 4, 9, 11–12.

10. Ryan, 4.

11. Ibid., 3.

12. Gilman, 8, 16, 24; Ryan, 4–5.

13. Gilman, 8, 10, 21.

14. Ibid., 16.

15. Gilman, 14–15, 18–19, 26.

16. Ryan, 5.

17. *Ruttger's Bay Lake Lodge, Deerwood, Minnesota,* MHS Pamphlet Collection, Crow Wing County Box 2. The Ruttger resorts then included Ruttger's Bay Lake Lodge, Deerwood; Ruttger's Sherwood Forest Lodge, Brainerd; Birchmont Lodge, Bemidji; Pine Beach Lodge, Brainerd; Shady Point Lodge, Pequot Lakes. A detailed timeline can be found at http://www.ruttgers.com (accessed 20 May 2007).

18. Jack Ruttger, Narrator, Margaret Robertson, Interviewer (Minnesota Resort Industry Oral History Project Collection, 1991), 4, OH 79.8 MHSL.

19. Max "Buzz" Ruttger Jr., Narrator, Theresa Ruttger, Interviewer (Minnesota Resort Industry Oral History Project Collection, 1997), 13, OH 79.9 MHSL. Max's parents, Max and Rosie Ruttger, owned two motels in Florida and shuttled back and forth between Minnesota and Florida for resort seasons.

20. Max Ruttger, 10–11; Randy Ruttger, Narrator, Theresa Ruttger, Interviewer (Minnesota Resort Industry Oral History Project Collection, 1998), 3, OH 79.10, MHSL.

21. Theresa Ruttger, Narrator, James E. Fogerty Interviewer (Minnesota Resort Industry Oral History Project Collection, 1997), 3–4, 13, OH 79.11, MHSL.

22. Theresa Ruttger, 12, 16.

23. Ruttger's Pine Beach Lodge, Brainerd, Minnesota, Records of Ruttger Resorts, F612.C95 MHSL; Max Rutter, 26, and Theresa Ruttger, 31.

24. Theresa Ruttger, 19, 20, 32.

25. Theresa Ruttger, 28; Randy Ruttger, 2.

26. "Cedric Adams, in This Corner," reprinted from the *Minneapolis Star,* 18 May 1960, Bar Harbor Nite Club, *Bar Harbor Beacon* 1 (June 1960): 1, MHSL Pamphlet collection. Emphasis in original.

27. Theresa Ruttger, 37.

28. Ibid., 42–45.

29. Jack Ruttger, 9, 10, 12.

30. *Ruttger's Bay Lake Lodge*, F612.C95, Pamphlet Collection, Crow Wing County, MHSL.

31. *The Negro Travelers' Green Book* (1956), 71–80. For histories of African American–owned resorts, see Lewis Walker and Benjamin C. Wilson, *Black Eden: The Idlewild Community* (Lansing: Michigan State University Press, 2002); and Marsha Dean Phelts, *An American Beach for African Americans* (Gainesville: University Press of Florida, 1997).

Patricia L. Pilling, "Segregation: Cottage Rental in Michigan," *Phylon* 25, no. 2 (1964): 191–201, describes the custom of segregated resorts in the Midwest in 1962.

32. "Transcript of an Interview with Norman P. Lyght," 25 June 1974, 10–11, OH 43.11, MHSL; William Flagg, Narrator, James E. Fogerty, Interviewer (Minnesota Resort Industry Oral History Project Collection, 1994), 6, 12–13, OH 79.2, MHSL.

33. Flagg, 3–14, 16, 18.

34. Ibid., 13, 18.

35. Leonard Dinnerstein, *Antisemitism in America* (New York: Oxford University Press, 1995), 92–93, 151–52, 158; Phil Brown, *Catskill Culture: A Mountain Rat's Memories of the Great Jewish Resort Area* (Philadelphia: Temple University Press, 1998), 11.

36. Brown, *Catskill Culture,* 41–44.

37. Abraham D. Lavender and Clarence B. Steinberg, *Jewish Farmers of the Catskills: A Century of Survival* (Gainesville: University Press of Florida, 1995); Irwin Richman, *Borscht Belt Bungalows: Memories of Catskill Summers* (Philadelphia: Temple University Press, 1998), 10–11, 63–64.

38. Richman, *Borscht Belt,* 31.

39. Ibid., 74–75, 81, 88–89, 98–99, 113–14.

40. Ibid., 121.

41. Joel Pomerantz, *Jennie and the Story of Grossinger's* (New York: Grosset & Dunlap, 1970), 301; *Grossinger News,* 9 November 1954; "Salute to the Grossinger Family," Fiftieth Anniversary Commemorative Program [1964], both Folder 14, RG 1195, Center for Jewish History.

42. Pomerantz, *Jennie,* 253, 255, 277, 303; Tania Grossinger, *Growing Up at Grossinger's* (New York: David McKay, 1975), 62.

43. Pomerantz, *Jennie,* 298–99; Grossinger, *Growing Up,* 19–20, 22; see also Rachelle H. Saltzman, "Rites of Intensification: Eating and Ethnicity in the Catskills," *Southern Folklore* 55, no. 3 (1998): 205–23. For the importance of dietary practices to maintaining Jewish culture in America, see Jenna Weissman Joselit, *The Wonders of America: Reinventing Jewish Culture, 1880–1950* (New York: Henry Holt, 1994), chap. 5.

44. Pomerantz, *Jennie,* 289, 292–93.

45. Ibid., 307–8.

46. Grossinger, *Growing Up,* 25, 29–31.

47. Brown, *Catskill Culture,* 82–84.

48. Joey Adams with Henry Tobias, *The Borscht Belt* (New York: Bobbs-Merrill, 1959); Brown, *Catskill Culture,* 186–89.

49. *The Goldbergs,* 17 August 1954, DuMont Television Network, 4-AAE-4472, Film and Television Archive Research Center, UCLA, Los Angeles. See entry "Gertrude Berg" and Michelle Hilmes's entry on *The Goldbergs* in *Encyclopedia of Television,* ed. Horace Newcomb, Museum of Broadcast Communications, available at http://www.museum.tv/archives/etv/index.html (accessed 9 July 2007).

50. Benjamin R. Epstein and Arnold Forster, *"Some of My Best Friends . . . "* (New York: Farrar, Straus and Cudahy, 1962), 456–58; "Discrimination in Hotels: A Cause for Crisis?" *Hotel Monthly,* May 1962, 28.

51. Edwin J. Lukas to CRC Offices Group Relations Agencies, 19 August 1953, American Jewish Committee, Folder, "Communal Issues, Public Accommodations, New York, 1948–1960," Box 28 GEN 347.17.13, Center for Jewish History, New York City.

52. Epstein and Forster, *Best Friends,* 46–47, 49; Dinnerstein, *Antisemitism,* 38.

53. Richman, *Borscht Belt,* 181–82, 188–92.

54. Deborah Dash Moore, *To the Golden Cities: Pursuing the American Jewish Dream in Miami and L.A.* (Cambridge, Mass.: Harvard University Press, 1993), 23, 26–27, 31–33, 35; Moore and Dan Gebler, "The Ta'am of Tourism," *Pacific Historical Review* 68, no. 2 (1990): 193–212.

55. Bureau of Outdoor Recreation, Department of the Interior, *Northern New England Vacation Home Study—1966* (Washington, D.C., 1966); John D. Bloodgood, "Troubles Stay Behind," *Better Homes and Gardens,* August 1962, 6; Richard Lee Ragatz, "Vacation Homes in the Northeastern United States: Seasonality in Population Distribution," *Annals of the Association of American Geographers* 60 (September 1970): 447–55.

56. "The Lake," 2 October 1991, *The Wonder Years,* T16959, Museum of Television and Radio, Los Angeles; http://www.imdb.com/title/tt0094582/ (accessed 13 August 2007).

57. *Dirty Dancing,* Vestron Pictures, 17 August 1987, http://imdb.com/title/tt0092890/business (accessed 13 August 2007).

58. Susan J. Douglas, *Where the Girls Are: Growing Up Female in the Mass Media* (New York: Random House, 1994); Kirse Granat May, *Golden State, Golden Youth: The California Image in Popular Culture, 1955–1966* (Chapel Hill: University of North Carolina Press, 2002); Anne B. Thompson, "Rereading Fifties Teen Romance," *The Lion and the Unicorn* 29 (2005): 373–96; Robyn McCallum, "Young Adult Literature," in *Oxford Encyclopedia of Children's Literature,* ed. Jack Zipes (New York: Oxford University Press, 2006), e-reference edition available at http//www.oxford-childrensliterature.com/entry?entry_t204.e3482 (accessed 25 June 2007).

59. Ernest Havemann, "Vacations: Danger Time for Marriage," *Ladies' Home Journal,* July 1968, 30–32.

Epilogue

1. More recent scholarship on the 1960s cautions against seeing young social movements of the decade as wholly revolutionary and instead emphasizes the pluralism of cultural styles and forms of resistance and acceptance of the status quo. See especially George Lipsitz, "Who'll Stop the Rain: Youth Culture, Rock 'n' Roll, and Social Crises," in *The Sixties: From Memory to History,* ed. David Farber (Chapel Hill: University of North Carolina Press, 1994), 206–34.

2. Lizabeth Cohen, *A Consumers' Republic: The Politics of Mass Consumption in Postwar America* (New York: Knopf, 2003); Beth Bailey, "Sexual Revolution(s)," in Farber, *Sixties,* 235–62.

3. David Firestone, "Tourism Industry Pins Hopes on Heritage and Culture," *New York Times,* 4 November 2001; Glenn Collins, "A Nation of Travelers Hard to Pin Down," *New York Times,* 8 September 2002; Joe Sharkey et al., "The Travel Industry Changes Its Vacation Plans," *New York Times,* 20 April 2003; Susan Catto, "Hitting the

Road, at Home," *New York Times Online,* 20 April 2003; Kate Zernike, "Supersizing Family Get-Togethers," *New York Times Online,* 6 June 2004.

4. Candace Choi, "Forget the Baby Sitter," *Salt Lake Tribune,* 9 April 2007; Charles Strum, "Family Driving: The New Model," *New York Times Online,* 15 May 2001; Stephanie Mencimer, "You Call This a Vacation," *New York Times,* 12 May 2002; Beth J. Harpaz, "Resolve to Take a Long Vacation," *Salt Lake Tribune,* 2 January 2005; Kelley Holland, "You've Earned a Vacation. But Dare You Take It?" *New York Times,* 25 March 2007; Timothy Egan, "The Rise of Shrinking Vacation Syndrome," *New York Times,* 20 August 2006.

5. Caren Osten Gerszberg, "The Family Vacation, Reinvented," *New York Times,* 13 May 2007; Jennifer Alsever, "The Latest in Hotel Pools: 3 Acres, with Slides, Indoors," *New York Times,* 10 April 2005; "Teach Your Children Culture, Wildlife and the Value of a Dollar," *New York Times Magazine,* 9 June 2002; Wayne Curtis, "Motel Paradiso," *Atlantic,* June 2007, 125.

6. Kevin Sack, "View from the Saddle," *New York Times,* 10 June 2001; Debbie Seaman, "A Ranch for Those on the Fence," *New York Times,* 21 July 2002; Gene Sloan, "Adventure Travel for Families Snowballs," *USA Today,* 10 August 2007; Tom Wharton, "Sometimes It's Tough to Keep the Magic Alive," and Wharton, "Disneyland a Pricey Proposal for Families," *Salt Lake Tribune,* 5 June 2005.

7. NPS attendance is down 5 percent from last year and as much as 15–45 percent at certain parks. See Peter Fish, "Old Faithful Versus the Xbox," *Sunset,* July 2007, 104; Michelle Higgins, "Canyons and Geysers Are Still Within Reach," *New York Times,* 8 July 2007; Jennifer Conlin, "National Parks Put Elk and Bison on the Menu," *New York Times,* 8 April 2007; "Kamping Trends, 2006," available at http://koapressroom.com/storystarters (accessed 31 May 2007).

8. Suzanne Berne, "A Breather for Parents and Kids," *New York Times,* 4 August 2002; Christine S. Cozzens, "Beside a Wisconsin Lake," *New York Times,* 25 July 2004; Amy Gunderson, "Pitter-Patter of Little Feet Grows at Resorts," *New York Times,* 10 April 2005; Seth Kugel, "Why We Travel, Bahamas," *New York Times,* 25 February 2007; Amy Gunderson, "Clearing the Decks, and Staterooms, for the Whole Clan," *New York Times,* 25 February 2007.

9. Bob Tedeschi, "More Choices for Vacation Home Renters," *New York Times,* 13 February 2005; Family Travel Files E-zine, available at http://ww.thefamilytravelfiles.com (accessed 12 November 2007); Fred Bierman, "Wishyouwerehere.com: Blogs from the Road," *New York Times Online,* 27 November 2005; Joanne Helperin, "Top 10 Family Road Trip Must-Haves," Edmunds.com, available at http://www.edmunds.com/reviews/list/top10/103117/article.html (accessed 12 November 2007).

10. Rebecca Gardyn, "The New Family Vacation," *American Demographics,* August 2001, 43–47; Beth Grenfield, "Gay Getaways: The New Wave," *New York Times Online,* 14 July 2006; Fred A. Bernstein, "For Gay Parents, a Big Week in the Sun," *New York Times,* 22 July 2007. See also "Demographics Explain about Two-Thirds of Everything," *Travel Insights,* April 2006, 16–18, Travel Industry Association of America, available at http://www.tia.org/resources/PDFs/Travel_Insights_2.pdf (accessed 12 November 2007).

11. David Brooks, "Pain, Agony, Despair: Flying with Children," *New York Times,* 24 July 2005; Laura Bly, "Are We There Yet?" *USA Today,* 19 July 2007; Joe Sharkey, "Kids on the Plane? Maybe I'll Have that Drink," *New York Times,* 22 July 2007; Marc Weingarten, "Las Vegas 2003: Forget the Chips, Try the M&Ms," *New York Times Online,* 25 April 2003; Amy Virshup, "South Beach, the PG Version," *New York Times,* 13 February 2005; A. O. Scott, "Adventures in Dreamland," *New York Times,* 13 May 2007.

12. Robert Sullivan, *Cross-Country* (New York: Bloomsbury, 2006); Mike Leonard, *The Ride of Our Lives: Roadside Lessons of an American Family* (New York: Ballantine Books, 2006); W. D. Wetherell, "A Rough Trip across the Generation Gap," *New York Times,* 5 January 2003; "Letters on Travel," *New York Times,* 19 January 2003.

Bibliography

Archival Collections

Archives Center, National Museum of American History, Washington, D.C.
Auto Club of Southern California, Los Angeles, California
Autry National Center, Los Angeles, California
Benson Ford Research Center, The Henry Ford Museum and Greenfield Village, Dearborn, Michigan
California State Automobile Association, San Francisco, California
Center for Jewish History, New York City, New York
Cotsen Children's Library Collection, Princeton University, Princeton, New Jersey
Disneyland Collection, Anaheim Public Library, Anaheim, California
Film and Television Archive Research Center, UCLA, Los Angeles, California
Look Magazine, Prints and Photographs Division, Library of Congress, Washington, D.C.
Maymie Richardson Krythe Scrapbook Collection, Seaver Center, Natural History Museum of Los Angeles County, Los Angeles, California
Minnesota Resort Industry Oral History Project Collection, Minnesota Historical Society Library, St. Paul, Minnesota
Moorland-Spingarn Research Center, Howard University, Washington, D.C.
Museum of Television and Radio, Los Angeles, California
National Association for the Advancement of Colored Persons (NAACP), Papers, Library of Congress, Washington, D.C.
National Park Service Records, Record Group 79, National Archives and Records Administration II, College Park, Maryland
Rand McNally Map Collection, Newberry Library, Chicago, Illinois
Schlesinger Library, Radcliffe Institute, Harvard University, Cambridge, Massachusetts
Schomberg Center for Research in Black Culture, New York City, New York
Shades of L.A. Collection, Los Angeles Public Library

Published Works

Abbott, Carl. *Political Terrain: Washington, D.C., from Tidewater Town to Global Metropolis.* Chapel Hill: University of North Carolina, 1999.
Adams, Joey, with Henry Tobias. *The Borscht Belt.* New York: Bobbs-Merrill, 1959.
Aikman, Lonnelle. "U.S. Capitol, Citadel to Democracy." *National Geographic Magazine* 102, no. 2 (1952): 143–92.
Akerman, James R. "American Promotional Road Mapping in the Twentieth Century." *Cartography and Geographic Information Science* 29 (July 2002): 175–91.
———. "Blazing a Well-Worn Path: Cartographic Commercialism, Highways Promotion, and Automobile Tourism in the United States, 1880–1930." *Cartographica* 30 (1993): 10–19.

———. "Private Journeys on Public Maps: A Look at Inscribed Road Maps." *Cartographic Perspectives* 33 (Winter 2000): 27–47.

American Automobile Association. *Americans on the Highway.* Washington, D.C., 1950.

Anderson, Benedict. *Imagined Communities: Reflections on the Origin and Spread of Nationalism.* Rev. ed. New York: Verso, 1991.

Angelou, Maya. *The Heart of a Woman.* New York: Random House, 1981.

Aron, Cindy S. *Working at Play: A History of Vacations in the United States.* New York: Oxford, 1999.

Athearn, Robert G. *The Mythic West.* Lawrence: University Press of Kansas, 1986.

Atwood, Albert W. "Washington, Home of the Nation's Great." *National Geographic Magazine* 91, no. 6 (June 1947): 699–738.

Autry, Gene, with Mickey Herskowitz. *Back in the Saddle Again.* New York: Doubleday, 1978.

Avila, Eric. "Popular Culture in the Age of White Flight: Film Noir, Disneyland and the Cold War (Sub)Urban Imaginary." *Journal of Urban History* 31, no. 1 (November 2004): 3–22.

Baranowski, Shelley, and Ellen Furlough, eds. *Being Elsewhere: Tourism, Consumer Culture, and Identity in Modern Europe and America.* Ann Arbor: University of Michigan Press, 2001.

Barringer, Mark Daniel. *Selling Yellowstone: Capitalism and the Construction of Nature.* Lawrence: University Press of Kansas, 2002.

Belasco, Warren James. *Americans on the Road: From Autocamp to Motel, 1910–1945.* Baltimore: Johns Hopkins University Press, 1979.

Berg, Manfred. "Black Civil Rights and Liberal Anticommunism: The NAACP in the Early Cold War." *Journal of American History* 94 (June 2007): 75–96.

———. *The Ticket to Freedom: The NAACP and the Struggle for Black Political Integration.* Gainesville: University Press of Florida, 2005.

Better Homes and Gardens. *Family Camping.* Des Moines, Iowa: Meredith Publishing Co., 1961.

Biel, Alice Wondrak. *Do (Not) Feed the Bears: The Fitful History of Wildlife and Tourists in Yellowstone.* Lawrence: University Press of Kansas, 2006.

Biondi, Martha. *To Stand and Fight: The Struggle for Civil Rights in Postwar New York City.* Cambridge, Mass.: Harvard University Press, 2003.

Boas, Max, and Steve Chain. *Big Mac: The Unauthorized Story of McDonald's.* New York: E.P. Dutton & Co., 1976.

Bodnar, John, ed. *Bonds of Affection: Americans Define Their Patriotism.* Princeton, N.J.: Princeton University Press, 1996.

———. *Remaking America: Public Memory, Commemoration, and Patriotism in the Twentieth Century.* Princeton, N.J.: Princeton University Press, 1992.

Boettger, Suzaan. *Earthworks: Art and the Landscape of the Sixties.* Berkeley: University of California Press, 2002.

Bogle, Donald. *Primetime Blues: African Americans on Network Television.* New York: Farrar, Straus and Giroux, 2001.

Borne, Lawrence R. "Dude Ranching in the Rockies." *Montana: The Magazine of Western History* 39, no. 3 (1988): 14–27.

———. "Western Railroads and the Dude Ranching Industry." *Pacific Historian* 30 (1986): 47–59.

Bracken, Peg. "Taking a Family Vacation." *Saturday Evening Post,* 13 June 1959, 25.

Brauer, Ralph, with Donna Brauer. *The Horse, the Gun and the Piece of Property: Changing Images of the TV Western.* Bowling Green, Ohio: Bowling Green University Popular Press, 1975.

Bremer, Thomas S. *Blessed with Tourists: The Borderlands of Religion and Tourism in San Antonio.* Chapel Hill: University of North Carolina, 2004.

Brown, Phil. *Catskill Culture: A Mountain Rat's Memories of the Great Jewish Resort Area.* Philadelphia: Temple University Press, 1998.

Bryson, Bill. *I'm a Stranger Here Myself: Notes on Returning to America after Twenty Years Away.* New York: Broadway Books, 1999.

Buscombe, Edward, and Roberta E. Pearson, eds. *Back in the Saddle Again: New Essays on the Western.* London: British Film Institute, 1998.

Butsch, Richard, ed. *For Fun and Profit: The Transformation of Leisure into Consumption.* Philadelphia: Temple University Press, 1990.

Caro, Robert A. *The Years of Lyndon Johnson: Master of the Senate.* New York: Knopf, 2003.

Chafe, William H., Raymond Gavins, Robert Korstad, et al. *Remembering Jim Crow: African Americans Tell about Life in the Segregated South.* New York: The New Press, 2001.

Chidester, David, and Edward T. Linenthal, eds. *American Sacred Space.* Bloomington: Indiana University Press, 1995.

Christiansen, Dr. and Mrs. N. W. *A Trip through Yellowstone Park: Interesting Events Portrayed in Music.* Long Island, N.Y.: Belwin, 1953.

Clarke, Sally H. "Unmanageable Risks: *McPherson v. Buick* and the Emergence of a Mass Consumer Market." *Law and History Review* 23 (Spring 2005): 1–52.

Clifton, Gordon K. *Golden Book of Automobile Stamps.* Toronto: Musson Book Company, 1952.

Cohen, Lizabeth. *A Consumers' Republic: The Politics of Mass Consumption in Postwar America.* New York: Knopf, 2003.

Coleman Company. *More Fun Outdoors with Coleman.* Wichita, Kans., ca. 1953.

Confino, Alan. "Collective Memory and Cultural History: Problems of Method." *American Historical Review* 102 (December 1997): 1386–403.

Coontz, Stephanie. *The Way We Never Were: American Families and the Nostalgia Trap.* New York: Basic Books, 1992.

Cronon, William, George Miles, and Jay Gitlin, eds. *Under an Open Sky: Rethinking America's Western Past.* New York: Norton, 1992.

Davis, Clark. "From Oasis to Metropolis: Southern California and the Changing Context of American Leisure." *Pacific Historical Review* 62, no. 3 (1993): 357–86.

Davis, J. Allen. *The Friend to All Motorists: The Story of the Automobile Club of Southern California through 65 Years, 1900–1965.* Los Angeles: Automobile Club of Southern California, 1967.

Davis, Susan G. "Landscapes of Imagination: Tourism in Southern California." *Pacific Historical Review* 68 (May 1999): 173–92.

———. *Spectacular Nature: Corporate Culture and the Sea World Experience.* Berkeley: University of California Press, 1997.

Dinnerstein, Leonard. *Antisemitism in America.* New York: Oxford University Press, 1994.

Douglas, Susan J. *Where the Girls Are: Growing Up Female in the Mass Media.* New York: Random House, 1994.

Dudziak, Mary L. *Cold War Civil Rights: Race and the Image of American Democracy.* Princeton: Princeton University Press, 2000.

Dunn, Edward D. *Double-Crossing America by Motor: Routes and Ranches of the West.* New York: G. P. Putnam's Sons, 1933.

Ehrheart, William J. "The World's Most Famous Movie Ranch: The Story of Ray 'Crash' Corrigan and Corriganville." *Ventura County Historical Society Quarterly* 43, no. 1–2 (1999): 3–39.

Epstein, Benjamin R., and Arnold Forster. *"Some of My Best Friends . . . "* New York: Farrar, Straus, and Cudahy, 1962.

Farber, David. *The Age of Great Dreams: America in the 1960s.* New York: Hill & Wang, 1994.

———, ed. *The Sixties: From Memory to History.* Chapel Hill: University of North Carolina Press, 1994.

Feilitzsch, Heribert Frhr. V. "Karl May: The 'Wild West' as Seen in Germany." *Journal of Popular Culture* 27, no. 3 (Winter 1993): 173–89.

Findlay, John M. "Far Western Cityscapes and American Culture since 1940." *Western Historical Quarterly* 22, no. 1 (February 1991): 19–43.

Flink, James J. *The Automobile Age.* Cambridge, Mass.: MIT Press, 1988.

———. "Three Stages of Automobile Consciousness." *American Quarterly* 24 (October 1972): 451–73.

Foster, Mark S. "In the Face of 'Jim Crow': Prosperous Blacks and Vacations, Travel and Outdoor Leisure, 1890–1945." *Journal of Negro History* 84, no. 2 (1999): 130–49.

Frank, Thomas. *The Conquest of Cool: Business Culture, Counterculture, and the Rise of Hip Consumerism.* Chicago: University of Chicago Press, 1997.

Franz, Kathleen. "The Open Road: Automobility and Racial Uplift in the Interwar Years." In *Technology and the African-American Experience,* edited by Bruce Sinclair, 131–53. Cambridge, Mass.: MIT Press, 2004.

Futrell, Jim. *Amusement Parks of New York.* Mechanicsburg, Pa.: Stackpole Books, 2006.

Gabler, Neal. *Walt Disney: The Triumph of the American Imagination.* New York: Knopf, 2006.

Gallup Poll [computer file]. *Public Opinion, 1935–1997.* Wilmington, Del.: Scholarly Resources, 2000.
George-Warren, Holly. *Public Cowboy No. 1: The Life and Times of Gene Autry.* New York: Oxford University Press, 2007.
Gerstle, Gary. *American Crucible: Race and Nation in the Twentieth Century.* Princeton: Princeton University Press, 2001.
Graburn, Nelson H. "The Anthropology of Tourism." *Annals of Tourism Research* 10 (1983): 9–33.
Grant, Julia. *Raising Baby by the Book: The Education of American Mothers.* New Haven: Yale University Press, 1998.
Graves, William. "Washington, the City Freedom Built." *National Geographic Magazine* 126 (December 1964): 735–81.
Gray, Ralph. "Vacation Tour through Lincoln Land." *National Geographic Magazine* 101 (1952): 141–84.
Greenberg, Jack. *Crusaders in the Courts: How a Dedicated Band of Lawyers Fought for the Civil Rights Revolution.* New York: Basic Books, 1994.
Grossinger, Tania. *Growing Up at Grossinger's.* New York: David McKay, 1975.
Gudis, Catherine. *Buyways: Billboards, Automobiles, and the American Landscape.* New York: Routledge, 2004.
Hale, Grace Elizabeth. *Making Whiteness: The Culture of Segregation in the South, 1890–1940.* New York: Pantheon, 1998.
Haley, Alex. *Roots.* New York: Doubleday, 1976.
Hays, Samuel P. *Beauty, Health and Permanence: Environmental Policies in the United States, 1955–1985.* New York: Cambridge University Press, 1987.
Heller, Nancy. Interview by author, 27 December 2006, New York City.
"Highway Hotels and Restaurants." *Architectural Record* 114 (July 1953): 158–77.
Hodes, Martha. *Black Women, White Men: Illicit Sex in the Nineteenth-Century South.* New Haven: Yale University Press, 1997.
Holm, Bill. *Cabins of Minnesota.* St. Paul: Minnesota Historical Society Press, 2007.
Hurley, Andrew. *Diners, Bowling Alleys and Trailer Parks: Chasing the American Dream in the Postwar Consumer Culture.* New York: Basic Books, 2001.
Ise, John. *Our National Park Policy: A Critical History.* Baltimore: Johns Hopkins University Press, 1961.
Isserman, Maurice, and Michael Kazin. *America Divided: The Civil War of the 1960s.* 2nd ed. New York: Oxford University Press, 2004.
Jacobs, Meg. *Pocketbook Politics: Economic Citizenship in Twentieth-Century America.* Princeton: Princeton University Press, 2005.
Jakle, John A. *The Gas Station in America.* Baltimore: Johns Hopkins University Press, 1994.
———. *The Tourist: Travel in Twentieth-Century North America.* Lincoln: University of Nebraska Press, 1985.
Jakle, John A., and Keith A. Sculle. *Fast Food: Roadside Restaurants in the Automobile Age.* Baltimore: Johns Hopkins University Press, 1999.

Jakle, John A., Keith A. Sculle, and Jefferson S. Rogers. *The Motel in America.* Baltimore: Johns Hopkins University Press, 1996.

Jenkins, Elmer, ed. *Guide to America.* Washington, D.C.: Public Affairs Press, 1947–48.

Johnson, Michael L. *Hunger for the Wild: America's Obsession with the Untamed West.* Lawrence: University Press of Kansas, 2007.

Johnson, Susan Lee. *Roaring Camp: The Social World of the California Gold Rush.* New York: Norton, 2000.

Jonas, Gilbert. *Freedom's Sword: The NAACP and the Struggle against Racism in America.* New York: Routledge, 2005.

Joselit, Jenna Weissman. *The Wonders of America: Reinventing Jewish Culture, 1880–1950.* New York: Henry Holt, 1994.

Kahane, Charles Jesse. *An Evaluation of Passenger Safety: The Effectiveness and Benefits of Safety Seats.* Washington, D.C., 1986.

Kammen, Michael. *Mystic Chords of Memory: The Transformation of Tradition in American Culture.* New York: Knopf, 1991.

Kasson, John F. *Amusing the Million: Coney Island at the Turn of the Century.* New York: Hill & Wang, 1978.

Keates, J. S. *Understanding Maps.* 2nd ed. Essex, England: Longman, 1996.

Keene, Frances W. *Travel Fun Book for Boys and Girls.* Pelham, N.Y.: Seashore Press, 1954.

Kerber, Linda K. "The Meanings of Citizenship." *Journal of America History* 84 (December 1997): 833–54.

Knapp, Sally. *New Wings for Women.* New York: Thomas Y. Crowell Co., 1946.

Kowalke, Ron, ed. *Standard Catalog of Ford, 1903–1998.* 2nd ed. Iola, Wisc.: Krause Publications, 1998.

Kozol, Wendy. Life*'s America: Family and Nation in Postwar Photojournalism.* Philadelphia: Temple University Press, 1994.

Kruse, Kevin M. *White Flight: Atlanta and the Making of Modern Conservatism.* Princeton: Princeton University Press, 2005.

Landry, Bart. *The New Black Middle Class.* Berkeley: University of California Press, 1987.

Lane, Carol. *Traveling by Car: A Family Planning Guide to Better Vacations.* New York: Simon and Schuster, 1954.

Larsen, Paul Clifford. *A Place at the Lake.* Afton, Minn.: Afton Historical Society Press, 1998.

Lassiter, Matthew D. *The Silent Majority: Suburban Politics in the Sunbelt South.* Princeton: Princeton University Press, 2006.

Lavender, Abraham D., and Clarence B. Steinberg. *Jewish Farmers of the Catskills: A Century of Survival.* Gainesville: University Press of Florida, 1995.

Leonard, Mike. *The Ride of Our Lives: Roadside Lessons of an American Family.* New York: Ballantine Books, 2006.

Lewis, Tom. *Divided Highways: Building the Interstate Highways, Transforming American Life.* New York: Penguin, 1997.

Liets, Lois, illustrator. *Annie Oakley Roundup Coloring Book, with Lofty and Tagg.* Racine, Wisc.: Whitman Publishing Co., 1955.

Limerick, Patricia Nelson. *The Legacy of Conquest: The Unbroken Past of the American West.* New York: Norton, 1987.
Linenthal, Edward T. *Sacred Ground: Americans and Their Battlefields.* Urbana: University of Illinois Press, 1991.
Lipsitz, George. *Time Passages: Collective Memory and American Popular Culture.* Minneapolis: University of Minnesota Press, 1990.
Love, John F. *McDonald's: Behind the Arches.* New York: Bantam Books, 1986.
Lowenthal, David. *Possessed by the Past: The Heritage Crusade and the Spoils of History.* New York: Free Press, 1996.
Lutz, Catherine A., and Jane L. Collins. *Reading National Geographic.* Chicago: University of Chicago Press, 1993.
Koutsky, Kathryn, and Linda Koutsky. *Minnesota Vacation Days: An Illustrated History.* St. Paul: Minnesota Historical Society Press, 2005.
MacCannell, Dean. *The Tourist: A New Theory of the Leisure Class.* 1976. Reprint, Berkeley: University of California Press, 1999.
MacDonald, J. Fred. *Who Shot the Sheriff? The Rise and Fall of the Television Western.* New York: Praeger, 1987.
MacDonald, J. Fred, Richard W. Etulain, and Glenda Riley. *The Hollywood West: Lives of Film Legends Who Shaped It.* Golden, Colo.: Fulcrum Books, 2001.
Marcus, Greil. *The Old, Weird America: The World of Bob Dylan's Basement Tapes.* New York: Henry Holt, 1997.
Marling, Karal Ann. *As Seen on TV: The Visual Culture of Everyday Life in the 1950s.* Cambridge, Mass.: Harvard University Press, 1994.
———. *The Colossus of Roads: Myth and Symbol along the American Highway.* Minneapolis: University of Minnesota Press, 1984.
———, ed. *Designing Disney's Theme Parks: The Architecture of Reassurance.* New York: Flammarion, 1997.
Mathison, Richard R. *Three Cars in Every Garage: A Motorist's History of the Automobile and the Automobile Club in Southern California.* Garden City, N.Y.: Doubleday & Co., 1968.
May, Elaine Tyler. *Homeward Bound: American Families in the Cold War Era.* New York: Basic Books, 1988.
May, Kirse Granat. *Golden State, Golden Youth: The California Image in Popular Culture, 1955–1966.* Chapel Hill: University of North Carolina Press, 2002.
McGirr, Lisa. *Suburban Warriors: The Origins of the New American Right.* Princeton: Princeton University Press, 2001.
Meyerowitz, Joanne. *Not June Cleaver: Women and Gender in Postwar America, 1945–1960.* Philadelphia: Temple University Press, 1994.
Milanich, Nara. "Whither Family History: A Road Map from Latin America." *American Historical Review* 112 (April 2007): 439–58.
Mintz, Steven, and Susan Kellogg. *Domestic Revolutions: A Social History of American Family Life.* New York: Free Press, 1988.
Moore, Deborah Dash. *To the Golden Cities: Pursuing the American Jewish Dream in Miami and L.A.* Cambridge, Mass.: Harvard University Press, 1993.

Moore, Deborah Dash, and Dan Gebler. "The Ta'am of Tourism." *Pacific Historical Review* 68, no. 2 (1990): 193–212.

"Negro Market Highlights in Three Cities: Weekly Earnings of Negro Families, 1945." *Sales Management* 58 (20 May 1947): 20.

The Negro Motorist Green Book. New York: Victor H. Green & Co., 1949.

The Negro Travelers' Green Book. New York: Victor H. Green & Co., 1956, 1958.

Nicolaides, Becky M. *My Blue Heaven: Life and Politics in the Working-Class Suburbs of Los Angeles, 1920–1965.* Chicago: University of Chicago Press, 2002.

Orton, Ann Whiting. Interview by author, 19 July 2006, Salt Lake City, Utah.

Outdoor Recreation Resources Review Commission. *National Recreation Survey.* Washington, D.C.: Outdoor Recreation Resources Review Commission, 1962.

Park, Shelly M. "From Sanitation to Liberation: The Modern and Postmodern Marketing of Menstrual Products." *Journal of Popular Culture* 30 (1996): 149–68.

Partridge, Bellamy. *Fill 'er Up! The Story of Fifty Years of Motoring.* New York: McGraw-Hill, 1952.

Patterson, Doris T. *Your Family Goes Camping.* New York: Abingdon Press, 1959.

Perillo, Lucia Maria. *The Oldest Map with the Name America: New and Selected Poems.* New York: Random House, 1999.

Phelts, Marsha Dean. *An American Beach for African Americans.* Gainesville: University Press of Florida, 1997.

Pilling, Patricia L. "Segregation: Cottage Rental in Michigan." *Phylon* 25, no. 2 (1964): 191–201.

Pomerantz, Joel. *Jennie and the Story of Grossinger's.* New York: Grosset & Dunlap, 1970.

Pomeroy, Earl. *In Search of the Golden West: The Tourist in Western America.* New York: Knopf, 1957.

Ragatz, Richard Lee. "Vacation Homes in the Northeastern United States: Seasonality in Population Distribution." *Annals of the Association of American Geographers* 60 (September 1970): 447–55.

Rand McNally & Co. *Rand McNally Western Campground and Trailering Guide.* 1970.

Richman, Irwin. *Borscht Belt Bungalows: Memories of Catskill Summers.* Philadelphia: Temple University Press, 1998.

Rodnitzky, Jerome L. "Recapturing the West: The Dude Ranch in American Life." *Arizona and the West* 10 (1968): 111–26.

Rojek, Chris. *Capitalism and Leisure Theory.* London: Tavistock, 1985.

Rothman, Hal K. *Devil's Bargains: Tourism in the Twentieth-Century American West.* Lawrence: University Press of Kansas, 1998.

Rugh, Susan Sessions. "Branding Utah: Industrial Tourism in the Postwar American West." *Western Historical Quarterly* 37 (Winter 2006): 445–72.

———. *Our Common Country: Family Farming, Culture, and Community in the Nineteenth-Century Midwest.* Bloomington: Indiana University Press, 2001.

Runte, Alfred. *National Parks: The American Experience.* 3rd ed. Lincoln: University of Nebraska Press, 1979, 1997.

———. "Promoting the Golden West: Advertising and the Railroad." *California History* 70, no. 1 (Spring 1991): 62–75.

Ruth, Kent. *How to Enjoy Your Western Vacations.* Norman: University of Oklahoma Press, 1956.

Saltzman, Rachelle H. "Rites of Intensification: Eating and Ethnicity in the Catskills." *Southern Folklore* 55, no. 3 (1998): 205–23.

Sandage, Scott A. "A Marble House Divided: The Lincoln Memorial, the Civil Rights Movement and the Politics of Memory, 1939–1963." *Journal of American History* 80 (June 1993): 135–67.

Scharff, Virginia. *Taking the Wheel: Women and the Coming of the Motor Age.* New York: Free Press, 1991.

Scholten, Susan. *The Geographical Imagination in America, 1880–1950.* Chicago: University of Chicago Press, 2001.

Schroeder, Doris. *Annie Oakley in Double Trouble.* Racine, Wisc.: Whitman Publishing Co., 1958.

Sears, John F. *Sacred Places: American Tourist Attractions in the Nineteenth Century.* New York: Oxford University Press, 1989.

Seiler, Cotton. "'So That We as a Race Might Have Something Authentic to Travel By': African American Automobility and Cold-War Liberalism." *American Quarterly* 58 (December 2006): 1091–117.

Sellars, Richard West. *Preserving Nature in the National Parks: A History.* New Haven: Yale University Press, 1997.

Shaffer, Marguerite S. *See America First: Tourism and National Identity, 1880–1940.* Washington, D.C.: Smithsonian Institution, 2001.

Shapiro, Aaron. "'One Crop Worth Cultivating': Tourism in the Upper Great Lakes, 1910–1965." Ph.D. dissertation, University of Chicago, 2005.

Sharp, Harry, and Paul Mott. "Consumer Decisions in the Metropolitan Family." *Journal of Marketing* 21 (October 1956): 149–56.

Slotkin, Richard. *Gunfighter Nation: The Myth of the Frontier in Twentieth-Century America.* New York: Atheneum, 1992.

Soule, George. "The Economics of Leisure." *Annals of the American Academy of Political and Social Science* 313 (September 1957): 16–24.

Sozen, Joyce, ed., *Travel Fun for Kids.* New York: Maco Publishing, 1966, 1967.

Spellman, Susan V. "All the Comforts of Home: The Domestication of the Service Station Industry, 1920–1940." *Journal of Popular Culture* 37, no. 3 (2004): 463–77.

Spigel, Lynn. *Make Room for TV: Television and the Family Ideal in Postwar America.* Chicago: University of Chicago Press, 1992.

Sullivan, Robert. *Cross-Country.* New York: Bloomsbury, 2006.

Sunset Books. *Gold Rush Country: Guide to California's Mother Lode and Northern Mines.* Menlo Park, Calif.: Lane Publishing Co., 1957.

Talley-Jones, Kathy, Letitia Burns O'Connor, and Dana Levy. *The Road Ahead: The Automobile Club of Southern California, 1900–2000.* Los Angeles: Auto Club of Southern California, 2000.

Tatham, Julie. *Cherry Ames: Dude Ranch Nurse.* New York: Grosset & Dunlap, 1953.

Thelen, David. *Memory and American History.* Bloomington: University of Indiana Press, 1990.

Thompson, Anne B. "Rereading Fifties Teen Romance." *The Lion and the Unicorn* 29 (2005): 373–96.

Thornbrough, Emma Lou. "Breaking Racial Barriers to Public Accommodations in Indiana, 1935 to 1963." *Indiana Magazine of History* 83 (December 1987): 419–61.

Tompkins, Jane. *West of Everything: The Inner Life of Westerns.* New York: Oxford University Press, 1992.

The Travelers' Green Book. New York: Victor H. Green & Co., 1961, 1963.

Travelguide, Inc. *Travelguide.* New York, 1952, 1954, 1955.

Trillin, Calvin. *Travels with Alice.* New York: Ticknor & Fields, 1989.

Tsai, Eugenie, and Cornelia Butler, eds. *Robert Smithson.* Berkeley: University of California Press, 2004.

U.S. Census Bureau. *Historical Statistics of the United States,* Part 2, Series Q. Washington, D.C., 1975.

U.S. Department of the Interior, Bureau of Outdoor Recreation. *Northern New England Vacation Home Study—1966.* Washington, D.C., 1966.

U.S. Department of Labor. Bureau of Labor Statistics. *Collective Bargaining Provisions, Vacations: Holidays and Week-End Work.* Bulletin 908-2. Washington, D.C., 1948.

U.S. House of Representatives. *Hearings before Subcommittee No. 5 of the Committee on the Judiciary, House of Representatives, 88th Congress,* First Session, Serial No. 4, Part III. Washington, D.C., 1963.

U.S. National Highway Traffic Safety Administration. *Federal Motor Vehicle Safety Standards and Regulations.* Washington, D.C., 1999.

U.S. Senate. *Hearings before the Committee on Commerce,* 88th Congress, First Session on S. 1732, Title II, Part 1, Serial 26. Washington, D.C., 1963.

Van de Water, Frederic F. *The Family Flivvers to Frisco.* New York: D. Appleton and Company, 1927.

Verral, Charles Spain. *Annie Oakley, Sharpshooter.* New York: Simon and Schuster, 1956.

Vostral, Sharra V. "Masking Menstruation: The Emergence of Menstrual Hygiene Products in the United States." In *Menstruation: A Cultural History,* edited by Andrew Shail and Gillian Howie, 243–58. New York: Palgrave Macmillan, 2005.

Walker, Lewis, and Benjamin C. Wilson. *Black Eden: The Idlewild Community.* Lansing: Michigan State University Press, 2002.

Washington, James Melvin, ed. *I Have a Dream: Writings and Speeches that Changed the World.* San Francisco: HarperCollins, 1992.

Weems, Robert E. *Desegregating the Dollar: African-American Consumerism in the Twentieth Century.* New York: New York University Press, 1998.

Weiss, Jessica. *To Have and To Hold: Marriage, the Baby Boom and Social Change.* Chicago: University of Chicago Press, 2000.

Weitzman, Andrea Corwin. Telephone interview by author, 6 August 2007.

Wells, George Stevens. *Guide to Family Camping.* Harrisburg, Pennsylvania: Stackpole Books, 1973.

Whalen, Charles W., and Barbara Whalen. *The Longest Debate: A Legislative History of the Civil Rights Act of 1964.* Washington, D.C.: Seven Locks Press, 1985.

White, Roger B. *Home on the Road: The Motor Home in America.* Washington D.C.: Smithsonian Institution, 2000.

Whittlesey, Lee H. *Death in Yellowstone: Accidents and Foolhardiness in the First National Park.* Boulder, Colo.: Roberts Rinehart, 1995.

Wiese, Andrew. *Places of Their Own: African American Suburbanization in the Twentieth Century.* Chicago: University of Chicago Press, 2004.

Williams, John. *This Is My Country, Too.* New York: New American Library, 1966.

Wilson, Kemmons. *The Holiday Inn Story.* New York: Newcomen Society in North America, 1968.

Wiltse, Jeff. *Contested Waters: A Social History of Swimming Pools in America.* Chapel Hill: University of North Carolina, 2007.

Wolcott, Victoria W. "Recreation and Race in the Postwar City: Buffalo's 1956 Crystal Beach Riot." *Journal of American History* 93 (June 2006): 63–90.

Wrobel, David. *Promised Lands: Promotion, Memory, and the Creation of the American West.* Lawrence: University Press of Kansas, 2002.

Wrobel, David M., and Patrick T. Long. *Seeing and Being Seen: Tourism in the American West.* Lawrence: University Press of Kansas, 2001.

Yoggy, Gary A. *Riding the Video Range: The Rise and Fall of the Western on Television.* Jefferson, N.C.: McFarland & Company, 1995.

Yorke, Douglas A., Jr., John Margolies, and Eric Baker. *Hitting the Road: The Art of the American Road Map.* San Francisco: Chronicle Books, 1996.

Zelinsky, Wilbur. *Nation into State: The Shifting Symbolic Foundations of American Nationalism.* Chapel Hill: University of North Carolina Press, 1988.

Index